Restructuring Schools, Reconstructing Teachers

Restructuring Schools, Reconstructing Teachers

RESPONDING TO CHANGE IN THE PRIMARY SCHOOL

Peter Woods,
Bob Jeffrey, Geoff Troman
and Mari Boyle

OPEN UNIVERSITY PRESS
Buckingham • *Philadelphia*

Open University Press
Celtic Court
22 Ballmoor
Buckingham
MK18 1XW

and

1900 Frost Road, Suite 101
Bristol, PA 19007, USA

First Published 1997

A catalogue record of this book is available from the British Library

ISBN 0 335 19816 3 (hb)   0 335 19815 5 (pb)

Library of Congress Cataloging-in-Publication Data
Restructuring schools, reconstructing teachers : responding to
change in the primary school / Peter Woods ... [*et al*.].
    p.   cm.
    Includes bibliographical references (p.   ) and index.
    ISBN 0–335–19816–3. — ISBN 0–335–19815–5 (pbk.)
    1. Elementary school teachers—Great Britain—Case studies.
2. Education, Elementary—Great Britain—Case studies.   3. School
management and organization—Great Britain—Case studies.
4. Educational change—Great Britain—Case studies.   I. Woods,
Peter.
LB1776.4.G7R47   1997
372.941—dc21   97–8655
                                                            CIP

Typeset by Graphicraft Typesetters Limited, Hong Kong
Printed in Great Britain by Biddles Ltd,
Guildford and King's Lynn

Contents

Acknowledgements

We are grateful to the headteachers, teachers and other staff of all the schools involved for their time, openness, insights and cooperation in the research that has led to this book. Nick Hubbard and Barry Cocklin have given valuable support, and have contributed data to Chapter 5 and Chapter 3 respectively. We have benefited from comments from a number of people, and would like to record thanks particularly to Jennifer Nias, Marion Dadds, Martyn Hammersley, Roland Vandenberghe, Michael Hubermann and Andy Hargreaves. Special thanks are due to Maria for her invaluable encouragement and continuing intellectual and emotional support; Joe for sustenance, debate and insight; and Kath and Bronwyn for all their expert help. We have received valuable secretarial support from Aileen Cousins, Lynn Tilbury and Jan Giddins.

This book brings together the results of research from four projects, all funded by the ESRC, whom we thank for their support. The projects are: (1) 'Creative Teaching in the National Curriculum' (1991–1995; ESRC Reference R000233194); (2) 'The Effects of Restructuring on Teaching as Work' (1993–1997; R00429334361); (3) 'Child-Meaningful Learning in a Bilingual School' (1994–1997; R000235123); and (4) 'The Effects of Ofsted Inspections on Primary Teachers and their Work' (1995–1997; R000236406); The Centre for Sociology and Social Research at the School of Education, The Open University, has also provided valuable support.

Some chapters or parts of chapters have appeared in print previously. Part of Chapter 1 was originally published as 'The rise of the new professionals? The restructuring of primary teachers' work and professionalism', *British Journal of Sociology of Education*, 17(4), 1996: 473–87. Part of Chapter 2 appeared as 'Stepping' into the future: new forms of organisation in the primary school', *Journal of Education Policy*, in press. Part of Chapter 4 appeared as 'The composite head: coping with changes in the primary headteacher's role', *British Educational Research Journal*, 22(5), 1996: 549–68. An earlier version of Chapter 6 was presented as a paper entitled 'Intensification and teacher stress' at a conference on Teacher Stress and Burn-out at Marbach, Germany, 1995. We thank the editors and publishers of these papers for permission to reuse this material here.

Introduction

We have been exploring the nature and consequences of the radical changes
that have been occurring in primary schools in recent years, and the coping
strategies and adaptations made by teachers and headteachers to these
consequences. We draw on research that has been carried out in seven primary schools for periods varying from two to five years between 1991 and 1997.
Five of the schools are in London and the two others are in contrasting areas
in the Midlands. We have used a qualitative approach, involving close association with the schools concerned over a lengthy period, observation of lessons
and other school activity, frequent and sustained interviews and conversations with teachers and others at various times and in various situations, and
documentary analysis. Throughout, we have been concerned to give voice to
teachers and headteachers, and we make full use of their testimony in the
book. Further information about methods is given with the individual chapters, as required.

We begin, in Part A of Chapter 1, by discussing the general context within
which the present impetus for change originated and which continues to
provide its motive force. In common with other institutions and systems, education is under pressure to transform in response to worldwide economic,
technological, social and political developments. We trace through how this
macro factor has prompted the restructuring of schools and of teachers' work,
how it has influenced school organization and teacher roles. We also examine the process of 'reculturing' – the way in which inroads are being made
on what has hitherto been one of the most intransigent feature of school life,
teacher culture. We note how conceptions of the 'good teacher' can change
over time and consider the expectations of the current role. The key question is what effect this is all having on schools and pupil achievement, and
whether it is making things better or worse. Is it likely to improve schools,
enskill teachers and raise standards? Or is it constraining schools, deskilling
teachers and debasing education? Educational researchers and comment-
ators differ in their views on this. There are arguments and evidence to support both sides, and it is possible that both trends are occurring simultaneously, and in contest with each other. We consider the relationship between
these trends in the course of the book. In Part B, we develop a model

suggested by our data through which these questions might be tackled. Primary teaching has been shown to be rooted in a number of dilemmas which all teachers confront in the classroom (Berlak and Berlak 1981; Alexander 1984). We identified some new dilemmas in the aftermath of the introduction of the National Curriculum, and of other related developments. But we also noticed a foreshortening of choice for the teacher in resolving dilemmas and this appeared to be one way in which the character of primary teaching, in all its compartments – not just classroom teaching – was undergoing fundamental change. Where this was significant, we term the experience a 'tension'. Where there was felt to be very little choice at all, we term it a 'constraint'. In some schools, teachers were still working in creative ways with the curriculum. They were tackling old and new dilemmas creatively, and transforming them into positive action. In this sense, teachers' professionalism was being enhanced. We have illustrated this in previous reports (Woods 1995; Woods and Jeffrey 1996b). Elsewhere, however, teachers were experiencing tensions and constraints. The general trend from dilemma to tension and constraint runs as a theme throughout the book.

In Chapter 2 we examine how changes in the area of personal and professional relationships have developed. While ostensibly along the lines of more freedom, democracy and collegiality, in reality these changes are towards more constraint. In the first section we draw on a number of schools in our research to show teachers were experiencing a managerialist discourse which focuses more on the systems of organization than actual teaching and learning in the classroom. At the same time, they were under pressure to develop a more collaborative culture. A feature of some primary schools before the changes took hold used to be the democratic nature of these cultures (Nias *et al.* 1992). However, in our schools, the more bureaucratic aspects of managerialism, such as paperwork and meetings, were dominating. This trend is bringing a change to the nature of collaborative arrangements, and affecting teachers' creativity in and out of the classroom. How and why things come to be this way are key questions. In the second section, therefore, we discuss one headteacher's attempts at restructuring a school's organization and culture along collaborative lines. It is clear that teaching takes place at various levels. The manifest, surface layer appears to operate in a straight linear fashion, from the formulation of policy through to the conceptualization and operationalization of practice. However, beneath this layer there is a harder reality where efforts to resolve tensions and get round constraints turns micropolitical action into a fine art. We wanted to consider how the primary school had changed organizationally, i.e. the meso level, following the macro and micro levels of Chapter 1. However, we found it impossible to uncouple the structure of the school from the politics of its establishment. In this sense, school organization is more of a process, a dynamic thing, that is available for negotiation and renegotiation. The second part of Chapter 2, therefore, developed into a study of micropolitics. Using one of our case study schools, we examine how the head engineered changes in the management and work culture. It was his way of resolving the new dilemmas that had arisen for him, but it meant new forms of constraint for others. We conclude that change probably entails an increase in, and refinement of, micropolitical action, which acts against more genuine collegiality and also individuality.

In the next two chapters, we turn to the teacher's role in the new organization. The teacher role has altered in size, content and, possibly, status. With respect to the first, teachers have been given more responsibilities without losing any of the former, and without any change in working conditions, which leads Campbell and Neill (1994b: 163) to talk of 'role inflation'. With respect to content, there is more emphasis, notably, on managerial aspects of their role, such that now some talk of 'teacher-managers'. The results of these changes, for some, mean new opportunities and 'extended professionalism' (Hoyle 1974); for others, the changes mean loss of control and creativity and a more restricted professionalism. In Chapter 3, we consider how teachers across all our projects are adapting to new official conceptions of the 'good' teacher. We show that there is a wide range of experience, from enhanced transformation (where the changes are experienced mainly as an escalation of dilemmas in the situation, requiring refined professional action), through various forms of tension to constraint, where, at the extreme, the ability to cope is minimal. The experience of role conflict in these latter cases, we argue, is better envisaged as 'role tension', since it involves strong emotions and conflict within the inner self (as opposed to the situation), which is demonstrably counterproductive for educational practice.

We go on, in Chapter 4, to examine adaptations to the primary headteacher role in a similar manner. Again, this role has undergone radical change. The managerial aspects here are even more emphasized – heads are seen by the Government* as the prime agent in the schools for the implementation of the reforms. This poses an interesting question. If heads are indeed the 'leading professional' (Davies 1987) within the school, and hence best equipped with adaptational and transformational skills, how will they experience the real changes? Some have obviously found them insuperable constraints, and have taken early retirement. The numbers of heads doing this have escalated in the years since the Education Reform Act of 1988 (see Chapter 6). To what degree are those that remain experiencing role dilemmas, and what degree role tensions? Again, we found a varied response among our heads, and here we present three strongly contrasting types, discussing the principles that guide them, the strategies they adopt, and the feelings that accompany them. We compare the heads across the current main functions of the role – guardian of the institutional bias, gatekeeper, manager, leading professional and cultural leader. All three of the heads have received strong approval from the Office for Standards in Education (Ofsted) inspectors and

---

* The 'Government' here refers to the Conservative Government, 1979 to 1997.

other significant personnel, and are regarded as 'good' heads. This shows that, while there may be an apparently closely and clearly prescribed headteacher role, and thus one official type of 'good' head, in effect, many types are possible within those parameters. There are ways of preserving one's values while meeting requirements, though, it has to be said, at some cost to one's physical and emotional state.

Continuing this theme of widely variable adaptation, we go on to consider three very different responses to school inspections from individual teachers. The institution of a new mode of inspection under Ofsted in 1992, designed to embrace all schools within a regular pattern of rigorous and systematic evaluation by new teams of inspectors, was a further measure in the Government's declared drive to improve educational standards. It is a critical measure, for it threatens to reduce that area of negotiability that had allowed teachers hitherto a degree of discretion in implementing the Government's policy. It stands, therefore, to increase the areas of tension and constraint. Some believe that this is what is required for educational improvement, but on the evidence of the previous work on creative teaching as cited above, we believe this view to be misguided. So how have teachers experienced the new form of inspection? Again, we found some variability. In Chapter 5, we take three individual teachers – a head, a deputy head and a classroom teacher – and examine their widely differing reactions to inspections that had recently occurred in their schools. We examine their experiences in relation to three criteria that emerged from the research: (1) the nature and degree of intensification experienced in preparing for the event; (2) the realities of the event constructed by the teachers; and (3) the meanings of the event for the teacher's self. For the classroom teacher, the inspection was almost a non-event, and she could hardly wait to return to 'normal'. For the headteacher, it was the biggest boost to her confidence that she had received since becoming a head. For the deputy head, the inspection induced trauma of the worst kind, but brought about a reconstruction of self through a circuitous route in ways not determined by the Government's policy. We discuss the implications for enhanced, or constrained, professionalism.

One of the ways for teachers to avoid such negative trauma is by shifting identity and status from professional to technician, which they appear reluctant to do. But if no way out is discovered, teachers become even more liable to suffer stress and burn-out. The incidence of these states has increased dramatically since 1988, the year of the Education Reform Act, and was all too evident in the schools of our research. Creative teachers seem particularly at risk (see Woods 1990). In Chapter 6, we consider this escalation against the background of restructuring, intensification and the Government's reforms. We trace the effects of these macro factors deriving from global trends and the Government's policy through to meso levels consisting of institutional and other middle-range factors, and micro levels comprising social factors within the teacher's biography and person. The interaction between the three is the field upon which teacher experiences are played out. In order to study this interaction, we bring together two approaches that we believe have particular relevance – interactionism and some recent formulations about 'deprofessionalization' and 'intensification' of teachers' work. The latter provide a view of how recent macro developments bear on stress, and the former on how they are actually experienced by teachers and how we might conceptualize those experiences.

Hargreaves (1994a) argues that the present age in teaching is characterized by *struggle*. There are forces and groups intent on deprofessionalizing teachers and their work, while there are others seeking to redefine teachers in more positive ways. Teachers themselves occupy the key position in this conflict. It is important, therefore, in the pursuit of enhanced professionalism, that teachers engage with the changes, rather than being taken over by them. In order to do that, they need to understand the origins and nature of the changes, and their own responses to them. This book is a contribution towards that endeavour.

Sounds like, "We'll teach you – understand it the way we do – and then "engage" – but it is us who should be 'learning' their language, their implicit meanings – not teaching them.

CHAPTER 1

Restructuring and the growth of constraint

In Part A, we consider the general historical, political and educational context in which change has been taking place. In Part B, we develop a framework through which we will examine the actual impact of the changes on teachers in schools and classrooms.

PART A: THE RESTRUCTURING OF PRIMARY TEACHERS' WORK

Introduction: the context of restructuring

Schools, together with many other institutions in society, are undergoing radical change, in a process that has come to be known as 'restructuring'. Restructuring is a current international phenomenon in developed economies. Basically, it is a response to the globalization of capital and communications, the rapid growth of information and technological developments, changed modes of economic production, economic crisis and increasing moral and scientific uncertainty (Harvey 1989; A. Hargreaves 1994a). With regard to education, Lawton (1992) argues that the Government's legislation for restructuring is motivated variously by the following:

- A crisis in legitimation: In advanced capitalist economies, there is public doubt that educational systems can carry out their job adequately (Habermas 1976).
- Concern about effectiveness: The labour and economic problems of the early 1980s and high levels of youth unemployment suggested that educational systems were providing neither an adequate nor relevant education.

Studies showing declining test scores in international league tables stimulated concern that some Western economies were not developing human capital.

- Concern about efficiency: There was increasing evidence that investing more money in education does not necessarily increase educational standards or increase the Gross National Product.
- The managerial revolution: The 'traditional bureaucracy with its emphasis on centralised decision making, control, uniformity, close supervision and commitment to standard operating procedures' (Lawton 1992: 145) is associated with inefficiency. The key to improvement is seen to be the application of more management and management systems. Rather than bureaucratic, the new manager is the autonomous and entrepreneurial school-based leader.
- A populist movement: There is a groundswell of popular support for ideas concerning parents having a greater control over, and choice in, the education of their children. Parents as consumers are seeking the best buy in education. Parent power is in the ascendant (Dale 1989).
- A crisis in capitalism: Western democracies are currently facing an accumulation crisis. Drives for profitability involve an emphasis on the public sector using resources efficiently and effectively in the context of cuts in public finance and expenditure.
- Provider capture: Professions such as medicine, teaching and the law have hitherto enjoyed a relatively large measure of professional autonomy and control. Critics argue that the sole providers of a service, such as teachers, accrue more benefits than their customers. Restructuring aims to redistribute benefits from the provider to the client.

The societies in which restructuring is taking place have all experienced economic recession and become increasingly uncompetitive in international markets since the oil crisis of 1973. Educational systems and teachers have been held to be the cause of economic failure by not producing a workforce with the appropriate skills for a rapidly changing world (Weinstock 1976). The failure of less radical attempts to reform schools has induced despair. Rudduck (1991: 28) has argued that, 'the tight weave of traditions and routines, combined with the loose coupling of their internal communication systems, can make schools almost as impermeable as a fortress'. The situation, therefore, seemed to call for radical action.

Restructuring in the United Kingdom

Restructuring in the UK has been characterized by the contradictory processes of decentralization and centralization.

Decentralization has involved the marketization of schooling (Ball 1994). By the Education Reform Act 1988, which instituted the Local Management of Schools (LMS), schools have become independent budget-holders. Their funding is linked to the number and ages of pupils on roll. The ability of parents, in theory, to choose the school their children will attend renders schools subject to market pressures. Parents are expected to choose the 'best' schools, thus encouraging all to improve educational standards. It is thought, too, in the light of the failure of central reform movements, that schools have greater capacity to improve themselves. The argument is that giving teachers the autonomy to exercise professional judgement in the management of finance, resources, curriculum and pedagogy increases the prospect of reforms paying off in terms of improved teaching and learning (A. Hargreaves 1994b). Such reforms have been introduced in a period of economic retrenchment, with schools being forced to consider their economy, efficiency and effectiveness (Audit Commission 1984).

Such measures, it is argued, will liberate schools from the bureaucratic grip and ideological meddling of local education authorities (Ball 1994). Giving funds directly to heads and governors would release entrepreneurial initiative which, again, would fuel a rise in educational standards (Grace 1996). In the neo-liberal discourse of marketization, smart schools produce a smart workforce. Legislated changes for increasing school autonomy in the way described, and creating an education market, have been vigorously promoted in the United States by internationally influential writers inspired by the moves to local financial management in the UK (see Chubb and Moe 1992). They advocate the removal of schooling from central and local state interference in order to make schools responsive to the market and thereby increase educational output in the form of high test scores. Public choice theorists, such as Chubb and Moe (1992) and Tooley (1993), see unrestructured schools as bureaucratic and in need of incentives and choice. Bureaucracy is considered to be the enemy of quality in education and the most effective schools are the ones where the 'handcuffs have been taken off the administrators' (Boyd 1996) so that they can manage the autonomous school more efficiently and devise their own vision, while responding to the choices that parents make in the schooling of their children.

At the same time as these decentralization measures, however, the Government, through the Education Reform Act 1988, instituted a large amount of centralization through a mandated National Curriculum and system of testing. Published test scores aim to provide a basis for both parental choice of school and school accountability to the community. Four-yearly inspections by the Office for Standards in Education (Ofsted) provide public accountability. The work of teaching is increasingly codified in the Ofsted criteria (1993a, 1995b), and therefore easier to assess and grade by the inspectors. Teaching methods are coming increasingly under scrutiny, with pressure on teachers to adopt a more traditional style congruent with one supported by the state (Clarke 1991; Department of Education and Science 1992a; Woodhead 1996).

Restructuring does not have to take this form. In the United States, for instance, restructuring has been largely a response to removing the bureaucracy and political interference of the municipal state, and faith in teachers to implement reform has been retained. There has been a 'resurgence in and respect for the dignity, quality and sophistication of teachers' practical knowledge and judgement' (A. Hargreaves and Dawe 1989: 4–5). Restructuring as recommended by groups such as the US Carnegie Forum on 'Education and the Economy' would 'respect and support the professionalism of teachers to make decisions in their own classrooms that best met local and state goals while holding teachers accountable for how they did that' (A. Hargreaves 1994a: 241). Murphy and Evertson (1991) suggest components of restructuring which include: school-based management; increased consumer choice; teacher empowerment; and teaching for understanding. The National Governors' Association (1989) recommend that 'curriculum and instruction be redesigned to promote higher order thinking skills and the decentralization of authority and decision-making to site level, more diverse and differentiated roles for teachers and broader systems of accountability' (cited in A. Hargreaves 1994a: 241).

By contrast with these basically teacher empowering developments, teachers in the UK have been excluded from the partnership for policymaking created in the post-war social democratic settlement (Lawn 1995). Their participation in curriculum and assessment policymaking has been restricted to a number of token consultation exercises (Haviland 1988). Indeed, Bash and Coulby (1989) argue that many of the restructuring reforms seem based on a deep distrust of teachers, and Ball (1990) identifies a 'discourse of derision' being constructed about teachers by New Right 'think tanks', media and politicians. 'Progressivism' in teaching and initial teacher education (Lawlor 1990) and 'trendy teachers' have been the targets of ridicule since the Black Papers of the late 1960s. From this viewpoint, teachers are seen as the cause, rather than the solution, to educational crisis (Ball 1990). Teachers have received a 'bashing', too, from academics who see them as witting or unwitting agents of capital and instrumental in reproducing the inequalities of capitalism (Mac an Ghaill 1996). These attacks have been accompanied by official support for a return to 'traditional' teaching and 'real' schooling (Boyd 1996). This has seen the introduction of a subjects-based National Curriculum, and repeated calls for increases in whole-class teaching and ability grouping, in the form of streaming or setting (Clarke 1991; Department of Education and Science 1992a; Woodhead 1996).

The idea of the restructured school

System-wide changes are intended to stimulate the transformation of the internal organization and culture of the school. The restructured school is seen by some as the self-managing, autonomous or empowered school (Caldwell and Spinks 1988; D.H. Hargreaves and Hopkins 1991). Market forces emphasize the role of headteachers as business leaders while retaining their traditional responsibility for educational management. Traditional primary school leadership has been criticized for supporting hierarchical structures, and for slowness in responding to change (Alexander 1992). In the role of entrepreneurial leader, heads can respond creatively and flexibly to rapid changes in the external environment of the school. They direct and manage human and material resources in order to maximize pupils' learning. Faith in management to organize restructuring of the institution, to devise technically based solutions and implement radical reforms has been central to many of the recent changes. There is a moral ascendency of managerialism (Inglis 1989, Walker and Barton 1987). Consequently, the Department for Education and Employment now sponsors headteacher training for heads and intending heads, leading to a national qualification for headship (Haigh 1995b).

While the Government seemed to encourage a top-down management style, other supporters of the self-managing school saw the head operating as team leader in flattened management hierarchies. Leadership using these structures is in the mould of Human Resource Management and Total Quality Management with their associated quality assurance systems (Menter *et al.* 1995). Human Resource Management, for instance, 'harnesses the occupational/organizational culture to the delivery of efficiency and quality (Menter *et al.* 1995a: 6). Rational planning is to the fore; headteacher 'vision' is embodied in the prime management tool of the school development plan. In this new managerialist discourse, managers are to be leaders of 'vision'. Advocates of this view (Peters and Waterman 1982; Purkey and Smith 1985) claim that they should have, 'the capacity to articulate and win commitment to a vision for the school and ensure that vision is internalised in the structures, processes and procedures which shape everyday activity' (Angus 1994: 21).

Reculturing

The management of consent and collaboration is a key role for leaders of self-managing schools. Schools are urged to become 'more like businesses' (Coopers and Lybrand 1988), and post-industrial businesses have flattened hierarchies in which all workers are 'empowered' to participate in management. In their idea of the 'empowered school', D. Hargreaves and Hopkins (1991: 15) argue that 'management is about people. Management arrangements are what empower people. Empowerment, in short, is the purpose of management'. They see management in an holistic sense with teachers, headteachers, parents and governors engaged in a type of collaborative management which often requires 'a change of school culture' (ibid.: 17). Previously the primary school had been criticized because of its culture of individualism which impeded innovation (D.H. Hargreaves 1994). Class teachers operating individually and in isolation in their classrooms were seen to be badly placed to respond creatively to change (Alexander 1984). Fullan's (1988) answer to school and teacher development lies in 'cracking the walls of privatism'. However, as Fullan (1991: 114) observes, 'Changing structures is easier to bring about than changes in values, beliefs, behaviour and other normative and cultural changes'. These changes, therefore, need support. Following Werner (1982), Hargreaves describes 'support strategies' (ibid.: 255) for reculturing, which create release time so teachers work together; assist them in collaborative planning; encourage teachers to try a new experience, a new practice or grade level; involve teachers in goal-setting; and create a culture of collaboration, risk and improvement.

Reculturing, it is claimed, is likely to be better at changing classroom practice than 'quick cultural fixes' (ibid.: 256). The form of organizational structure and culture known as the 'moving mosaic' promises to 'foster vigorous, dynamic and shifting forms of collaboration through networks, partnerships and alliances within and beyond the school' (ibid.: 257). However, reculturing in its negative form is merely a way of 'managing' school cultures so that teachers cheerfully comply with structural goals and purposes already fixed by the bureaucratic center [*sic*] (ibid.: 256).

Central to reculturing is collaboration, which contrasts with the individualism of the old order (D.H. Hargreaves 1980). New organizational structures and cultures require flexible and differentiated teachers to work in them (Lawn 1995). They need to be able to work on their own, but also, increasingly, to work together. In the school improvement (D.H. Hargreaves 1994; D.H. Hargreaves and Hopkins 1991; Caldwell and Spinks 1988) and teacher development literature (Nias 1989; Biott and Nias 1992), there is a pronounced emphasis on collaboration through which teachers develop new skills by sharing professional knowledge. This view is supported by a number of official policy documents (Department of Education and Science 1992a; Ofsted 1994) and in the Ofsted criteria for inspection (Ofsted 1995b). We examine some attempts to develop collaborative cultures in Chapter 2.

Intensification

Apple (1986) argues that, in late twentieth-century capitalist societies, work intensifies as capital experiences an accumulation crisis and pressure for efficiency mounts in public and private sectors. Intensification leads to reduced time for relaxation and reskilling; causes chronic and persistent work overload; reduces quality of service; and separates the conceptualization from the execution of tasks, making teachers dependent on outside expertise and reducing them to technicians (A. Hargreaves 1994a: 118–19).

The introduction of new roles and responsibilities, an extended curriculum, new assessment tasks and the need for retraining (Campbell and Neill

1994a) all contribute to intensification. What for some was 'a dream at conception' turned into a 'nightmare at delivery' (Campbell 1993). It is clear that there has been massive work overload, a loss of spontaneity and or reflective time, an increase in stress (see Chapter 6), a burgeoning of bureaucracy (Campbell and Neill 1990; Campbell *et al.* 1991a; Pollard 1991; Osborn and Broadfoot 1992; Pollard 1994; Pollard *et al.* 1994). Some argue that the way teachers think and feel has also been exploited. They have been caught in the 'trap of conscientiousness' (Campbell *et al.* 1991b), doing their best to meet the prescribed targets but compromising the quality of learning and their own health.

The official answer is not to lighten the load, but to express concern that teachers are not working hard enough and to suggest lengthening the working day and week (Ofsted 1994). These changes are taking place in the context of less favourable funding of primary, compared to secondary, schools (House of Commons 1986) and continual annual financial cuts. These have resulted in increased class sizes (*Times Educational Supplement* 5 July 1996a), teacher redundancies and a growth in the number of teachers applying for early retirement (Smithers 1989; see also Chapter 6). School closures and teacher dismissals are becoming more of a reality (*Times Educational Supplement* 5 July 1996b). Note, however, that while most researchers agree that some intensification has taken place, not all agree that deprofessionalization is a necessary consequence, as we discuss later.

Changing forms of control of teachers' work

It has been argued that previous centre–periphery reforms which were intended to transform schools failed because the schools enjoyed a relative autonomy (Dale 1989), allowing a large degree of slippage between central policymaking agencies and the schools where policy was implemented. Within schools, teachers also had a certain autonomy, and adapted innovations in line with their professional ideologies This led some to refer to schools as 'organised anarchies' (March and Olson 1976). Some thought this epitomized in the case of the William Tyndale Junior School. Prior to the mid-1970s, control of the education system 'rested on assumptions of shared values and norms, priorities and practices throughout the educational system rather than explicit rules' (ibid.: 126). However, teachers at William Tyndale in 1975 caused a scandal by seeking to institute their own brand of education. Dale (ibid.: 126) describes the way the teachers used the control they enjoyed to introduce changes in the school:

> At the economic level they were quite explicit in opposing the centrality of schools' human resource service to the economy. Their job was not to provide 'factory fodder'; they saw themselves as preparing human

beings rather than human capital. They sought, too, to undermine the class structure as far as possible in their policies and practice, rather than reinforce it, which they saw as the inevitable outcome of schools' traditional sorting and selection function.

The teachers were eventually suspended and the school closed. The whole affair demonstrated that 'neither the school managers nor the parents, neither the politicians nor the officers of ILEA [Inner London Education Authority] appeared to be able to control what the teachers were doing' (ibid.). This was because teachers had a 'licensed autonomy', which was 'renewable upon the meeting of certain conditions. Just how those conditions were met was subject to broad limitations' (ibid.: 130). The Tyndale teachers had clearly pushed 'licensed autonomy' beyond its limits.

Following the public inquiry there was a 'political will' to 'clip the wings' of teachers and bring the system under closer control (ibid.: 145). One of the lessons which had been learned was that 'schooling was too important to be left to teachers' (ibid.: 135). There followed a 'fundamental shift in the area of control from 'licensed autonomy' to . . . 'regulated autonomy' (ibid.: 132). Under the latter, control would become

> tighter, largely through the codification and monitoring of processes and practices previously left to teachers' professional judgement, taken on trust or hallowed by tradition. This shift has come to be equated with the move to greater accountability.

The codification and monitoring achieved through new accountability systems, Dale argues, changed the game teachers were expected to play from 'catch me if you can' to 'jumping through hoops' (ibid.: 143).

Prior to 1979, the state aimed to achieve control through schools' adherence to the curriculum aims and objectives of local education authorities and general inspection by Her Majesty's Inspectors. In reality, inspectors had an advisory rather than inspectorial role, and because of their comparatively small numbers, very few schools could be inspected. In the period following 1979, educational policy became increasingly concerned with the control of the system. These trends crystallized in the Education Reform Act 1988 and have underpinned policy since. Centralized educational policy now defines the work of teachers. It exercises control over teacher training through the stipulation of teacher competencies and has legislated a National Curriculum and a standardized, national system of assessment, with regular inspection by the privatized inspectorate.

Control in the schools is exercised through management, considered by policymakers as the means of implementing the reforms in the schools, and also to act as a 'panacea for easing the tensions' (S.J. Ball 1994) of restructuring. While managers are cast as the agents of change they can only fulfil this role by changing themselves. Thus, in the new order, headteachers retain their traditional powers (in fact they have increased considerably), but delegate some duties and responsibilities to senior management teams and curriculum coordinators. Despite these changes, the purpose of management, it is argued, remains the same – to gain teachers' commitment to change and motivation for work, while exercising control over them (Friedman 1977; Grace 1996). These functions of management were recognized by a former Secretary of State for Education when he acknowledged that, whilst control was necessary to 'ensure that standards throughout the country are brought up to the level of the best', the implementation of the reforms 'depend[s] on the professional skills of teachers' (MacGregor 1990: 5).

While the radical reform of schooling has its advocates, it also has its critics (see Angus 1994). A. Hargreaves (1994a: 243) for instance, notes that the discourses and practices of restructuring are sometimes employed to make top-down reforms which are 'force-fed' to teachers 'slightly more palatable'. He is also alert to the fact that the 'very term, restructuring, has been adopted from the corporate context where it first emerged' (ibid.). There it had been a synonym for the 'management of recession and retrenchment' (ibid.). In schools it can be used by the 'most cynical proponents of restructuring as a euphemism for downsizing school staffing and resources and downgrading the services they can offer' (ibid.). Ball (1994) has argued that, despite the rhetoric of autonomy and empowerment, new systems of management are a powerful and pervasive way of controlling teachers' work, and that self-management is a form of covert 'indirect steering' by the state (Kickert 1991). Internal systems of monitoring, review and teacher appraisal, ostensibly devices to promote efficiency and standards, provide a self-policing mode of accountability. Such self-surveillance is more effective, too, because in this context 'resistance sets the dissenters against colleagues not policies' (Ball 1994: 54).

Smyth (1991) notes the paradox in a situation where teachers are being urged to work collegially at the same time that educational decision-making is increasingly centralized. Smyth (ibid.: 324) concludes that the culture of collegiality, almost mandatory in the self-managing school, is 'part of a broader strategy to harness teachers more effectively to the work of economic reconstruction'. Since teachers are no longer required by the state to engage in professional debates concerning the ends of education, but are merely expected to implement the plans of others, collegial work can be considered as a form of 'indirect rule' by the state (Ozga and Lawn 1988). Thus, by this argument, teachers come to collaborate in their own oppression.

Restructuring the primary teacher's role

Official definitions of the 'good teacher' prior to the changes emphasized the 'personal qualities' of teachers (Department of Education and Science

1983, 1985; Broadhead 1987). With the changes, and prefigured a decade before the Education Reform Act itself in an influential HMI document of 1978, came a tightly specified list of teacher competencies. The most prom-inent of these are the skills of 'matching', differentiation, subject expertise, coordination, collaboration, management and supervision; the most significant general change in the teacher role has been that from 'teacher' to 'teacher manager'.

'Matching' refers to the teacher's ability to match tasks given children to their abilities by 'providing children with learning experiences which take due account of their varying characteristics, and yet which are guided by a common set of principles' (Richards 1987: 191). The closely related concept of differentiation refers to teachers meeting the needs of the full ability range by 'providing children with learning experiences which take due account of their varying characteristics and yet which are guided by a common set of principles' (ibid.). The teacher's subject expertise refers to their knowledge, qualifications and experience in a curriculum subject and the quality of their teaching of that subject. HMI (1978) claimed these two factors interrelated in the production of high pupil achievement. They also considered that the effective teacher would be capable of sharing her subject expertise with her colleagues, working cooperatively with them and taking some responsibility for their training and supervision. By the mid-1980s, HMI were advocating increasing the management strategies of evaluation, appraisal and strategic planning (Department of Education and Science 1985).

These trends received a considerable boost with the Education Reform Act 1988. The influential discussion paper, *Curriculum Organisation and Classroom Practice* (Department of Education and Science 1992a), conveyed a model of the 'good' teacher as not restricted to one having competency and qualities to facilitate work in classrooms, but one that also has managerial competencies. There is frequent emphasis on subject knowledge and teaching expertise and the stressed importance of the subject coordinator as the key factors in both implementing the National Curriculum and raising national standards. Lawn (1991: 72) claims that:

> The duties, responsibilities and performance of the teacher have become more closely defined. The craft skills of teaching have become codified, subject specialism is a requirement, curriculum content and its assessment have been tightly specified. Teaching has been redefined as a supervisory task, operating with a team of teachers and [probably] with an allowance for leading and managing them, work is related to the overall development plan or whole school management policy.

The 'management' trend was emphasized still further by the Office for Standards in Education (Ofsted 1994). They recommended more and better management of teachers' work. The key to this was seen to be the curriculum coordinator, redesignated here as 'subject managers', because 'coordinators [was considered] too limited a description' (ibid.: 9, para. 37). Review, monitoring, evaluation, appraisal and curriculum audit are activities that HMI felt that the subject managers should be more involved in. In their *Handbook for the Inspection of Schools*, Ofsted (1993a) set out the 'Framework' that would guide inspectors in evaluating teachers. Throughout the 'Framework' the words of 'standards' and 'quality' occur frequently and teaching and learning are to be judged in terms of them. Management is evaluated according to its 'efficiency' and 'effectiveness'. The 'Framework' retains the prescriptions concerning subject specialism, match and differentiation. Thus, 'teacher quality' is now defined in terms of technical competencies as opposed to personal qualities (Lawn 1988). Indeed, the attributes that previously teachers may or may not have had, for example cooperativeness, are now, in official discourse, obligatory technical requirements of the job (ibid.: 162; see also Smyth 1991). The sum effect is that primary teachers have been restructured as teacher/managers. The increasing emphasis on technical competencies associated with managerial and bureaucratic roles rather than the personal qualities of the official 'good' teacher may reflect a general trend towards a more intensified technical–rational era. Seddon (1991), Arnot and Barton (1992) and Furlong (1992) argue that a new professionalism is being constructed in the new government controlled programmes of teacher education, which deprofessionalize teachers, in the old sense, and construct the 'official' technicist teacher.

We examine teachers' responses to the new role requirements in Chapter 3, and headteachers' responses in Chapter 4.

Consequences of restructuring

How far are we witnessing the demise of the 'professional' and the rise of the 'technicist' teacher? This is an issue on which the research evidence is uneven. The changes have elicited complex and contradictory responses from teachers (Grace 1996). Teachers filter the policies of change through their existing professional ideologies, perspectives and identities (Broadfoot and Osborn 1988; Woods 1993, 1995). This produces a variety of adaptations in the teacher workforce ranging from compliance with the new policy through mediation and accommodation to resistance and rejection. Pollard *et al.* (1994) identify an 'emergent professionalism' among teachers, who largely comply with the reforms and see them as necessary measures to remedy deficiencies in the system. D.H. Hargreaves (1994), too describes a 'new' professionalism in which teacher isolationism is broken down and a culture of collaboration arises. He claims that this is an unintended consequence of the Government's policy which was designed to stimulate competition. Webb and Vulliamy (1996) describe how teachers readily adopted the challenging new roles and responsibilities. Osborn (1995) suggests that teachers are now coming to terms with their restructured work and are developing new professional skills. Campbell and Neill (1994b), although noting the rapid intensification of primary teachers' work, claim this has not led to deskilling and deprofessionalization but to an enhanced professionalism. Cooper and McIntyre (1996) found the National Curriculum to be an effective stimulus to collaborative planning, shared professional learning and the development of teachers' professional craft knowledge. Increased professionalism in the areas of assessment (Gipps *et al.* 1995) and early years' education (Evans and Penney 1994) has been reported.

Alternatively, Grace's (1996) analysis of headteacher responses to the restructuring of their work shows how the marketization of schools, requiring managerialist strategies to implement, throws up many values dilemmas for the heads. Bowe *et al.* (1992: 5) argue that the new controls over teachers and their work, discussed earlier, produce complex changes in which the 'trust, commitment, cooperation and common purpose of teachers is being lost or jeopardized'. Mac an Ghaill (1992) argues that, in secondary schools at least, the teacher's 'occupational culture is in crisis, with the emergence of intensely differentiated and polarised bifurcated teaching ideologies' (ibid.: 178). Elements of these analyses both support and oppose the 'technification of teaching' thesis (Apple 1986). As Barton *et al.* (1994: 535) point out, 'important questions remain, including how successful are the attempts to control teachers and schools and what forms of opposition are teachers developing'. This is a major focus for the rest of the book.

PART B: FROM DILEMMAS
TO CONSTRAINTS

Introduction

Restructuring in the UK has had profound effects on teachers' work. There is ample testimony to overload, especially since the institution of the National Curriculum in 1988; to increased bureaucracy; and to heightened pressures of competition and accountability (Campbell and Neill 1994a). Primary teachers have had to acquire knowledge and skills in new subject areas, in assessment and in managing (Pollard *et al.* 1994; Gipps *et al.* 1995). These developments, we argue, are changing the nature of teachers' work from one characterized by the problematic but relatively free resolution of *dilemmas*, to one in which teachers begin to feel more oppressed by *tensions* and *constraints*. We have seen how restructuring has provided a fertile seed bed for these. Within formal expectations, teachers have to be both teachers and managers, schools have to be autonomous yet controlled, teachers have to collaborate yet compete, work individually and collegially, are excluded from policy implementation yet vital for putting the reforms in place. Add into this their own values and interests, and other sources and another layer of tensions arise over, for example, what should be taught and how.

The portrayal of primary teachers' work in the classroom as consisting in an almost continuous need to resolve a series of dilemmas was first popularized by the Berlaks in the 1970s (Berlak *et al.* 1976; Berlak and Berlak 1981). They noticed a number of apparent inconsistencies and contradictions in their teachers' behaviour, such as telling one child what to do while allowing another to make up her own mind. They postulated a framework consisting of a number of dilemmas in the general areas of 'control', 'curriculum' and 'society', which they felt conceptualized the complexity of teachers' meanings of classroom situations and the ways in which they were variously expressed in action. Basically, 'the teacher is drawn to some degree toward both poles of a dilemma' (ibid. 1976: 89), such as whether to treat the child as a 'whole child' or as 'student'; or to focus on knowledge as content or as process; or to opt for equal or differential allocation of resources. The Berlaks were interested in identifying 'specific patterns of resolution in behaviour' of these dilemmas. They use the term 'transformations' to describe resolutions of dilemmas 'where the pulls of both poles are joined.' The term designates 'those (rare) instances when the contending presses of the culture at least for the moment are synthesized and thus overcome' (ibid. 1981: 133). In other words, the problems, conflicts and difficulties associated with dilemmas are transformed into positive educational outcomes.

The Berlaks felt this model reflected teacher activity more adequately than polarized models, such as traditional–progressive, or formal–informal, since it typically contained aspects of both. In sociological terms, the model enabled analysis of how the construction of meanings by the teacher within the classroom resolved issues arising at the level of society. They argue that such dilemmas are inherent within liberal democratic society, emanating from the Enlightenment. They allow for a diversity of beliefs and some room for manoeuvre and negotiation in decision-making, such as would not be available in an authoritarian society imposing a single orientation upon schooling where teacher behaviour is almost totally determined by government policy.

A large number of alternative resolutions to the dilemmas noticed by the Berlaks is possible. For example, 'a teacher can follow different patterns of resolution for different children, and at different times of the year, or for different subjects or learning experiences' (ibid.: 91). On the matter of 'learning', there are decisions to be made on whether or not to learn, and what, when and how. In each case, teacher or child, or both, might decide. The Berlaks noted a variety of patterns of response, teachers being guided by certain principles. For example, the teacher may take most of the decisions in the 'basics', while leaving more scope for children's decisions in the non-basics. Or they might decide 'what' while leaving the child some discretion as to 'when'; or fix general parameters within which children make choices; and so on. There are almost endless possibilities – which faithfully reflects the complexities of teaching and the conflicts set up by the impacting of a number of opposing factors meeting in the moment-to-moment activity of the primary classroom. A complication is that teachers do not seem always to be aware of what is going on. In general (Berlak and Berlak 1981: 133),

> sometimes teachers' patterns of resolution seemed to be consciously chosen, deliberate efforts to put social and educational values into practice, though these choices were always qualified by situational constraints, some of which teachers recognized and discussed openly; at other times, teachers' patterns seemed almost totally mindless, sheer habit, or formed by cultural and social experiences and forces, or by internal needs of which they were but dimly aware.

The Berlaks' 'dilemma language' was certainly more appropriate for understanding what went on in primary classrooms in the 1970s than the dichotomous models which had predominated up to that point. But is it still appropriate? Alexander (1995), while finding the general idea suggestive, has criticized some aspects of the Berlaks' formulation, specifically their failure to produce evidence of teachers' awareness of the dilemmas as depicted by the researchers; and secondly for having too hard-and-fast categories – a charge the Berlaks themselves made about polarized models. To complement the Berlaks' work, Alexander draws from Argyris and Schon (1974). They see dilemmas arising from a professional's espoused theory versus theory in use, which causes an intellectual tension or inconsistency leading to discomfiture, which teachers try to avoid by deploying strategies, such as redirecting blame for any inconsistency to others rather to oneself, keeping the two sets of theory firmly apart (Keddie 1971), selectively suppressing elements producing the inconsistency (Alexander 1995: 24). Alexander consequently prefers the more generalized notion of 'competing imperatives', which, he argues, captures a sense of tension deriving from many sources and levels and encapsulates both the Berlaks' and Argyris and Schon's formulations. He claims that the teacher is at the intersection of many competing imperatives, and that they become more conscious of them as they become more experienced. Four sets or sources of 'competing imperatives' arise in his data:

● Openness and flexibility versus structure and predictability (in curriculum content, pedagogy and school building).
● Incremental, broad, undetailed planning versus full and long-term planning.
● Teacher as intervener versus non-interventionist.
● Grouping-management pressures versus the perceived need to group on a differential curriculum or activity basis; and how to distribute one's time and attention among the groups.

Changes in dilemmas

There have been changes in the nature and source of dilemmas, in professionalism in relation to dilemmas, and in the emphasis on the macro element. We shall consider each of these in turn.

Changes in the nature and source of dilemmas

Alexander (1995: 262) notes changes in teachers' experiences of dilemmas in three separate studies that he has conducted over the years. Pre-1988, his research indicated the following were prominent:

- Classroom organizational issues (such as use of space and resources; and a tension between themes and subjects).
- Management of learning issues (groupwork; distribution of the teacher's time among class).
- School issues (headteacher or school policy as opposed to ideas of the individual teacher).

The 1992 study revealed four problem areas:

- Assessment of the National Curriculum.
- Record-keeping.
- The range, quantity and content of the National Curriculum.
- Pressures to modify teaching, especially to introduce more whole-class teaching.

Alexander makes these points:

- Pre-1988, dilemmas were mainly about pedagogy.
- Post-1988, dilemmas were mainly about curriculum content and pupil assessment.

A dilemma can be transformed into a certainty over time; for example, teachers were ambivalent about comprehensive planning, predictability and structure in 1986. However, by 1992, they had become essential features of teaching. Alexander concludes, therefore, that while some dilemmas are intrinsic to teaching; others are induced by the political climate or fashion of the day – relating, perhaps, to different conceptions of the 'good' teacher.

The source as well as the nature of dilemmas has changed. In 1986 and 1988, teachers experienced pressures to conform to 'informal' ideas and practices from within the professional culture of primary teaching, mainly from heads and advisers. In this sense, problems and dilemmas were within the school and classroom, and teachers often blamed themselves for difficulties they experienced. After 1988, the National Curriculum emanated from outside the world of primary teaching (which led in turn to teacher solidarity; frustration and stress could be directed outside the school and profession and towards government and government agencies).

Increased importance of professionalism

Following this last point, one could argue that professionalism has become more of a central feature of teacher dilemmas. Evans *et al.* (1994: 206–7), studying teachers of infants' reactions to the National Curriculum, felt that

> The prime source of teachers' dilemmas was the concept of professionality with which they were operating. The implementation of the National Curriculum required teachers to define their work more broadly than teaching children; they had to participate in professional development and training, collaborate in planning with colleagues, engage in agreement trials on assessment in which they had to justify their judgements of pupil attainment. Moreover, they had to develop a view of the political purposes of the curriculum . . .

Evans *et al.* argue that teachers were resisting becoming 'extended professionals', which implementing the National Curriculum was requiring them to become, preferring a more 'restricted' view. 'Extended professionals' according to Hoyle (1975, 1980), are 'concerned with locating their classroom teaching in a broader educational context, comparing their work with that of other teachers, evaluating their work systematically, and collaborating with other teachers'. The extended professional is theory-friendly, concerned about educational and teacher development, and sees 'teaching as a rational activity amenable to improvement on the basis of research and development'. The 'restricted professional' is more circumscribed, less interested in theory and development, more focused on the 'here and now' in classroom practice. Are teachers already deprofessionalized, therefore, such that they now resist opportunities to extend that are afforded them in the National Curriculum? Evans *et al.* (1994: 209) conclude that dilemmas deriving from the conflict over curriculum priorities will be the least resolvable; whereas 'dilemmas arising from reduced professional confidence and esteem, and from reduced sense of autonomy, may come to be read as temporary, self-indulgent or anachronistic in a post-corporatist world where public servants . . . are accountable directly to their employers and indirectly to their consumers.'

Equally, some see professionalism of prime importance, but take a contrary view to Evans *et al.* We argued earlier that the 'teacher development' offered by the National Curriculum might be seen largely as acquiring a range of competencies. The 'extended professional' might be expected to oppose development along such limited lines, and to opt for continuing to wrestle with the dilemmas that are an intrinsic part of the job, and which provide scope for intellectual extension. Maguire (1995: 130; see also Rudduck

1992), for example, argues that the current focus on teacher competencies elevates technical skills training above intellectual work:

> What may get lost in all this may be the interrogation of pedagogy, the tentativeness and the questioning which characterize the creative and informed professional teacher. If teacher education becomes recon-structed as a 'rational' task of attaining competences rather than a complex set of dilemmas which require reflexive consideration, then there may be very real consequences for teacher professionalism.

The existence of dilemmas is taken here as a sign of a healthy situation (Postman and Weingartner 1969: 204):

> To discount the contribution of dilemmatic choices to lifelong learning is to become urban ostriches. Instead, acknowledgement that dilemmas pervade our lives, and in doing so promote development, can produce people who are 'actively inquiring, flexible, creative, innovative, toler-ant . . . who can face uncertainty and ambiguity without disorientation'.

More emphasis on the macro element

A further development has been that the macro level of dilemma has be-come more apparent. Some of these dilemmas, such as whether to central-ize or decentralize, are evident in Chapter 1. From these, a number of other dilemmas develop – such as management versus teaching, competition or collaboration, teaching old skills or new skills – but all can be traced back to the Government's policy and beyond. As the Berlaks originally argued, the dilemmas experienced by teachers at classroom level are invariably to some extent (though not all – see Alexander above) expressions of central dilemmas of value, purpose and control which permeate society. A. Hargreaves (1994a, b) sees these as being embodied in four major areas of tension, what he calls 'dilemmas of restructuring – ones that have powerful implications for the purposes of restructuring and the directions it will take and for the processes of teacher development contained within it' (ibid. 1994a: 57). They are:

- Vision or voice? (the development of a common vision and shared goals versus the encouragement of teachers' voices, which may be dissident).
- Mandates or menus? (reflecting the shift from 'single and relatively stable belief systems to multiple and rapidly shifting ones' (ibid. 1994a: 63).
- Trust in processes or trust in people ? (trust in 'the qualities and conduct of individuals' versus trust in 'the expertise and performance of abstract systems' (ibid. 1994b: 252).
- Structure or culture? (that is, planning for change mainly through restruc-turing the curriculum versus encouraging development through building on existing beliefs, practices and working relationships).

In considering solutions to these dilemmas, Hargreaves (1994a: 74), while clearly sympathetic to the second items in the list above, does not see it as a matter of 'either/or'. For example, teacher culture depends on the kind of school structure that is in place. If we wish to encourage new cultures, we may have to institute new structures.

> The reality of restructuring is that these structural prerequisites of teacher collaboration may need to be imposed so that teachers can create continuous cultural change and generate future structural change themselves.

How far that is a realistic vision of the future is another matter. These seem to us to be abiding dualities. From time to time, the emphasis changes, with the eternal quest being the most productive balance between the two. In recent years, the weight has swung significantly towards the first items in Hargreaves' list. The result is that dilemmas are to some extent experienced differently from how they were in the Berlaks' day, as we discuss below.

Some definitions

Before considering how our data inform the dilemmas model, we find it useful to consider the terms of the debate in a little more detail. This interrogation will then enable us to demonstrate how, in some respects, conflicts within teaching remain the same as they were in a previous generation, and in some respects have become different. We find it convenient to distinguish between dilemmas, tensions and constraints. These are all imperatives that press on the teacher and cannot be ignored. They have to be confronted and demand action. Sometimes the imperatives are 'competing', as in 'dilemmas' and 'tensions'; sometimes the competition becomes one-sided, and the imperatives squeeze and force in one direction regardless of the teacher's wishes, as in constraints. We shall examine each of these in turn.

Dilemmas

Miller (1994) sees a dilemma as 'a particular type of predicament which occurs when the pressing alternatives available, or serious obligations we face, seem so evenly balanced that it is hard, sometimes impossible to make a choice' (reported in Denicolo 1995: 3). Miller suggests (1994: 30–31) that dilemmas are

- everyday occurrences, yet pressing and serious to the participants, not trifling or inconsequential;
- conflict situations, presenting evenly balanced choices or obligations;

- conflicts derived from the incompatible demands of either a single principle or a pluralistic ethic;
- situations which cause unfavourable consequences, i.e. leaving some remainder, whichever alternative is selected; and are
- distinguishable from problems in that only the latter leave no remainder and are eliminated when solved. Dilemmas cause some personal concern and urgency, and may involve feelings of regret or guilt.

Taking this into account, together with previous work on dilemmas, we see them as having the following properties, which we discuss below:

- Awareness.
- Choice, but difficult.
- Situational.
- The options are evenly balanced and incompatible (Billig 1988).
- Necessity. This may be both *legal*, where a choice *has* to be made by law; and/or *moral*, where values inform the choice. The two may conflict.
- Usually, whatever the choice in dilemma resolution, it is seen as leading to unfavourable consequences. Denicolo (1995), however, prefers a formulation which allows the possibility of positive outcomes (see also Day and Hadfield 1995). We also take this view.

For something to be experienced as a dilemma, teachers must be aware or conscious of it being so. They are confronted by choice, which they are free to make, although at times it may be difficult to do. Billig (1988: 163) writes:

> What is involved is clearly not a straightforward issue of choice, of alternative courses of action, nor on the other hand a matter of intellectual puzzles or paradoxes . . . The characteristic of a dilemma which makes it significant for social analysis is that it is more complex than a simple choice or even a straightforward technical problem . . .

What makes decisions difficult is that the alternative courses are mutually exclusive. Thus, classroom teaching versus group teaching is not necessarily a dilemma – both may feature harmoniously within a teacher's repertoire. Similarly, many teachers have a measure of classroom autonomy and whole-school planning, and it might be claimed that in some circumstances, one reinforces the other. There has to be a profit or loss or both associated with any decisions made. Legal versus moral requirements are a familiar theme here.

We shall regard dilemmas as situational in the sense that they are largely resolvable by professional action. This is not to say that dilemmas are just intellectual problems to which one simply applies intelligence to solve. Dilemmas are lived experience – they are processes. Thus, the potential dilemma of teaching the whole class versus teaching individuals has to be resolved within the particular situation in the light of what has gone before and what will come after, in both immediate and longer term perspectives; and through the experience and perspective of the teacher concerned. In other words, dilemmas have a history, a future and a context. Decisions, therefore, are not easy, and require the knowledge, skill, experience and judgement of a successful teacher. Also desirable is an 'actively inquiring, flexible, creative, innovative, tolerant, liberal personality, who can face uncertainty and ambiguity without disorientation' (Postman and Weingartner 1971: 204). Dilemmas are not stressful by our definition (see Chapter 6, p. 145) – if they are, they are 'tensions' or 'constraints'. Thus, a reflexive, professional teacher can resolve whether to teach the whole class or individuals, on a pragmatic, fitness-for-purpose basis. Dilemmas involving the need to control, the need to befriend and the need to teach are resolved through cultivating the skill of 'orchestration' (Woods 1990). Dilemmas involving the difference between child as student and the whole child are resolved by the careful construction of a culture of teaching and learning to which both teacher and students subscribe.

To say that dilemmas are situational is not to objectify them. They are constructed through interaction between teacher and situation. Thus, what is a dilemma for one teacher can be a tension or constraint for another. For example, an inexperienced teacher is more likely to find the same situation tension-ridden than a more experienced one. Similarly, there is less risk of tension where one's values accord with a situation than where they do not. Billig (1988: 163) observes:

> The characteristics of dilemmas are revealed as fundamentally born out of a culture which produces more than one possible ideal world, more than one hierarchical arrangement of power, value and interest. In this sense, social beings are confronted by and deal with dilemmatic situations as a condition of their humanity.

Nor, if dilemmas are situational, are they unconnected to meso and macro spheres. Awareness of dilemmas means that they are frequently the subject of debate among teachers and subject to collective decisions. The discussion may take the debate out of the pragmatic world of the everyday and into the macro area, or more general principle from which the dilemma arises. For instance, at a staff meeting, held immediately prior to an Ofsted inspection, the main debate was over whether to spend time constructing samples of children's work for validation of individual assessments and as aids to comparative assessment, or whether to photocopy the work directly from the pupils' books. At one point, the deputy head wanted to discuss the whole matter of teacher judgement versus the necessary presentation of evidence. The debate began as a technical one, but developed into a more general, moral one concerning whether teacher judgements were acceptable, or whether teachers had to provide evidence concerning those judgements to satisfy managerial accountability. Darling (1993) argues that dilemmas need to be tackled at this level since their resolution does not necessarily lie within the classroom.

Tension

Billig (1988: 163) describes dilemmas as 'social situations in which people are pushed and pulled in opposing directions'. However, to distinguish these from a different kind of imperative, we prefer to regard these as tensions. Tensions pull or stretch, perhaps in many opposing directions at once, and are less amenable than dilemmas to professional action. Stress and strain is the result. Tension is the product of trying to accommodate two or more opposing courses of action where choice is limited or circumscribed. Thus, dilemmas become 'tensions' where factors beyond the teacher's control impede decision-making. The teacher resolves tensions strategically, often on a political rather than educational basis. Whereas dilemmas are situational, requiring professional action for resolution, tensions invade the inner self, arouse stronger emotions, are more personal than professional, and are added problems for those teachers who combine self with the teacher role, as many primary teachers do (Nias 1989). We might draw a contrast again, therefore, between (1) the more usual kinds of role conflict or role strain (D.H. Hargreaves 1972), which, like dilemmas, are capable of being accommodated within the primary teacher culture, and (2) role tension, which causes problems and arouses emotions of a new order. Again, tensions are processes and interactions, so a similar set of circumstances can be experienced as complementary to the role by one teacher, and as role tension by another. We discuss some of these instances in Chapters 3, 4 and 5.

Constraint

If dilemmas are situational and tensions personal, constraints are structural, in the sense that they are beyond personal resolution within the immediate context. Constraint implies compulsion, force, repression of natural feelings. Constraint operates against the choice of perceived better alternatives. It thus restricts the free resolution of dilemmas and removes even the element of choice involved in tensions, and determines their transformation in particular ways. This is not to say that all constraint is counterproductive. Like other activities in social life, teaching has to take place within certain parameters. But, heretofore, teachers have enjoyed a degree of negotiability in the implementation of policy (Ball and Bowe 1992; Fitz 1994). This appears to be becoming squeezed. We consider some forms of constraint that attend the drive for more collaboration among school staff in Chapter 2. We discuss and illustrate cause, occurrence and nature of constraint in the production of teacher stress in Chapter 6.

Barthes's (1976) distinction between 'readerly' and 'writerly' policy texts might clarify the difference among these imperatives further. The individual has more scope for interpretation in the latter, little in the former. Whether a text is one or the other depends to some extent on the interaction between reader and text. The outcome depends to a large extent on what Helsby (1995: 324–5) calls 'professional confidence', which

> implies a belief both in one's authority and in one's capacity to make important decisions about the conduct of one's work. To some extent these beliefs are shaped by custom, by training and by previous experience, but they may be undermined by challenges to, or disturbances in, the existing system and practices.

Helsby's evidence showed a fall-off in professional confidence since 1988. Her teachers experienced a 'loss of autonomy, an increase in prescription and a loss of trust' – in other words, a growth of constraint. As the space for choice diminishes and confidence drops, so erstwhile dilemmas are experienced more and more as tensions and constraints. Teachers feel forced into doing things when they feel strongly that it would be more morally sound and more genuinely educationally productive to be doing some other contrasting activity. The result is frustration, overload, stress, ingenious adaptation – as we illustrate in later chapters.

Dilemmas in context

Table 1.1 summarizes, in very broad terms, the model suggested by our data. We distinguish between dilemmas, tensions and constraints, mainly on the degree of choice available to the teacher. They tend to have different locations, and different kinds of outcome, predominant in different periods. The model might be linked with the 'opportunities to teach and learn' (OTAL) model expounded in Woods (1990), which suggested three major types of teaching according to opportunity – creative, where teachers are afforded opportunities to exercise their skills (transforming dilemmas); coping, where opportunities are more limited (seeking to resolve tensions); and survival teaching, where opportunities are non-existent or under threat, or running counter to aspirations (subjugation under constraints).

We should stress that these are tendencies, and not absolutes. It is not a static model. Though in general we would argue that teaching has become more tension-ridden and constrained and less dilemmatic, things can move in the reverse direction. We give one illustration of how this can be done in Chapter 5 (a 'reconstruction of self'). Also, all three types of pressure have been experienced to some degree or other in all three periods indicated. As

Table 1.1 Teaching imperatives

Imperative	Experiential site	Degree of choice	Outcome	Period
Dilemma	Situational	Free	Creative resolution	Pre-ERA*
Tension	Personal	Limited	Strategic coping	Post-ERA
Constraint	Structural	Little or none	Survival Personal adjustment Resistance Stress	Post-Ofsted

* ERA, Education Reform Act 1988.

we have noted, too, these experiences differ according to teacher stance. For one teacher, a situation might be experienced as a dilemma that is experienced as a constraint by another teacher. In sum, as far as our research is concerned, there have been three main changes since the time of the Berlaks' research:

- As dilemmas have proliferated and intensified, so has teachers' ingenuity at transforming them into certainties. The Berlaks felt that transformations were rare, but we found them a common feature of *creative teachers'* work. We have shown in earlier studies (Woods 1995; Woods and Jeffrey 1996b) how teacher ingenuity is a match for some new, some old, dilemmas which teachers had to face.
- Some of what used to be dilemmas, however, have developed into tensions and/or constraints. The studies reported in this book show a marked move towards tension and constraint.
- Teacher dilemmas now appear to differ in *kind*, being more value-based. The debate engendered by the reforms of recent years has increased consciousness of dilemmas in general, and of their existence at different levels.

We illustrate these developments in the schools of our research in the rest of the book.

CHAPTER 2

Collaborating under constraint

INTRODUCTION

Teacher ingenuity at devising transformations, as illustrated in Woods and Jeffrey (1996b) is not enough to cope with all of the difficulties that confront them. In some areas, teachers are experiencing tensions and constraints where formerly there may have been dilemmas. As Pollard *et al.* (1994: 240) note:

> Rather than providing a legislative framework through which they could offer and fulfil their professional commitment, the reforms introduced constraint and regulation into almost every area of teachers' work.

The restriction of choice in these areas forces them, often against their will, towards one pole of the imperative. The effect of this is towards restricted professionalism. This is evident in the area of *collaboration*, a key aspect of teacher culture in recent years.

In response to the demands for restructuring, the 1980s saw a shift from the old paternalistic and authoritarian styles of management in primary schools towards collaborative approaches to whole-school change (Wallace 1988). Nias *et al.* (1989, 1994) give one illustration of such an approach in the 'culture of collaboration' they identified in three of the five primary schools of their research. Such cultures were marked by valuing both individuality (person above role) and interdependence, by awareness of belonging to a group and a collective sense of responsibility. These aims were secured through valuing openness (freedom to admit mistakes, display anger, guilt, grief, etc.) and a sense of mutual security. They also noted strong leadership. There is potential for professional development here through the free exchange of opinions. Nias *et al.* (1994: 272) point out that 'collaborative staffs tended to be both happy and resilient'. They would provide excellent forums for the transformation of dilemmas.

Elsewhere, Nias (1989: 167) talks of 'bounded professionals':

> [These] have whole-school perspectives and an interest in collabora-
> tion and collegiality but are largely atheoretical and school-bounded
> in their approach to other educational issues. Like 'extended profes-
> sionals' they derive satisfaction 'from problem-solving activities and from
> a greater control over their work situation' (Hoyle 1974: 18), but like
> 'restricted professionals' they also find great rewards in successful class-
> room practice.

One response to the new managerialist demands that have been made since
these analyses, has been the development of what A. Hargreaves (1994b) terms
'contrived collegiality'. This involves collaboration, certainly, but contrasts
with that identified by Nias in that 'teachers' collaborative working relationships are not spontaneous, voluntary, development-oriented . . .' (ibid.: 195).
They are, rather, administratively regulated, compulsory, implementation-
oriented, fixed in time and space, and predictable (see also Warren-Little
1987; Wallace 1991).

There is currently a great deal of rhetoric about collaborative school planning, but considerable problems about its implementation (Osborn and Black
1994). Given this, one might expect a range of different responses, with a
number of compromises and trade-offs. In her study of a primary school
immediately following the Education Reform Act of 1988, for example, Acker
(1990b) noted signs of a change from a culture of collaboration to one showing signs of bounded professionality. There was still critical and reflective
discussion, but now more on immediate practical problems which the teachers
needed to solve. 'The tensions as teachers struggled to come to a compromise
between the old and the new ways seemed clearly evident . . .' (ibid.: 268).
Pollard *et al.* (1994: 93) observed that

> enforced collegiality can sometimes lead to a lack of ownership in the
> planned work and hence a loss of interest and spontaneity. On the
> whole, however, most of the teachers welcomed the increase in collab-
> oration and partnership with colleagues, and felt that it added a new
> dimension to their professionalism.

Elsewhere (ibid.: 240) they note a development of collegiality in some schools,
but mainly as a form of resistance to the Government's reforms, rather than
as a means of working towards goals shared with the Government. The general trend, however, was away from collaboration in managing change to more
managerial and directed approaches (ibid.: 75). Similarly, Webb and Vulliamy
(1996: 158) in their research, identify a form of tension 'between collegial and
top-down managerial approaches to whole school change'. They noted the
breaking down of the old individualist culture, and increased cooperation
among colleagues in a number of areas; but 'equally strong if not stronger
forces appeared to be combining to promote directive management styles by

headteachers, which undermine the feasibility and credibility of teachers working together collegially . . .' (ibid.: 158–9).

We also noticed a mixed response from our teachers. On the one hand, the introduction of the National Curriculum has stimulated their appreciation of new forms of collaboration: 'It took a bit of getting used to, actually working in a team, but in the end we could see that people had so much to offer.' However, in other respects, increasing managerialism is creating new tensions in the area for teachers, and imposing constraints on their own preferred mode of development. We use case studies here to examine

- some of the complexities and contradictions involved in the notion of 'collaboration',
- the nature of tensions and constraints in this area, and how they are experienced and tackled,
- the dynamics of developing a collaborative culture, and
- the educational significance of these developments.

In Part A, we examine teachers' experiences of collaboration in some of our study schools where 'enforced' collaboration has the effect not only of defeating its own objectives at the formal level, but also of killing off any genuine collaboration that had operated informally in their schools. An interesting question is: if contrived collegiality is a result of the changes, how actually does it come about, especially if the original intention was to encourage more genuine collaboration? What are the corrupting elements in the process, and to what extent are they a product of the constraints of centralist policies? In Part B, therefore, we consider a head's attempt in one of our schools to replace the stark individualism and separatism of the previous order with a new collaborative culture. Whatever the educational merits of collaboration, the most prominent feature of the process of establishment was the micropolitics the head felt obliged to deploy to achieve his aims, which appears to run counter to the kind of collaborative spirit formerly identified by Nias *et al.* (1989). The chapter thus illustrates the anti-educational consequences of enforced collaboration, and provides insight into the processes that, in spite of these anti-educational results, constrain schools towards that end.

PART A: COLLABORATIVE CONSTRAINTS

How constrained collaborative cultures can become is illustrated in several of the schools featuring in our research. What is actually constrained, in what way, and with what educational consequences? We seek answers to these questions by focusing on three prominent areas of constraint indicated by our research: overkill, shortfalls and institutionalized discourses.

Table 2.1 gives some basic information about the schools and teachers who have informed this section.

Table 2.1 Collaborative constraints. Schools and teachers involved

School	Teachers and their experience
Livery 200 pupils. A small inner-city school. 50 per cent free dinners	Laura (15 years) (Years 2 and 3), Luke (20 years) (Year 5) Catrina (20 years) (Deputy Head – floating) Anita (10 years)
Hillside Over 300 pupils. Mid-sized suburban school. 30 per cent free dinners	Gwen (25 years) (Year 6)
Girthwaite Over 300 pupils. Mid-sized estate school. 50 per cent free dinners	Marilyn (25 years) (Year 6)
Flatley School Over 600 pupils. Large inner-city school. 73 per cent free dinners	Grace (25 years) (Year 4) Shula (13 years) (Year 3)
Panstation School 200 pupils. Small inner-city school. 73 per cent free dinners	Nadine (4 years) (Year 2)
Lowerside School 200 pupils. Small inner-city school. 63 per cent free dinners	Bernadette (20 years) (Year 2)

Collaborative overkill

The innovations have entailed an escalation in the number of meetings teachers are required to attend. This schedule is a typical example:

> 'Monday we have senior management meetings, then we have Tuesday's staff meeting. This Wednesday we have key stage coordination meetings and Thursday lunchtime we have a school administration meeting . . . We used to be able to support the administration of the school on one meeting a month.'

> (Laura)

There are many more coordinators' meetings, informal meetings with parents and governors' meetings and subcommittees at which staff have to explain and account for school policies in specific areas, which, for the most part, teachers accept as part of their accountability. In spite of teachers being interested in being part of the decision-making processes in the school, the amount of time taken up by these processes impinges on their classroom practice.

> '[I] didn't get home until twenty to nine last night, and the time that I was in school before the Governors' meeting was a staff meeting. It

wasn't me planning and organizing my classroom, getting ready for today. Consequently, by twenty to nine I've had it, my brain has been active all day . . . So it does impinge on your teaching because no longer are you spending the time in preparation that you did. Last week I had meetings every night.'

(Marilyn)

Marilyn is a member of the senior management team and has a host of responsibilities – teacher governor, language coordinator, upper school co-ordinator – as does Grace, who initially welcomed working as a team, and who is the deputy head of a large school, but even she wants to have time in her classroom on her own:

'Actually, that's the time of day I'm happiest, at the end of the day when they've all gone home and I potter and I'm thinking about the next day. That's my kind of productive time, and then I can go home and rest. But when they ask me to do things that take up my time and make me tired and I find of no value, it makes me angry. It's like you're not allowed to say that. You feel that you could be crucifying yourself by coming out with statements like that, but I don't care any more, and I want to say it loud and I want to scream, that's the way I feel.'

(Grace)

Teachers come to Laura for resources and to discuss other issues at awkward times and interrupt her preparation because *their* time has been taken up with meetings:

'Catrina came in because she wanted to discuss some issue with me, then Anita came in and wanted to discuss something about the class, but I was thinking: "I've come in at eight o'clock to really make sure my classroom's resourced, so that I've got needles and cottons and every-thing's ready." But I didn't get it done, and it wasn't because I wasn't trying. It was just because there were other demands.'

(Laura)

Nadine expresses the tension of being part of the corporate management (Corrie 1995) and giving enough time to their busy demanding classrooms:

'I would like not to have to resist management pressures. I spend all night worrying about how to say "Let's not have a lunchtime meeting" . . . You are thinking all the time of ways around what you are doing. Pulling yourself in different directions. Standing firm and then worry-ing about what they want you to do. It's continuous thinking.'

(Nadine)

The 'pulling in different directions' is indicative of the problem of encroach-ment into teachers' mental spaces, as is the distinction teachers make between productive curriculum meetings and other managerial demands which constrain the development of the former, as Grace observes:

> 'It takes time, but it isn't only that. We have other meetings to do with other aspects of the school. If we could just focus in and forget about all the other crap, the recordings and everything else and just really put the emphasis on the quality of teaching ... But you have to put every other aspect you have in place. Your special needs [are] taking so much time, plus making sure discipline is in order, dealing with the full range of curriculum areas, and add to that staffing and the budget. There's constantly so many other things.'
>
> (Grace)

Focusing-in is a key quality of productive collaboration, but an overabundance of managerial demands prevents appropriate focusing:

> 'Well, you spend so much time in bloody planning, it's a lot of effort before you actually start. You're doing the planning for next term the term before you've finished the topic you're doing. You're heavy into doing, say, Tudors and Stuarts and you have to start thinking about Ancient Greeks. It's constant.'
>
> (Grace)

In collaborative terms, managerialism can lead to unproductive practices. Shula, from the same school, talks in terms that indicate that overplanning can lead to undercommitment. The staff met in departments, and the planning for the term was shared out in pairs, each of which prepared work for two-week periods in order to try to construct an integrated curriculum worked by everyone. Whilst many liked the arrangement, others were sceptical:

> 'Eve and I did the preparation for our department for the first week back. I hold little hope that it will be the same for all the other pairs and combinations who plan after that. As far as I know, people are happy with the arrangements, but it means that the people who are lazy have an easier ride. That's the nature of people, isn't it ... ? Where does their responsibility come in, when do they have to look at a document? If someone's always producing something for you, what makes you go and look at a document? You don't if it's all produced for you, organized; you never have to open a folder because it's already done.'
>
> (Shula)

Easen (1994) suggests that collaborative team meetings have little effect on the substance of primary teachers' daily lives except in terms of accountability, and that a better model of a collaborative culture would be to recognize primary teachers as highly collaborative *and* highly autonomous. The consequences of overprescription from the school collaborative group is that the collaborative process itself becomes seen as less than sincere and less authentic.

Collaborative shortfalls

The quality of the experience matters as well as having time in which it can happen. For example, Gwen loves school journeys, in spite of being on duty 24 hours a day, the dominating activity is with children: 'You're with children, you like children, because it's a real experience for them rather than talking about things. It's a lot of social things with the children.' At school level, collaboration and corporateness can become ends in themselves. If choices are only allowed over trivial matters or matters that restrict the implementation of the teachers' values, then there are further constraints placed on teachers, not just in terms of time and space, but in teachers' commitment to 'extended professionalism':

> 'Yesterday, we talked about the job description in the business meeting and what it entailed. From this we compiled a list on the wall as to the extra jobs we should be doing like collecting coffee cups and watering plants. Now I agree that for the smooth running of the school those things have got to be done, but it seemed to me that the main issue was the statements in the job description. But we ended up discussing, for half an hour in our lunchtime, whether we should take coffee cups back to the staffroom or not. Sometimes I find it really frustrating.
>
> 'It's ever so difficult to come to any sort of decision about the running of the school when you've got 14 or 15 people who have got opposed views as to the colour of a school sweatshirt. How many hours of discussion need to take place? All these decisions! Everybody should be involved, should feel they're involved and have, I think the word these days is to have "ownership". So because of that, we need to spend a lot of time discussing it. I personally feel it's a waste of time and I would rather somebody took this decision. I may or may not agree with it but I would live with that and I'd like to get on with my job. I actually feel that when it comes to discussing what sort of report forms we have in the back of our assessment folders, I don't have strong feelings. I'll fill any sort of form in they want. I don't want to discuss it because I know that people aren't going to agree, and at the end of the day, the people who feel most pressured will just shut up but feel disgruntled. I'm coming to the conclusion that democracy isn't always useful and I'm horrified that I'm thinking that sort of thing. This is really a movement towards benign dictatorship or something. I don't know. I'm as confused about this as anybody, but I am beginning to see so much time spent inefficiently arguing about such trivialities and seeing the complaints and the tempers running high, the aggravations and the damage it does to relationships, it's not worth going through the facade of democracy.'
>
> (Gwen)

There is also a facade of power. Laura illustrates the diminution of choice typical of constraints:

> 'More power to do what? More power to spend your diminishing budget and choose what not to spend it on? More choice about which staff to cut, more choice about whether to have ancillary helpers or stock, shall we do without an Nursery Assistant or shall we buy a new computer? These are the sorts of choices we've got now, and is this power?'
>
> (Laura)

Collaborative processes may not necessarily arrive at the best result, and where they damage a great deal of an experienced teacher's values, then they not only constrain the teacher, but they may cast further doubt on the efficacy of the collaborative process. A school staff made a democratic decision to adopt a local education authority scheme of work that incorporated all aspects of the National Curriculum. The older, more experienced members were sceptical of the advantages of the plan, but they and the headteacher were committed to a democratic way of working and they were conscious of the feelings of the new teachers who outnumbered them.

> 'I went along with it because I felt that the new teachers wanted to see some kind of structure [and] because I felt for the kind of sanity of people in the school at the moment. Not having any experience to go on themselves, apart from what they learnt in college, they didn't see what we were doing right.'
>
> (Luke)

Laura, in the same school, summarizes the situation after a year of operating the scheme:

> 'The ideal of all the staff being involved in the decision-making is that it sounds a really nice one, but you often have a situation where you might have people who are just not qualified to make the decisions, aren't aware of the importance or the results of their decision-making. They don't realize what a straitjacket such a prescriptive planning document can be and now they do and they can't believe they voted for it. It's democratic, but maybe it wasn't appropriate, and maybe somebody like the head, who has got many years' experience, might be more properly suited to make that decision.'
>
> (Laura)

Debates and discussion are central to collaborative processes but if the only agenda is concerned with choices that are concerned with trivia and cost-cutting exercises, or there is no time to research fully the benefits and drawbacks of new systems, then teachers' commitment to collaboration becomes threatened.

Institutionalized discourse

An important feature of the collaborative culture is the informal discussions and conversations that take place in 'back regions' (Goffman 1968), outside the arena of formal lessons and institutional and curriculum processes. Laura thinks there is still a measure of this:

> 'I think there still is a simple normal network because we're social creatures, and we still pop into classrooms and chat and say, "Hey, that's really nice, I like the way you've done that, I could use that, I'll do it different." We still get this input from each other.'
>
> (Laura)

However, the *nature* of talk between teachers has become a focus of concern as Laura observes:

> 'Meetings are now institutionalizing the conversations between teachers. Normally, teachers used to go and relax in the staffroom for half an hour and have a chat about what was going on. Schools used to function on this and it was a relaxed and nurturing way of swapping information. Now we have meetings because we have to keep records of the way information is being exchanged. What we're really doing is institutionalizing the informal discourse. It's almost as though it doesn't count unless you've had a meeting about it and written up the minutes.'
>
> (Laura)

This is another constraint on teachers' ways of working. The swapping of teaching ideas becomes the property of the corporate discourse:

> 'I said, "Hey! Look at this, what do you think of this? You could do this with your class." She replied, "Oh yes, could you bring it up in the meeting?" And I thought, "Well, not really, because I just haven't got time to do that. I'm just mentioning that this is a really rich and useful activity you could do." '
>
> (Laura)

Candide explains why she was more motivated by an idea that arose spontaneously,

> 'Because this one was alive, it wasn't just a cold piece of paper. It was alive, it was getting excited about the idea and then me trying them and getting excited about them and then Frances doing them . . . Because if something comes from collaboration with your colleagues, like working in partnership and it comes from you, you've got ownership to make that work, and when that works you're excited about it.'
>
> (Candide)

Whilst the spontaneity might still be around to some extent, Marilyn notes a subtle change in the content of talk, even in the informal situations:

'It's more centred around behaviour and National Curriculum. I think that's a change that's crept up on you without you perhaps realizing that it was happening. It's a change in the conversation in the staff-room. There aren't so many of those impromptu get togethers as there used to be.'

(Marilyn)

The institutionalizing of the informal discourse means more time is spent in formal meetings to the detriment of classroom work. Collaboration becomes counterproductive. Laura would like to discuss an aspect of maths pedagogy at one meeting, but is aware that this will take even more time, and there is other work to be done in the classroom before the school is locked up for the day. So it does not get discussed:

'Now I could talk to members of staff about maths teaching at other times in an informal way but it isn't validated anymore . . . We're insti-tutionalizing what was the normal conversation, the exchange of skills, the support, it's all becoming institutionalized, supported by, or weighed down by the paperwork.'

(Laura)

She feels:

'The informal network was stronger, because there's only so much energy. You just get tired after a while, and because there was more time to talk, you felt more relaxed about things in the past and so there was more time, not only to support members of staff who did need it, but to notice members of staff who needed it . . . Whereas now one is more likely to fill in a form and write down what the problem is, and it's sometimes quite difficult for somebody to articulate what their prob-lem is, because in a sense, if you can articulate what the problem is you've solved it. So it takes quite a lot of talking around to find out what it is.'

(Laura)

She also notes that, in the past, meetings may have helped in a therapeutic way by allowing discussions of how people feel about their work. The situa-tion now takes a purely problem-solving approach:

'When there's a meeting to discuss curriculum matters, there's very little point in having a meeting to have a whinge. Though it's thera-peutic and everybody needs it, you have a meeting to suggest positive solutions to problems, so in a sense these meetings are rarely thera-peutic. Now if you've got a member of staff who is needing support for all sorts of different reasons, this isn't really meeting the needs of that member of staff.'

(Laura)

Shula, deputy head, also feels that the dominant management style is a problem-solving one rather than an individual and therapeutic one:

'My perception now is that people come to me with a problem because I'm seen as a specialist. Whether it's to do with a specific child or whether it's to do with a particular area of equipment, they expect me to tell them how to deliver it. They are expecting an answer. They're not expecting "I don't know," whereas before I could say things like, "It doesn't work for me either." This is because of the pressure of the curriculum, because you've got to get through so much, because people are themselves worried because they don't think they're giving enough depth to the work. So I've become more of a specialist in solving-problems, and quickly. It's meant that, whereas in the past I might be thinking about how the children will learn or how groups will interact or the effects of a particular child on the group dynamics or whatever, I find I can't afford the time to really play around with it in my head. I need to get in there, listen to the problem, ask pertinent questions and be able to say, "Right, how about trying this," and they trot off quite happily because you've given them something to do. I don't think that you should just necessarily talk about a problem. We should have time for a little counselling session here.'

(Shula)

Shula has highlighted the human aspect of managing, which has become lost in the intensification that constrains her work. Efficient managerialism comes to mean quick solutions to various problems so that the next one can be addressed and tackled. This whole process may then create more problems in the wake of ineffective short-termism. As A. Hargreaves (1994a: 138) notes:

Reform is often guided by the belief that every problem has a solution. Perhaps the real challenge of reform as a continuous process, though, is acknowledging that every solution has a problem. This is the ultimate perversity of postmodernity.

When primary teachers criticize more collaboration at school level, they may not just be attempting to hang on to more autonomy and resisting 'extended professionalism', as argued by Evans *et al.* (1994). They may be responding to current 'imperatives' of primary teaching and considering the consequences of a managerialist approach that favours more collaboration in the interests of a more corporate institution, and which may not be totally productive in terms of pupils' learning. The constraints illustrated here are indicators of more of a contrived collegiality.

PART B: CONTRIVING A COLLABORATIVE CULTURE

How do such cultures come to be established? In this section, we explore aspects of the process of change in the organization and culture of one primary school which has collaboration as a central aim. 'Meadowfields' caters for 450 pupils in the $4\frac{1}{2}$ to 11 age range. It has a staff of 17 teachers, and enjoys a good reputation in the community and with the local education authority. We are concerned with developments in the school during the period 1986–1994. We focus on the head's attempts to transform the school culture from one characterized by teachers' individualist practices, to one in which collaborative working and whole-school decision-making was institutionalized. We shall explore this head's more general adaptation to his new role in Chapter 4.

From the 'pyramid' to the 'moving mosaic'?

Our analysis is based upon data derived from conversations, interviews with and observation of the headteacher, James Davies (who was appointed in 1986), teachers and learning support assistants in Meadowfields school over an 18-month period in 1995–1996. Under the previous head, the school had a good reputation in the community for discipline, traditional values and high academic standards. The school was run on regimental lines, with a 'top-down' management model. Scale posts were few and were allocated to the 'team leaders' of each of the units. Team leaders had some power but were largely conduits for the head's curriculum and organizational decisions, and had attained scale posts for reasons of seniority and organizational responsibility more than curriculum responsibility. The head maintained surveillance and control of the curriculum by touring classrooms and correcting teachers: 'We don't do art in the mornings here' (comment to a teacher found doing art at the 'wrong' time of day); 'We don't do things that way here' (comment to a teacher trying to introduce more informal teacher–pupil relationships). On some occasions the deputy head was instructed to 'have a word' with an erring teacher. Despite the extent of pedagogic and curricular control, the teachers enjoyed a 'relative' classroom autonomy in curriculum knowledge and teaching methods. Collaborative work between the teachers did not take place. Even trying to 'borrow' resources from a colleague was out of the question. A strict division of labour existed between teachers and classroom assistants. The work of these ancillaries was restricted to making tea, cleaning paint brushes, mixing paints and preparing displays, while the teachers worked in isolation in their classrooms, being solely responsible for teaching and learning. Parents were kept at arm's length, indeed 'discouraged from coming into the school'.

The previous head clearly belongs to the 'headmaster tradition' in English schooling, one which maintained a 'powerful culture of school leadership' (Grace 1996: 76). He operated a 'robust autocracy' (ibid.) and articulated a discourse central to which were notions of 'my school', 'my teachers' (Alexander 1984). This tradition 'has been an obstacle to the development of more democratic and participative forms of school governance' (Grace 1996: 76).

James Davies was appointed head of Meadowfields in 1986. This was his first headship. He had taught in primary schools since 1968 and had wide experience of primary education as a class teacher and deputy head. Central to his plans for change were teacher collaboration and involvement in whole-school decision-making. His first attempts, before the Education Reform Act 1988, were met with resistance by the 'old professionals' (Riseborough 1984; Pollard 1987; Troman 1996a) – staff committed to the old regime and very reluctant to change – who adopted a range of wrecking tactics, including much complaining, challenges to the head's authority, disrupting policy working groups, lobbying senior members of staff and stubborn continuance of old practices.

James came to feel, therefore, that cultural change would require more direct intervention on his part. An early initiative was to find a way of removing a powerful symbol of the old organizational culture – the school bell. Under the old regime, this had signalled the end of lessons every 25 minutes and the whole school moved to different teachers:

> 'After the first month I just couldn't cope with the bell any longer. I called a staff meeting and I said I was actually going to stop the bell. Then, of course, there was a huge resistance from the older members of staff because they wouldn't know when it was time to do all the things they had to do. I said they could take the decision if they wished and it was a narrow majority that they decided in favour of the bell. We did have a vote on it because I was confident that they wouldn't want the bell. I was wrong . . . Anyway I got a fire officer in a week later and he told me, the bell shouldn't be rung because it was a fire hazard. So I went to the following staff meeting and said that it wouldn't be rung and they threw their arms in the air and I said, "Well it's not my decision." So everybody had to have clocks on the wall and watches and we went from there. But that was the first thing I did that a group of them didn't like, because they felt it was almost devious that I brought this fire officer in. Actually he was a mate of mine so I knew that he'd say what he'd said.'
>
> (James)

The school bell affair shows how James, to use his own words, daily 'walks the tightrope' between staff involvement in decision-making and strong cultural management. The staff were not afforded the opportunity to engage in a dialogue about or vote on whether to have the generalist teaching organization.

They were given some involvement in the relatively minor issue concerning the bell, though even here, in the end, James had his way. Beneath a rhetoric of democracy James was quite clear that his desire for cultural change would be satisfied:

> 'I had to really reorganize the attitude of the staff and I had to bring in my new ideas. It was about re-educating the majority of the staff. And a lot of them didn't want it because they had been here a long time and they were coming up to retirement. They weren't really interested in having staff meetings and inservice training and all that sort of thing. They didn't see the point in that. Everything was going swimmingly before and they didn't see the point in trying to change it all.'
>
> (James)

James still walks the tightrope when he decides which staff meetings and working party groups to attend, choosing when to stay away to let staff have a say on 'safe' issues, and when to attend to provide some positive steering. During 18 months' fieldwork in the school, the staff were not once observed voting on issues.

Being unable to determine the nature and direction of organizational and cultural change or to survive using strategies of 'secondary adjustment' (Goffman 1961; Riseborough 1993), the 'old professionals' sought retirement or posts in other schools. They were replaced by teachers more able to function in the transformed school. As James explains:

> 'What I had to do was to start to appoint people who would look at things in such a way that they saw their role as part of a team and that the team was the whole school together. It wasn't just a question of me making all the decisions but that they would have a role to play in that sort of thing. We looked at appointing people with good backgrounds and experience in curriculum areas but also proven leadership skills and working within groups and teams at other schools. The governors, by this time, grasped the fact that I was saying 'this isn't *my* job, its *our* job'. It's a team thing and you're part of the team as well because we've got to do this.'
>
> (James)

Subsequent strategies for developing this culture, but maintaining control as cultural manager, were to be seen in James delegating tasks to colleagues who were close to him, and setting up working parties and collaborative teaching teams. However, these groups do not engage in serious challenge of school policy, nor are they required to make major decisions concerning organization, budgeting and staffing. These decisions are taken by James.

However, while collaboration at the formal, policymaking level was somewhat contrived, an informal collaborative culture began to blossom in these early years of James's headship among the 'new professionals' – teachers willing to countenance change, though not uncritically. They attested to the quality of this new informal culture since James became head:

'It works informally because the relationships are such that you can go and talk to people. So you have respect for other people's professionalism. And you know if you need something, you know who to go to and you know you will get the kind of response you need to have, and you know the other person will give the time to help you. I think it's mutual trust and respect.'

(Grace, Year 1 and senior teacher)

'Within our situation, with the sort of support we give each other, I think its possible [implementing the National Curriculum]. If we hadn't that sort of situation I don't think we could have done it.'

(Sarah, Year 4 senior teacher)

'I work with a team that is absolutely brilliant. We just work well together. I think in all my teaching career this has been the best team I have ever worked with. It's just that everybody works together. There is none of this, "I'm doing this and not telling anybody about it", it's just a big exchange of ideas and sharing of things. You ought to see us after school having a cup of tea and a gossip. It's not just gossip as in relating what's happening in the rest of the world – but what is happening in our class that day and who is having problems. So if you have got a child with a problem then somebody else would perhaps have an idea about it or suggest ways to tackle the problem. Somebody will say, "I used so and so and it wasn't brilliant." If somebody has a worksheet or something we automatically share them. It saves you such a lot of time.'

(Pat, Year 1)

'My life is transformed. I feel so different. It's just lovely. It's just such a pleasure. It's hard work but you know we all get on, all the people we work with get on so well together. Everybody is very cooperative, everybody is very sharing.'

(Frances, Year 4)

Here are signs of more genuine collaboration of the kind observed by Nias *et al.* (1989). However, not all of the relationships were harmonious. Frances is aware that there are teachers in the school with whom she could not work collaboratively. While James acknowledges that 'there's a lot of good collaboration in that people share and are willing to ask for support', he also is aware that the composition of year teams is important:

'Lillian and Karen sharing that open-plan Terrapin made things work superbly. They planned well together – but they get on well together.

Now I could put two other teachers in there and it would be a total disaster. I wouldn't even attempt it.'

(James)

There is an indication here that the informal collaborative culture had not, in James's own words, 'just fallen from the sky'. It was 'the culture I laid down here when I came and removed the top-down system. So I think the culture of collaborative working has been set.' But it works at two levels, formal and informal, and in different ways at each. The latter, the more genuinely collaborative of the two, was soon to come under threat as external pressure for change mounted further.

Constructing the moving mosaic?

Following the Education Reform Act of 1988, further organizational and cultural transformations were attempted by the headteacher. These included the creation of a senior management team (SMT) and the introduction of a formal organizational structure designed to utilize the expertise of the subject coordinators. The intention behind both was to increase collaborative work in the school.

The Senior Management Team

All the teachers at the school, with the exception of a newly qualified teacher, had a curriculum responsibility which included the supervision and monitoring of the work of their colleagues. The school organization, therefore, had a flattened hierarchy in which efficiency might be achieved through flexibility, power sharing and teamwork. It was, however, the headteacher and members of the SMT who had the most responsibility and power. Within the SMT, all allowances (with the exception of the deputy head) are temporary. This gives the headteacher flexibility to switch financial incentives as management priorities change. Roles within the SMT, like allowances, are not fixed. While all SMT members each had curriculum and organizational responsibilities, other tasks changed as school priorities changed. Membership of the SMT was fluid to an extent, though there was a core of six permanent members. It was amongst this group, therefore, that it might be expected to find teachers who had sought increased responsibilities and a managerial role. Indeed, some of them had been appointed to the school as 'change agents' (Hoyle 1986), or 'strategic replacements' (Gouldner 1965) to assist in restructuring the existing occupational culture. One member of the SMT, the English/ Special Educational Needs (SEN) coordinator, was referred to by the headteacher, in this respect, as the 'first chisel in the rock'. Most members of the senior management team had entered teaching before the Education Reform Act of 1988. Only one of the SMT had received any training for management responsibilities. A general pattern seemed to be for them to acquire additional management responsibilities as their careers progressed in the school. Although the discourse of the SMT was about shared decision-making, teamwork and flattened hierarchy, they were perceived by other colleagues as 'the élite', 'the cherries on the cake', 'those that do' and 'the chiefs' (the other teachers referring to themselves as the 'indians'). Thus, the pyramid organization had been replaced by merely another form of hierarchy.

A changed formal organization

As we have seen in Chapter 1, there is widespread official advocacy of restructuring the coordinator's role to increase managerial work outside the classroom, in policy formation, whole-school planning, training and in the supervision and monitoring of their colleagues' work (see Troman 1996c). This work was best carried out by releasing coordinators from some of their classroom teaching responsibilities, but this had resource implications in a school facing budget cuts (Richards 1987). The pressure on James was further increased by an HMI report on the school which was critical of the head not using the expertise of coordinators through collaborative work with colleagues. James responded by restructuring the school organization, and by 'downsizing' (i.e. not renewing the contracts of two temporary teachers) and, thus, increasing class sizes. These measures were taken in order to release the deputy headteacher who would act as a 'floating' teacher. He explained:

> 'Barry [deputy head] is going to take on a role which will have a lot more to do with support teaching. Barry's role in all this is to be the key teacher to release those people who are going to work with other staff in trying to raise standards in all curriculum areas. He is able to say [to the teachers] that he is able to assess them on the basis of the work he is doing with them that the continuity is there and there is obvious progression.'
>
> (James)

James is suggesting here a kind of piggy-back surveillance. Barry is expected to monitor the work of the coordinators to release them in order that they monitor and supervise colleagues.

One other teacher, Deborah, a young and less experienced teacher, was identified as a potential floating teacher.

> 'The only kink in the chain is Year 5. That's the only three-class year group we have left. So Deborah [Year 5 teacher] is known as the 'X factor' – someone who can take the role of support teaching in virtually

every subject area that can actually follow up a group. So it doesn't matter if that person doesn't take specific subject responsibility.'

(James)

Additionally, the head wanted the coordinators to move each year to a different age group in order to work alongside different teachers and thereby spread their subject expertise amongst the staff. The new system required a new type of flexible professional who could adapt rapidly to the new roles and responsibilities. James did not consider it 'good practice for professionals to stay in one area too long because [he didn't] think you see the whole picture'.

Some teachers seemed to approve of the changes. For instance, the maths coordinator, commenting on Barry's support role, said: 'I think it's brilliant, I've got two half-days a week freeing me up for administration.' The music coordinator (Karen) and home/school links coordinator (Lillian) were attracted to the idea of gaining help from other subject coordinators working alongside them because they felt they lacked expertise and knowledge in certain National Curriculum subject areas. The English/SEN coordinator also saw advantages in coordinators moving each year to work with different colleagues. She was 'quite impressed by it as it stands'. However, she did recognize a major drawback of having an annual rotation of coordinators:

> 'Often good working relationships take time to develop and within school at the moment there are a couple of year groups where teachers have been together for two or three years and they feel that the second year is the best year. Because in the first year you're trying things out and the second year is the year you say, "Well, that didn't work very well, let's improve it." The sharing of expertise, the sharing of knowledge, yes that's how I can see it happening. But the development of good working relationships may suffer. I don't know.'

Moving or manipulative mosaic?

The intended structure of the new organization, to enforce team, collaborative and flexible work, and the unpredictability, uncertainty of the environment it was produced in, resemble the type of organization which 'fares well in the volatile conditions of postmodernity' (A. Hargreaves 1994a: 62). It is a form of organization referred to by Toffler (1990) as a 'moving mosaic'. This is characterized by 'flexibility, adaptability, creativity, opportunism, collaboration, a positive orientation to problem solving and commitment to maximising their [teachers] capacity to learn about the environment and themselves' (A. Hargreaves 1994a: 63). Hargreaves advocates this form for schools for it is claimed that flexible organizations have the capacity to promote professional learning, support collaborative working between colleagues in planning and decision-making, improve teaching and learning, empower teachers and respond to rapidly changing circumstances.

However, as Hargreaves points out, the moving mosaic can easily become manipulative. He adds the caveat that 'teachers' suspicions that organisational "flexibility" and the loosening of their roles and responsibilities may be used against them are not without foundation' (ibid.: 67). The 'flexibility' which is the central element of the moving mosaic has been used in industrial and commercial contexts for deskilling and downsizing workforces (Harvey 1990). Although the new organization, at James's school, contains elements of both types of mosaic described here, the argument that it is manipulative seems more compelling, for the following reasons.

It was the headteacher acting unilaterally who introduced the restructured system. It was not the outcome of collective decision-making, collaborative process or even democratic consultation. It was the head's creative response to rapidly changing circumstances, and not an untypical one. The tension between the collegial and top-down management styles is increasingly being resolved with heads using their executive powers without consultation (Pollard *et al.* 1994; Webb and Vulliamy 1996). However, in the context of the case study school, this was a major departure from the school development plan and from previous ways of working in the school. As such, this was the head-teacher's vision rather than one which was shared with teachers, governors and parents.

The new system seemed designed to create or accentuate role ambiguity. This was particularly so for the deputy. While some of the teachers, as we have seen, viewed his role positively, others did not share this perception. Whatever his formal position, in practice, the deputy head, Barry, was seen by some of the staff as a 'spy', acting as the head's agent, and by some as a supply teacher. One coordinator described him as the 'highest paid learning support assistant in the county'. Barry himself saw his new role as an opportunity of gaining some non-contact time himself on occasions when he did not have to cover for colleagues, and as a preparation for what he perceived as the next stage in his career – headship in another school. This also seems to have been partly James's view, as there was no room in his scheme of things for a deputy head:

> 'The problem is at the moment I still have Barry as my deputy and I would like him to get a headship. He needs to be moving on because that's vital to him and it's vital to me because I don't need a deputy. I need a senior management group with people who have been deemed to be the senior staff, who take the responsibilities for pastoral care, curriculum issues, and so on. And it's a shared responsibility rather than one job.'
>
> (James)

As with supply teachers generally, it was likely that the ambiguous role, Barry's lack of a geographical space which would serve as his base (he did not have a classroom or an office), and his lack of opportunity to develop a relationship with one class, would be factors which could accelerate his departure (Morrison 1996). The whole idea of a moving mosaic depends on the ability of workers to occupy multiple and shifting roles; also for them to adopt changing responsibilities as external changes dictate. When role diversity means there is too much for the occupier of the role to do, this causes tension and conflict (Campbell 1988: 230), not integration and collaboration.

Paradoxically, the new organization, although introduced for responsiveness, actually lacked the flexibility of the existing informal collaborative culture in the school. The unpredictability of working conditions within the primary school has always demanded a degree of flexibility from the teachers, especially as (Alexander 1984: 206),

> Education is value-laden, complex and debatable; children are only in certain respects predictable; teaching is idiosyncratic and uniquely compounded of the characteristics of teacher, taught and the situation within which they meet; some education outcomes are desired and worked towards but others are not known in advance not least because the educational claim to foster individuality and autonomy is in fact conditional upon allowing for and seeking the new and unpredictable response.

However, the flexibility required by the new organization at Meadowfields school is of a different order. It is 'controlled'. The new system requires the teachers to move through the age ranges as allocated by the headteacher. This will involve them in abandoning phase loyalties and, for the 'key' 'floating' teachers, the 'X' factors, subject loyalty as well. Before the new form of organization was introduced, the head and staff (individually) used to discuss staff deployment for the coming year. While the head normally bowed to the staff's wishes he did have the 'final say'. While this process was taking place over some weeks in the summer term, there was a great deal of discussion in the staffroom involving teachers worrying about where they would be teaching, and with whom they would be teaching, during the following year. When the process was over there seemed to be much relief as most teachers had their wishes acknowledged. Some of the teachers had strong phase loyalties and seemed committed to remaining within a particular year group. Other teachers appeared to have not so much phase commitment but be committed to avoiding certain phases: 'I'm sorry but infants are not my cup of tea.' In the new system, this degree of self-determination and control of work, potentially, will be lost as the teachers move automatically through the years.

Alternatively, the teachers saw that they would be supported in subjects in which they may have a weakness, and even welcomed the increased supervision and control of their work: 'We would be able to do it the way the coordinators want it doing.' The new flexibility was perceived as something which was required of professionals these days in order to ensure continuity and progression by understanding all the stages the children pass through. The art coordinator (a Year 6 teacher), for example, was working with Reception and Year 1 classes to familiarize herself with this phase:

> 'Assessment/INSET Coordinator Tamsin went initially to observe the way in which art is done in the infants. Finding out what children of that age are capable of and then, perhaps, using that to suggest ideas or help plan the next term's art, which will make use of the infant teacher's expertise but also take into account what the children are capable of.'
>
> (Mark, Year 1 and senior teacher)

The experience would, no doubt, give her some credibility when she eventually advised the infant teachers. She would not be in the position of Webb and Vulliamy's (1996: 89) coordinator who offered advice but was perceived to 'know nothing about infants'. There was an air of resignation about this too. Being flexible was just part of the job. Some, for example Barry, saw it as a career move so that when they apply for deputy headships or headships they could demonstrate their experience in all year groups and an ability to 'fit in anywhere'. The teachers felt that this would be expected of them – an indication that this might become part of the next ideology, replacing 'child-centred progressivism' as the *sine qua non* of primary expertise (Alexander 1992). Yet others saw it as a way of avoiding boredom and keeping professionally fresh. Karen, for instance, had taught Year 6 before her move to the infants:

> 'I never understood anyway how you could just teach Year 6. Yes, you might get absolutely brilliant at it, but you'd get bored with this National Curriculum. It's the same thing you're churning out year after year after year.'
>
> (Karen)

Certainly in an increasingly static workforce (Richards 1987) this system might provide opportunities for teachers continually to face new challenges within the same school. Teachers who were on temporary or fixed-term contracts gave the organization further flexibility, particularly in periods when budget cuts forced 'downsizing'.

It has been an intention of the Government's policy to make schools more like business organizations (Coopers and Lybrand 1988). In this respect the new form of organization at Meadowfields does resemble the type of flexible post-Fordist organization which can adapt quickly to changing circumstances and therefore needs flexible workers who are capable of rapid adaptations to new situations. This seems to be behind the notion of the 'key' teacher and 'floating' teacher or 'X' factor. The idea of the flexible teacher does seem to resonate with descriptions of the flexible and multi-skilled and cooperative worker (Winterton and Barlow 1994) who works in collaborative teams or 'quality circles', and can substitute for colleagues as the production process dictates, thus preventing breaks in the work flow and production process. For management, this type of worker can increase productivity, worker commitment to each other and the company, the self-surveillance and control of workers, and product quality, while lowering staff turnover.

This mode of organization, however, may prove to be ill-suited to the predominantly female workplace of the primary school. The educational system and the school organization presuppose a technical–rational and masculine conception of career, seeing it as linear and continuous. The new organization is, in this respect, inflexible. Female careers are often non-linear and disrupted owing to breaks for child-rearing. As one female teacher said: 'The system will break down as soon as somebody leaves to have a baby.'

Other sources of flexibility were at risk. Informally the teachers worked with colleagues in the same year and had in many cases become friends. The collaborative relationship worked because the teachers were working with someone who was part of their positive reference group (Nias *et al.* 1989). Informal collaboration consisted of teachers planning together, talking in the staffroom and around the school, meeting each other out of school and spending INSET (inservice training) days together. Lack of non-contact time to free coordinators to do administrative tasks had led the teachers to draw on resources provided by the collaborative culture in order to create time for this work. These ad hoc arrangements included: the release of coordinators during assembly and hymn practice; the use of students to cover lessons; the use of the researcher to cover lessons; and the headteacher taking classes. These have all been informal and untimetabled events which have come about through the negotiations and collaboration of the teachers concerned. Teachers 'swap' their classes with colleagues, usually in the same year team, in order to teach subject specialisms and compensate for subject weaknesses – 'You teach my music and I'll do your PE'. More formally, the teachers collaborate in working parties, staff meetings and committees. They choose which policymaking groups to belong to and their participation in these looks to be genuinely collaborative. However, in the new system, teachers have no choice with whom they work, and, as was attested earlier, some teachers could not work well with each other. Teachers have mentioned that it takes longer than a year (perhaps two years) to develop a good working and professional relationship with a colleague, yet the new system requires an annual move. This does seem to be borne out since the successful pairings of teachers have been among those who have been together for several years. They had become interdependent, like friends, or like 'finger and thumb' (Nias 1987). These arrangements were now under threat in a moving mosaic that was more managed than truly collaborative.

CONCLUSION

As we argued in Chapter 1, teachers are now defined as collaborative professionals. Indeed, collaboration is arguably the central element in the 'new professionalism' (D.H. Hargreaves). The capacity to collaborate is now not seen as a desirable personal quality which teachers either have or have not, it is a technical requirement of the work of teaching (Lawn 1991). Collaborative cultures which assist professional learning and at the same time are known to have educational gains (HMI 1978; Nias *et al.* 1989) have led to the concept being appropriated and sponsored by a management eager to implement the reforms. Increasing managerialism with its attendant accountability systems is now putting schools in the position of having to demonstrate that collaborative working is taking place as a part of policy implementation. Ofsted inspectors, for example, assess levels of collaboration (Webb and Vulliamy 1996), not by penetrating the relatively invisible informal collaborative cultures (they are only in school for one week), but by looking for more visible structures where collaboration is assumed to take place, for instance documents and records such as timetables and minutes following meetings, and in structures such as SMTs, working parties and 'moving mosaics'.

The case studies reported here have shown some of the problems and intricacies involved in applying the 'collaborative principle' in schools, and of tackling the 'structure or culture' tension noted in Chapter 1 (p. 17). Ostensibly, these principles are culture-led. In effect, the culture is taken over by the structure. At Meadowfields, the contrived democracy and collegiality are steered by the firm hand of James' cultural management. It seemed that James had started out with good intentions, and had succeeded in fostering a productive informal collaborative culture among his staff which contrasted markedly with the regime of the previous order, and was much appreciated by 'new professionals' in the school. However, in attempting to breed new attitudes among other staff, and under pressure from external agencies, he was led to take more directive action which yielded a more contrived collegiality. His position reflects a tension-ridden situation that many heads have found themselves in since the Education Reform Act 1988 and particularly since the introduction of LMS (local management of schools) (Pollard *et al.* 1994; Webb and Vulliamy 1996; Grace 1996). On the one hand, heads need to shape a culture of collaboration and develop the new differentiated and flexible roles for staff (Lawn 1995) in order to implement the reforms through building consensus and utilizing the professional strengths of the teachers. On the other hand, an official role expectation is that they will be strong, entrepreneurial leaders with vision and a developed capacity for unilateral decision-making (Grace 1996). Furthermore, they are legally responsible for the decisions which are made. The primary head also operates in a rapidly changing context and turbulent external environment. This is particulary notable with regard to finance and budgeting. In such conditions heads need to respond rapidly and 'do their best for the school' (Grace 1996). In this situation, the tensions are resolved often strategically and politically rather than on an educational basis. In this context, collaborative shared decision-making may get in the way of strong and flexible leadership. As James explained to one parent who was seeking, but was refused, involvement in whole-school decision-making: 'The bottom line is finance and staffing; I'm the one who must take the tough decisions.' James basically seemed to favour strong direction, and found a way in micropolitics of avoiding tension, and handling the problems as professional dilemmas. Other heads, more committed to more genuine collaborative cultures, may be less successful.

Clearly, in some circumstances teachers like and benefit professionally from working in informal collaborative cultures (albeit that some may initially be managed ones). We have seen, equally, prefigured at Meadowfields and more established among the schools and teachers in Part A of this chapter, that contrived collaboration raises problems for the teachers. Notable here is the constraint that this form of collaboration places on individual working. The class teacher's strong sense of professional responsibility to her class is being threatened by the requirement that she engages in contrived collaboration. This aspect of 'individuality' as opposed to 'individualism' is a powerful reminder of a culture of teaching which is being restructured in the direction of enforced collaboration. In this shift, not only individual working but genuine collaborative cultures which promise authentic school improvement are under threat. While primary teachers may welcome a workplace culture of collaboration if the range and quality of the collaboration and collegiality are considered appropriate, they will see it as contrived collegiality if it appears to involve intensification, overload, ineffectiveness, limited choice, inappropriate democratic procedures, the domination of an informal discourse and extended institutionalization as we have seen here. They see through the management rhetoric and expose the managerial myths of 'ownership', 'empowerment', 'collaboration' and 'participative decision-making'.

We have discussed here how professional relationships are being reconstructed in some schools as 'managed' collaborative cultures. We turn in the next chapter to teachers' responses to the reconstruction of the teacher role.

CHAPTER 3

Tensions in the new teacher role

'They've got this model of a good teacher from somewhere, but I'm not sure it's me.'

(Veronica)

INTRODUCTION: CHANGES IN THE TEACHER ROLE

The teacher role is inherently conflictual (Grace 1972), but the nature of the conflict varies with the social conditions of the time. According to Grace (1985), the expansionism and affluence of the 1950s and 1960s, together with a shortage of teachers had warranted a 'legitimated professionalism' (i.e. recognized by government), with teachers distanced from formal control, and enjoying a considerable measure of freedom and autonomy, and improved status and working conditions. Role conflict during that era was a popular subject for study (Wilson 1962; Musgrave 1972; Grace 1972; D. Hargreaves 1972), and no doubt a source of stress for some (Woods 1989). But, we would argue, it was largely of the dilemmatic variety. The conflict was in the situation, it was part of the professional role, and, as such, subject to professional appraisal and resolution. It is what makes teaching an art, involving 'combining roles, solving dilemmas, and inventing patterns of events and relationships' (Woods 1990: 143). The different expectations of different pupils, or of pupils and parents, or of one's headteacher and one's colleagues, presented everyday dilemmas, which teachers reflected upon and discussed as part of their job. A teacher who experienced conflict between role commitment or career aspirations – whether to stay in one's school or go for promotion elsewhere (Wilson 1962) – had control of the decision since the problem was not a threatening one, and was circumscribed within the teacher's own experience. Conflicts arising from incompatible positions within the role were amenable to skills of 'orchestration', as discussed in Chapter 2. Role conflict arising from values differences were 'essentially a conflict with society rather than self' (Grace 1972: 93). These are all dilemmatic situations, presenting urgency and difficulty, perhaps, but an intrinsic and accepted part of the somewhat diffuse professional teacher role. Dilemmatic role conflict is largely positive, in that progress made through the decision taken outweighs any negative residue.

The changed times of the 1980s and 1990s brought new conceptions of the teacher role. The state has clawed back its control, reduced the status of the profession, and, as we saw in Chapter 1, unilaterally redefined the concept of the 'good' teacher. The primary teacher is now expected to have subject knowledge, and a whole range of new skills, including managerial, collaborative and assessment skills. The National Curriculum and the new demands for planning and record-keeping have escalated workload levels (see Webb and Vulliamy 1996, for detailed examination of specific changes in responsibilities). Even pedagogy, heretofore the teachers' preserve, is coming under scrutiny, with teachers no longer being encouraged to be so 'child-centred' in their teaching, but to use traditional techniques more. Further, if control was 'invisible' in the 1950s and 1960s, it was now made very 'visible' (Grace 1985). New forms of accountability have made the new role more pronounced – expectations are greater, and procedures are in place to see how far they are met. Despite all this 'role inflation', working conditions for primary teachers remain the same (Campbell and Neill 1994a).

Role conflict arising from these new circumstances is altogether of a different order from that of the previous era for many teachers. Some teachers are making positive responses to the changes. Osborn *et al.* (1996: 149; see also Woods 1995; Woods and Jeffrey 1996a), for example, report of their sample:

> A significant minority of teachers felt that a new professionalism involving creative ways of working with individual children . . . was possible provided they had the confidence to shape the imposed changes to more professionally acceptable ends.

However, a number of teachers have not, as yet, found this possible. Their 'professional confidence' (Helsby 1995) has been shaken. They are experiencing role tension. Role tension is largely negative, having adverse effects on teaching and learning. That there has been a large degree of this since 1988 is beyond dispute. For many of the sample of Osborn *et al.* (1996: 139), in 1990, 'the impact of the changes on their work and role was perceived to be largely negative'. A number of the changes had intensified by 1992–1993, and for some 'the satisfactions derived from teaching were ebbing away while the frustrations were increasing' (ibid.: 142). A particularly strong conflict derived from the demands of the National Curriculum and the teachers' perceived needs of their children (ibid.: 148). Another, elsewhere, in relation to secondary schools though quite possibly applying to primary teachers (Gewirtz

1996), lay in teachers' complaining that they were losing the opportunity to work on an individual basis with students and being forced into whole-class teaching on a 'production line' (p. 15). This example neatly shows the difference between what was before a dilemma, and has now, through the diminution of choice, become a tension. The experience of role tension suggests the characteristics we advanced in Chapter 2, notably the assault on the substantial self (Ball 1972; Nias 1989), as opposed to situational siting. As D.H. Hargreaves (1972: 79) notes, role conflict is harder to reconcile where the basic self is involved. Also involved is the rousing of strong emotions. In both areas, primary teachers are especially vulnerable, through their strong investment of self in role (Nias 1989), and through their use of the emotions in their practice (Woods and Jeffrey 1996b). The two are connected. Once dilemmas become tensions, there is a movement from largely cognitive to largely affective response. Teacher emotions are disturbed in some way or other because tensions invade the self. In some cases they are severe enough to become constraints, forcing a decision of rejection (i.e. retirement) or personal adjustment (Becker 1977), that is simply accepting the changes. The only other possibilities are stress or burn-out.

Role tensions are not just psychological disturbances of the moment, but have sociological connections. They have their origins in restructuring at the macro level, and are mediated by institutional and personal factors. We discuss the social construction of teacher stress in Chapter 6. In this chapter, we are concerned with teacher feelings in relation to their change in role. Hitherto, the study of teachers has been overwhelmingly concentrated on their thinking. We are also interested in teacher thinking, but see this as indissolubly connected with feelings, which has come to assume prior importance with the changes. Strong feelings have been generated, and these have implications for teachers' ability to do their job. These are a more relevant subject for study, we feel, than a detailed examination of the new role itself. In some ways the notion of 'role' has come to be regarded as an outmoded function-alist concept in that it focuses attention on the demands of the position to be filled, rather than what individuals make of those demands. Official prescrip-tions of the 'good' teacher may make a useful benchmark, but we are inter-ested in how these demands are mediated, even perhaps resisted, by teachers.

This attention to process, self and feelings yields a rather different typology from those previously advanced (for example, Lacey 1977; Pollard *et al.* 1994; Woods 1995). Reviewing the data on the effects of role conflict on self, we find our teachers fall into four broad categories, with a number of subcategor-ies, that roughly accord with dilemmas, tensions and constraints. The broad categories are:

- Enhanced teachers. These teachers experience role conflict predomin-antly as dilemmas, and are enriched by their solutions to them. They feel able to employ their creative powers in their teaching and management.

However, there are some ambivalent teachers here, who find both enrichment and tensions in the reforms.

- Compliant teachers. These experience a mixture of role dilemmas and tensions. Their creativity is deflected from teaching and towards devising strategies to cope. But there is wide variation among them, with some, for example, being positively conformist and seeing the social world as predominantly dilemmatic, whereas others are more strategically compliant and/or more disturbed.
- Non-compliant teachers. These also experience role tension, and to a somewhat worse degree since they are uncompromising in their values and in their practice.
- Diminished teachers. Role conflict for these is predominantly constraint in effect. They feel devalued and disillusioned, and are either 'leaving' the system or 'sinking' beneath it.

In some ways, typologies misrepresent reality. They are too neat and orderly to reflect faithfully a complex world full of contradictions and inconsistencies, where an individual might subscribe to a number of the types given, even in the course of one day, according to such factors as particular aspects of the type, time, place, people associating with, domestic affairs, etc.; or where other important features that all hold in common, but not picked up in the analysis, run through the types. But it is a device we prefer, since it offers a way of organizing a mass of detail on teacher responses, concentrating on those major features indicated by our data, and considering the full range of those responses. We feel that we have kept faith with the interactionist approach of the studies in that the typology is grounded in the data and has undergone repeated refinement in order to accommodate all the teachers that have featured in the research informing this book. The typology is based on the major themes that have emerged from our discussions with and observations of these teachers. The association with these teachers for at least a year, and more in some cases, was long and intensive enough for us to feel reasonably confident that the type we have assigned them to represents their predominant mode of response. The representation is qualitative, and we have selected as our examples to illustrate the categories the teachers who gave the richest data – roughly half of our sample. We give the numbers of teachers in each category as a matter of interest, but the sample is not large enough to claim wider generalizability. However, it is significant that such a comparatively small sample yields such variable response, with serious implications for teaching and learning.

THE STUDY

We give in Table 3.1 some basic information about the schools and teachers featuring in this chapter. This includes school type, size, and pupil free-lunch

Table 3.1 Characteristics of schools and teachers

School	Teachers and experience
The Rural School 350 pupils with packed lunches	Tim (22 years)
Meadowfields The Town School. 450 pupils. 8.4 per cent free dinners	Elizabeth (25 years)
Cottingly The Village School. 210 pupils. 14 per cent free dinners	Bronwyn (25 years), Becky (20 years), Helen (2 years), Frank (26 years)
Flatley The Large Inner-City School. 73 per cent free dinners	Georgina (10 years), Rosemary (10 years)
Lowstate The Estate School. 50 per cent free dinners	Aileen (20 years), Angelina (25 years), Emily (5 years), Esther (20 years), Evelyn (15 years), Larry (15 years), Lional (25 years), Lucy (20 years)
Morghouse The Suburban School. 30 per cent free dinners	Naomi (18 years)
Trafflon The Small Inner-City School. 70 per cent free dinners	Carol (25 years), Cloe (25 years), Clare (25 years), Tania (20 years), Toni (20 years), Veronica (20 years), Victoria (4 years)

percentage; also teachers' names and years of teaching experience. Other relevant information about the teachers will be given in the appropriate place. We shall consider each category in turn. Most of our schools had either had an Ofsted inspection recently or were about to have one. We regard that as a critical event in the schools, which brought to a head many of the issues connected with change in the teacher role, how the teachers felt about them, and how they responded. We are mainly concerned, however, with general responses to role change in this chapter. We shall consider the particular effects of school inspection in Chapter 5.

Enhanced teachers (fifteen teachers)

There were two kinds of self-enhancement. In some cases there was unreserved support for new developments, and a relishing of new situations and challenges, with feelings of exhilaration and elevation. In other cases there was more ambivalence. Some developments were welcomed, others rejected.

Unequivocal enhancement (five teachers)

Tim, Larry and Becky represent this group. Prominent features of their approach to role performance were positive planning, engagement, self-determination and reinforcement.

Positive planning
These teachers were 'marked by a sense of optimism' (Musgrave 1972: 237). Tim is in his third year as deputy head at The Rural School, and is totally committed to a systematic approach to curriculum organization involving cross-year-group inputs which he describes as 'vertical pulling together'. He is elated by this approach and talks with ebullience about how central school planning has a cohesion. He approves of planning procedures because 'in the good schools, there is more working together and sharing of ideas'. He looks ahead with keen anticipation:

> 'The next step is that automatically from the curriculum map will come the schemes, and from the schemes will come assessment opportunity, and my idea is to actually have an assessment map where we highlight specific opportunities or progression and assessment of specific skills and concepts and then you can see the experiences the children should have had.'

> (Tim)

Becky (Year 2) who works in The Village School (Cottingly) and is a PE and art post-holder, enjoys

> 'courses, plans and action plans . . . Because the National Curriculum is standardized, we need standardized assessment and standardized planning. There was not enough equal access for pupils when we were totally teacher-topic driven. I'm not threatened by uniformity; it doesn't affect my creativity for delivery is at the centre of creativity, not content.'

> (Becky)

Engagement
It is part of their positive approach that they engage with colleagues, and with others, such as inspectors. They do not simply dictate to the one and answer to the other. Tim's long-term objectives arise out of observation of other schools and other management systems. He overcame potential problems of overload and achieved control firstly by 'having agreed objectives with staff – and then not being deflected from those' and secondly, by not taking on 'too many new initiatives rather than doing a smaller number really well and feeling some satisfaction and achievement from that'.

Part of these teachers' managerial role is to attend courses and become familiar with current management techniques. This was extremely beneficial for Becky during her Ofsted inspection,

> 'I'd seen Ofsted reports and worked on action plans and we'd actually observed lessons via videos and we had to mark them as they mark them, so I knew what was going to be going on so the Ofsted observation wasn't such a shock. If I got a job to start after Christmas and they said we've got an Ofsted in January, it wouldn't make me think, "Oh, I don't want to go".'
>
> (Becky)

Larry (Year 6), who works in The Estate School (Lowstate) and is a science post-holder, took an invitation to consult inspectors at its word, and

> 'was proactive and every occasion that I was proactive they responded immediately and came to see me . . . obviously if I hadn't engaged them I would have missed that opportunity.'
>
> (Larry)

Larry felt elated by the way he managed his Ofsted experiences. There were three occasions when he 'grabbed people to come in'. On one of these he was

> 'doing a good PE session and I could see an inspector floating around in the corridor and I opened the door and said, "Are you OK?" and she said, "Yes, but I've arrived at this classroom here and there's an inspector in that room," and I said, "Why don't you come in here and look at me?" [Otherwise] Every time they were there, I spelled it out, I made sure by engaging them, "Have you got everything you want? Is there anything you want to ask me? Had you noticed this? Was everything clear? Have you seen this?".'
>
> (Larry)

Self-determination

Tim has the confidence to assess his capabilities and argues that his experience in, and commitment to, educating children assists the possibility of managing the National Curriculum.

> 'Because I have a range of experiences behind me, I know what's important to me and although we have external pressures, I do my best to meet those expectations but I'm not driven from my principles too far. As far as I'm concerned, there's no tension, but I think other staff, because they haven't got that and because they want to do it the National Curriculum way, do feel it.'
>
> (Tim)

Thus, what is dilemmatic for Tim is tension-ridden for others less experienced. He is also able to orchestrate, and perform what he calls 'a balancing act between covering the excessive content of the National Curriculum because these children are going to be tested in the near future . . . and making sure that they have the entitlement to the curriculum that they deserve, and it's not presented in too dry a way.'

(Tim)

Larry is convinced that enhancement of the self lies with the teacher:

'The giving of a grade is in the hands of the teacher because it reflects your practice, so without any shadow of a doubt it must be up to the teacher. It is up to you as to whether you want to jump through those hoops.'

(Larry)

In spite of all the changes, Becky is still keen about the job and feels fulfilled by all of it. She is

'happy about what I'm doing in my class for my areas of responsibility, but not necessarily about all the other teachers in all areas of my responsibility, but I oversee this quality informally and the staff here are very easy to get on with . . . I never get up in the morning and think, "Oh, I don't want to go to school" . . . I get up and know that every day is going to be different.'

(Becky)

Reinforcement

Tim felt gratified by the commendation of Ofsted, especially when one of his managerial schemes was adopted,

'We now have a variety of statement banks that have been built in so you could have six different starters to a sentence and eight different endings for our assessment on computer . . . Ofsted said that we were easily covering our national obligations and they were very detailed reports.'

(Tim)

Becky was delighted that her detailed planning was used as a model:

'The headteacher actually changed over to the way I was doing it. She took my crib sheet and introduced it when I first came here. Then I went on this deputy heads' course and we started talking about learning objectives and assessment and planning and I did a big presentation on planning and record-keeping and she's incorporated it into our planning.'

(Becky)

Larry was elated with his Ofsted grade, and found the experience 'encouraging because we had a very professional person who had no knowledge of the school or of me, not coming with any particular viewpoint, coming in and confirming judgements I had made.'

(Larry)

Ambivalent enhancement (ten teachers)

Our second group of teachers also achieved self-enhancement through taking on managerial roles, but were more critical of managerial practices. This ambivalence can lead to more difficult dilemmas for them – and some role tension. They tended to be less 'positive', less 'engaged', as well as less committed to the changes than teachers in the first category. We examine this category through the experience of two teachers. Elizabeth works in The Town School (Meadowfields) and is an experienced teacher who has responsibility for maths. Toni works in The Small Inner-City School (Trafflon) and has been deputy head for five years. She has a considerable amount of responsibility for curriculum development and assessment throughout the school.

Developmental aspects
The aspects of the changes which the two teachers felt developed their selves and made them feel good about teaching were greater expertise and feelings of ownership and control.

ADVANCED EXPERTISE   Elizabeth sees the need for some sort of monitoring, and feels this calls for skill and sensitivity.

'I've asked to look at people's maths files and I've been able to help people with the resourcing of those. What's meant to happen now is that I'm going to be able to go into different areas to work with people. I don't know how it's going to work – it's going to be a bit delicate I think because I don't want to tread on anybody's toes . . . You really feel you're being seen with a critical eye and that's got to be avoided really. It's just the way you approach people. You work with them rather than showing them "this is the way to do it".'

(Elizabeth)

Toni's expertise has been advanced. She has learnt 'what a policy document is', and from having 'wasted her time doing it in a very long-winded way', can now do it in a day, and can 'sit down with others and help them'. She likes assessment profiling because she's 'bothered about whether the child has been shown to make progress'. She feels 'a better teacher now because the assessment has helped me break down the work so I can build it into the planning'. She feels professionalized by some of the managerialist processes:

'Last week I took all new planning sheets home, went through them, and funnily enough I quite enjoyed doing it because it made me feel that I have got some expertise ... I still get a buzz occasionally, like even this morning when Cloe said, as course coordinator, she needed some samples to show the end of Key Stage, I was able to provide three examples that I did last year with the children and I thought "Oh, it's really good fun this kind of thing, it's really good".'

(Toni)

OWNERSHIP AND CONTROL   Elizabeth enjoys her involvement at managerial level.

'It's nice to have a say in what goes on in school. I think I've been here long enough to know how things happen, how people tick and what's accepted and what's not and how to get around people or talk to people or whatever. I just like to be in the know as well.'

(Elizabeth)

She is unsure about other management practices around involvement, such as where governors and parents have attended meetings, but still sees ways in which all could benefit:

'Governors have got better management skills than we have. They're more aware of budgeting than we are. Perhaps we can palm off those skills to them and let us control what happens in school and the education side of it.'

(Elizabeth)

She enjoys the control aspects of being a subject manager:

'If I wasn't doing it, I'd be very irritated perhaps by what another coordinator would do. I'd feel that I wanted to be in charge of it.'

(Elizabeth)

She spoke with some pride about *her* maths policy:

'The first thing I did when I came here was to write the school's maths policy. I worked with a couple of other people to get some ideas together, but it was best working on your own though it was supposed to be involving everybody and everyone's ideas to make the whole thing work. It really wasn't feasible because there was no time to do it in school. It had to be done at home, so it's pretty much my document.'

(Elizabeth)

There is a personal element in Toni's enthusiasm for constructing policies, planning and record-keeping. She needs 'to write, whenever I've been taking any exam or whatever in my life I need to write because the action of writing makes it go in my mind'.

Negative aspects
These gather around the tensions caused by intensification and by attacks on ownership.

INTENSIFICATION　Elizabeth catalogues the increased pressures and the tensions caused:

> 'heavy workload . . . being asked to do too much . . . extra jobs . . . no finish/no end to it . . . pressure on you . . . all the time spent trying to do your best . . . now it's two topics a term and it's a nightmare . . . God, I haven't done this and I haven't done that and I've got to do that . . . feeling dizzy/shell-shocked at the end of the day . . .'
>
> (Elizabeth)

Toni tells a similar story. She wants 'to have more life', but feels that 'the job is trapping me'. In the term prior to an Ofsted inspection, she succumbed to illness, a rare event for her:

> 'It was stress and it made me very annoyed because I thought "I'm a fairly calm person and I'm taking this reasonably well but something's going wrong. Am I having a breakdown?"'
>
> (Toni)

She articulates the tensions between the following.

- 'An unrealistic workload' and 'being part of the management of this school'.
- Improvement in quality of teaching, but 'at what personal cost?'
- 'Piling the pressure on her teachers', against sympathy for the workloads they labour under.
- Starting work straight away on arriving home, or cooking a meal.
- Going out, or staying in and working.
- Being 'realistic, you are only human, you can only achieve so much', versus 'if I'm not actually vigorous and achieve something by the time it gets to the weekend, it is totally out of hand'.
- Being positive about the National Curriculum, and feeling negative about some of its effects.
- Going for a headship, against 'all that amount of responsibility'.

These are more than professional dilemmas. Moreover, they have a cumulative effect, so that what may appear to be trivial matters come to assume great importance. One's decision-making processes are affected, and choice becomes even more delimited. Toni is 'in a quandary about how to balance up my life'. She feels:

> 'a sort of heavy feeling approaching each evening, thinking, "Here I am in total silence, work work work," and I don't really know what the

answer is . . . I do get depressed about my non-existent social life while I'm at work . . . I do feel this heaviness when I enter my home, that sometimes my home is my prison because I'm there and I have to work and I refuse invitations . . . What I want is to get out of my job . . . If there was a way out, I would take it . . . I do enjoy it while I'm here and some of the management bits are great, but obviously there is frustration.'

(Toni)

Intensification, in the end, atrophies the self. Self-renewal and self-development get swallowed up in the endless, self-perpetuating demands of the system. With no outside stimulus:

'It must affect the quality of teaching and learning in this class if I arrive on a Monday morning and I haven't had that kind of weekend where I've done something different. I do need something to motivate me. We're not developing anything for ourselves as individuals so how can we be expected to be in the right frame of mind to help the children . . .'

REDUCED OWNERSHIP AND CONTROL   At one point, Elizabeth's maths policy was superseded by the local education authority, which she thought a retrograde step,

'It can't be very clear if it's just two sides. I think what I wrote – lots of very clever people's thinking on maths and how it should be taught – is very valuable as a school policy. To have something on two sides of A4 is meaningless but that's what we're supposed to be doing. If we're going to have to do it like that, why don't they just give us the sheet and say, "There you are".'

(Elizabeth)

The local education authority planning sheets also were 'not designed to take as much detail as we want to put on our planning', so

'. . . are causing us headaches now because if you fill them in in a very sort of skeleton manner they're no use to us in the classroom. You have to have your own plan with much more detail on that you can work from.'

(Elizabeth)

Toni sometimes wonders,

'Am I identifying things that really are there or, as an individual, are they being identified for me and I'm playing the game? Because I was thinking about myself when I was younger the other day, and I'm not the person I was when I was younger, it's kind of stamped out of me.'

(Toni)

The loss of control is exemplified in the long process of an Ofsted inspection:

'You have this vision of what you want to do with this school but that
vision doesn't become yours, does it? It becomes Ofsted's vision.'

(Toni)

As with some of Nias's (1991) teachers, Toni feels this loss of control as a
kind of bereavement.

'Last time I felt this upset in my life was when my father died five years
ago. It made me think of bereavement in a family for there are so many
other things coming out to do with like guilt, and when somebody dies,
they're gone, and you think, "What else could I have done?"'

(Toni)

It has also made her angry that

'the rug has been pulled from under me. I thought I was doing a good
job, though in my better moments I still think I am.'

(Toni)

Both teachers saw improved chances for themselves in their new role as
teacher managers. But they are humanistic rather than managerialist in
approach and this leads to tensions. These cause them to wonder at times
whether the enhancement outweighs the diminution of self. At the same
time, their brand of critical humanistic managerialism could be seen as a
positive base on which to develop managerial practices in primary schools.

Compliant teachers (twenty-nine teachers)

Compliant teachers are adapting, rather than enhancing, their selves, strategically realigning in response to tensions, though some are already accustomed
to take that approach. There is a sense of continuance, survival, even optimism,
but not development or enhancement. These teachers do not relish managerial opportunities and changes in role, but they accommodate, concur and
allow changes to impinge upon them. This was the largest category among
our teachers, but we identified wide variation among them, from 'supporting', to 'surviving', to 'disturbed' conformists.

The supporting conformists (ten teachers)

The supportive conformists are relaxed, composed, imperturbable, self-
possessed, even-tempered and moderate. They are rational, sensible and
equable. They feel generally satisfied they have done their best to incorporate the changes in role. They feel secure, assured, stable and have a generally
optimistic approach to work. They do not, therefore, experience role tension,
or even dilemmatic role conflict as other teachers do. An almost intuitive

pragmatism takes them to speedy resolution of difficulties. They seem to achieve these levels of equanimity through maintaining positive perspectives, routinizing managerial practices, distancing themselves from intensification and perceiving work as balanced. We take as examples Lional, Evelyn and Emily who teach at The Estate School (Lowstate) and Rosemary and Georgina who teach at The Large Inner-City School (Flatley).

Positive outlook
This is not the same as the positive outlook of the self-enhancers who are positive owing to advantages they can see for themselves. This positive approach is more a matter of 'meeting requirements'. Lional's (Year 6) perspective of his staff in the run up to Ofsted was that they 'felt reasonably secure about things'. Again, he had no misgivings about the consequences of the grading of teachers in his school. He did not see why 'it should make any difference', as he thought 'we shall see ourselves as being competent'. But again, he differed from many teachers in his school who found the whole situation distasteful and reacted strongly against the process. He did not even worry about the pupils letting him down. He said only a little to them the night before the inspection.

> 'I know we can rely on you to give a sensible answer if you're asked something. That's it really. I don't see any point in hyping it up.'
>
> (Lional)

Emily accepts without question most of the innovations and always sees some positive aspects to them,

> 'There are lots of things that need putting right, because things can easily get pushed away, so it's nice that they [inspectors] . . . can come in and tell us where we need to tackle things.'
>
> (Emily)

Like Lional, she does not think that a critical comment about her department will affect the staff.

> 'It's a school that everybody's together in anyway, we support each other so I don't think it will affect them. We do it because we know we're achieving, what we're achieving and what we're doing for the children. The parents support and they come in and they say, "Thank you" and all of the children love coming to school.'
>
> (Emily)

Like enhancers, they enjoy reinforcement. Lional's response to his Ofsted report was typically upbeat. It was: 'Nice to know that they regard us as a good school. Nice to get a pat on the back.' It was typical of Lional that he wanted everyone to focus on this, rather than the criticisms of one part of the school.

Routinizing managerial practices
Musgrove (1974: 45) notes:

> 'Although most people complain about the routine in their jobs, they
> would probably go mad without it. Without routine we are constantly
> dealing with unique, unprecedented, non-recurrent and non-standard
> events. This may be exhilarating; it is also exhausting.'

Routinization was a prominent strategy of the supporting conformists. There
was none of the ambivalence noted earlier, but nor was there any of the self-
enhancement. They avoided the 'exhaustion' – and also the 'exhilaration' –
in the interests of continuity and social order.

Lional is a maths post-holder with over twenty years' experience. He has
taken on some monitoring and believes that it is his job to check on the
progress of the children across the school but not to dictate teaching methods.
He does not want to judge teachers, or make them conform to any particular
practice through his monitoring, but accepts monitoring as a management
tool to ensure that a match between scheme and outcome becomes second
nature and routine. Typically, he welcomed the long lead in to an inspection, as it gave him time to get routines established, while not setting his
sights too high:

> 'all the sorts of routines, the record-keeping routines, the assembly
> routines. I guess we've felt that over the last year "We can just polish
> those up a bit and they'll be all right". I don't think you can really do
> more than that. You can't do anything too adventurous in a way, or
> revolutionize the school, so probably the right approach is to make the
> best of what you're doing at the moment.'
>
> (Lional)

Lional also feels that being able to pace himself lowers stress levels and work
should be seen as more routine than intensified. He is convinced that things
will get done, and is fairly confident about the schedule:

> 'There are things that people feel they've got to get done. I'll get them
> done. I've got some of them done this term, I'll get some of them done
> over the holidays, I'll get some of them done in the first four weeks of
> next term.'
>
> (Lional)

He runs for leisure, and feels this helps cope with the day's events. His
running is a metaphor for how he paces his work:

> 'I find that I get my best ideas running – keep on running! I just find
> it's relaxing. I tend to switch off while I run, and you just click over what's
> happened in the day. I would say I've paced myself quite deliberately

over the last month and probably before that. I've had a fair idea of what I'm going to need to do. I'm nearly there now.'

(Lional)

Evelyn (Year 6) is a language post-holder, relaxed about taking on management roles. For her, Ofsted meant having watertight plans, and she was happy for them to have a pre-Ofsted visit so they could acclimatize themselves to the real thing. This is another aspect of routinization, the belief that it is only a matter of practice to ensure people will cope with new situations. She saw Ofsted as a helpful pressure to get things done:

'I think it's pushing things, to tidy up paperwork that's left. If you've got a deadline, you do it. Once you've got a date, you go for it, don't you?'

(Evelyn)

The deadline is neither an opportunity to enhance the self nor a reason for panic or criticism, but a matter of incorporating it into the routine.

Distancing

These teachers were able to distance themselves from the role, unlike some other primary teachers (Nias 1989). Georgina (Year 1) has shared responsibility for maths in a large school, but she also has other responsibilities and events in her life:

'I go home and I have two children who want my attention and, school, you forget it. You can't be thinking of everything. I think it does help because I have to say, "Right, I will do 1½ hours tonight and what I don't do doesn't get done. I've got to have time at home with my kids and do what I need to do".'

(Georgina)

Rosemary (Year 6) feels it is important to distance stress.

'You just do your best, it's the same as any other day isn't it, teaching? You get on with it and that's that. Getting stressed about it is not going to help, is it? I think you need to be calm and relaxed and you get through it . . . I don't think I've changed much. I've always worked the same way and, I haven't done anything special. I just work as usual. That's me, you know. I try to calm others and stay on the right side of things.'

(Rosemary)

Emily does the same after a critical inspection visit,

'The only time I spoke about it was when somebody called me up and said: "Well, what do you think about it?" I didn't bother about it. I just said to my friend, "They come, but they're not there as far as I'm concerned when I'm in the classroom".'

(Emily)

Lional, like Larry, talked to the inspectors when they came into his room but from a sense of decency, rather than for self-enhancement. 'I saw it as something to survive not as a feather in my cap.' He wasn't bothered about being given a grade: 'I'm a practical person, I'll ride it.' And: 'I didn't feel harassed about people marking me through the week, so long as it is satisfactory, that's OK.' Similarly, Evelyn also spoke to the inspectors who came into her room, had some humorous conversation with them and was 'natural. I didn't stand back'. However, she was not interested in being given a grade as a teacher. 'I wouldn't have told the others my grade. I want to be seen as me.'

Balance

These teachers conceptualize events that might otherwise be in tension as ones that are actually balancing each other. Thus, Emily and her colleagues seem to take responsibility for the development of all the subjects in the school, unlike the modern trend to leave it to the post-holder (Webb and Vulliamy 1996), and she recognizes that they will be seen to be 'failing' in some areas.

'We know we're trying our best with new subjects, like design and technology. We've been on courses but we know where we're failing, and we're trying to put it right.'

(Emily)

Lional accepts

'that different people work in different ways. I know what sort of personalities other people are – you accept that.'

Evelyn could also see advantages in terms of uniform planning approaches and recognized the practical advantages for supply teachers. However, she was clear that 'I write things down to fulfil the requirements' even though she is good at planning, recording and organization. So she accepts the necessity for lots of written work but balances this up with the fact that it is required. Again, there is no real criticism or anxiety or anger, for this is the way it is. She and another member of staff, Lucy (featured later), planned a holiday to Morocco beginning on the Saturday after an Ofsted inspection, convincing themselves they would not be brought down by the process and that it was a matter of balancing the two events against each other.

Emily is aware that it is important to 'sell oneself', a new part of the role of a teacher. She does not think this is right, but it is *inevitable*, particularly with the way the Ofsted process occurs. Nevertheless, she thinks Ofsted has a role to play in terms of accountability and the school image. They 'are a good thing, they keep schools on their toes'.

The surviving conformists (ten teachers)

Surviving conformists are teachers who are critical of the process of change but who are determined to survive unscathed. They are doubters, dissidents, objectors to their new role. However, they are utilitarian, unsentimental, prudent and expedient. They often feel resigned and then recharged as another surge of adrenaline is discharged by an event or their efforts. They survive through a combination of supportive rhetoric, shifting positions and 'working the system'.

Supportive rhetoric

This form of rhetoric supports teachers' own educational values and counters current trends that appear in opposition to their values. The teachers seem to gain some comfort from *confronting* changing roles in these terms. Angelina, who does special needs teaching, is deputy head of The Estate School (Lowstate). She feels that the 'jumping through hoops' is the worst thing about much of primary teachers' new role, plus the vulnerability of primary teachers opening their classrooms and their practice to the outside world. She regrets the passing of 'fun' in teaching and the tight planning expected by Ofsted, for she feels this is debilitating if teachers feel they just have to plough on relentlessly instead of being brave and departing from the plans. She argues that teachers did their work for love in the past but now it is to produce evidence. She teaches working-class children because she sees herself as working-class and she wants to assist their development. She has a mission to teach but it is hard when parents expect too much. If she had to work as hard for the whole year as she did for Ofsted she would give up. She tires of the necessity to instigate uniform procedures and hopes that the day of the individual teacher has not passed. There is no 'promised land' for her to strive for now, and she had few visions left. It was just a 'grind to be got through'.

Cloe (Year 6) has taught at the same school for over twenty years and also has responsibility for science. She feels that a great deal of her individuality and enthusiasm is being sacrificed to a drive for uniformity: 'I'm becoming a vegetable to get things done.' Also: 'Children are becoming slots in a machine whereas we used to deal with the whole child.' She is also caught up in the dilemma/tension between 'corporate responsibility' and her individuality as a teacher. 'In a small school like this we are all expected to take up the management's woes for we are the management in reality.'

Lucy (Year 5) also teaches in The Estate School has a PE and dance post of responsibility. She feels:

'A lot of intuition is being forced out of our teaching. We can't respond to spontaneity so easily. The constraints are permanent. I could choose my own topic previously and now I'm having to teach what I'm told. There is a pressure to focus on the academic aspects of the curriculum and some of our children find it difficult. So the constraints are general.'

(Lucy)

She feels that the pendulum has swung too far the other way. 'It's an overreaction to the 1960s. There should be a happy medium.' She feels that Ofsted is 'putting teachers under a microscope' and that the grading system is an 'assault' upon teachers. She would rather have some personal comments about her teaching that she could work on.

Shifting positions

These teachers were willing to shift positions to accommodate change, as a temporary strategy. Angelina, in spite of her overall condemnation of the Ofsted process, found some comments in her Ofsted report useful, for it has enabled her to get things done that she thought were necessary but which were not being done. She is keen always to move on, after a short recuperation period. 'I was jet-lagged for a day, then my body caught up with my brain.' Once an event or a change is in motion she gets on and manages it. 'I don't like it but I can't alter it.'

Cloe's Ofsted report stated that 'literacy and mathematical standards of achievement were below the national average'. This had a profound effect on her, and she felt

'really pressurized because from somewhere I've got to produce SATs [Standard Assessment Tasks] results that will boost our standing . . . I was in tears at the staff meeting. I was dismayed by the head's reassurance that *we* would have better results this year. I could have screamed! It was the "we, we", and what it really boils down to is that "Cloe won't let it happen". Basically I'm the one where the buck falls.'

(Cloe)

The term following the Ofsted report Cloe was still not in good spirits, but she had found a way out. The mode of teaching required for the SATs

'is completely alien to my way of teaching – testing and teaching, teaching to test. However, my focus is on that really, and I don't give a monkey's uncle about anything else. If that's what they want, if they want better results, given the children I've got and the potential of the children, I will do my utmost to teach them how to pass an exam to the best of their ability and basically I'm spending the next fifteen weeks doing that.'

(Cloe)

In consequence, Cloe's SATs results following the inspection,

> 'were better because I acted like a function machine. You press a button and out comes the answer. I devoted most of that spring term to doing the whole science, English and maths curriculum that term. I went at it, bang, bang, bang, and if they hadn't got it tough titty. They had a lesson on this and a lesson on that and it was chalk and talk and thought for thought and you will learn and da da da da da da [*said rhythmically*] and we had a test on this and a test on that and we will have a test on something else. It was horrid. It wasn't much fun. I just went at it like a steam train.'
>
> (Cloe)

Having an aged mother to care for, and being forced herself to have a hysterectomy a few months after her stressful Ofsted inspection, she felt the time had come to ensure her survival.

> 'My attitude to teaching has completely changed since Ofsted. There is no reason for me to be here now except to collect a pay cheque. When I came into teaching that wasn't the reason. All those things have gone. There is no feeling that this is my vocation, my way of life, that I was meant to do this. I've accepted my lot. I've accepted that this is the way I have to do it. While I was still fighting it was so awful for I was so stressed by it. Now I accept that's the way I have to do it. Although it's depressing, you don't feel so stressed by it. You just get on and do it.'
>
> (Cloe)

Working the system

Goffmann (1961: 189) speaks of a set of practices among inmates of an institution that amount to 'working the system':

> Here, the spirit of the legitimate activity may be maintained but is carried past the point to which it was meant to go; we have an extension and elaboration of existing sources of legitimate satisfaction, or the exploitation of a whole routine of official activity for private ends.

Lucy had had a significant personal crisis nine years previously. She explained how she now maintained herself:

> 'I go along with rules, to keep my job. If I make it easier for them it will be to my benefit. I'm a believer in self. I have more confidence now, and if systems work for me, then that's OK. I used to bang my head against things. It didn't work. So now I live life. It's not just coping, it's living. If you communicate with people and let them know how you tick, it's better for you. I used to challenge things. Now I work the system.'
>
> (Lucy)

Lucy conforms because it helps her manage her fragile self. In doing so, she takes on new managerial roles. She ensured that she was well planned and organized for her school inspection. 'What was in my head I wanted to make clear to them in my files so I was super-organized.' She thought the inspection 'a breeze, I loved it. Would do it again tomorrow'.

Cloe has found some benefits to new ways of working,

> 'I am lucky in that I was junior secondary trained and I have a feel for the secondary way of doing things. So although it's hard, there have been aspects I've really enjoyed, like standing up and doing my main subject, geography. Doing rivers with my class. Really going into it and having them looking at the blackboard and me drawing diagrams and showing them how these things work and the kids all drawing them as well. I really enjoyed that side of it – but the rest of it is crap.'
>
> (Cloe)

In spite of her acceptance that there are pressures on teachers in this new climate, Angelina thinks teachers ought to be able to manage their emotions: 'After all, what can Ofsted do, shoot you?' She has her parents to stay in the middle of Ofsted to visit the Chelsea Flower Show, and she spends a lot of time calming people down. She urges people to take the longer view. She describes herself as the 'goalkeeper in the Ofsted game. I'm saving shots and own goals,' and she is not bothered that others play the centre forward role and get excellent grades. 'I'm not interested in grades. They are not part of my life plan. I just want to teach.'

The disturbed conformists (nine teachers)

This group of compliers battle for their professional identity, but in the short term not so successfully. Unlike the supporting conformists, who adopt the mode habitually, these are not happy with conformity. They would prefer to develop their selves, like the enhancers, but feel obstructed. Unlike the surviving conformists, they are not willing to 'shift positions', being committed to firm value beliefs. There is more anger and concern about their accommodation. Conformity is therefore a stop-gap measure. Bronwyn, Aileen and Carol represent this category. All these teachers are in their forties and have taught for more than twenty years. Bronwyn teaches in The Village School (Cottingly), Aileen in The Estate School (Lowstate) and Carol teaches in The Small Inner-City School (Trafflon). They all feel that they can adjust to most of the changes, though they have problems with some of them. Like the other conformists, there is a large measure of accommodation and working the system, but they are disturbed by the change in opportunities for professional development, the limitation of individuality and the assault on the educational values that they hold dear.

Accommodation

Bronwyn (Year 4) sees herself coping with a forthcoming Ofsted inspection, but her feelings are negative ones.

> 'I will cope with it, I will take it on board, I will do all the things I'm meant to do and I'll scrape and bow and I will back the headteacher to the hilt and I will back the school to the hilt. I won't let anybody down. But secretly inside myself I'm very, very angry that we're being made to go through this but I'm not quite sure at whom I'm being angry. Is it the Government? Is it the LEA? It must be the Government. We were dead scared when the LEA inspectors came round but now, of course, even that's not friendly any more, the big guys are coming in.'
>
> (Bronwyn)

Aileen (Year 2) is a 'worrier', and in order to ensure that she did not fail her Ofsted inspection, she spent many hours getting the work ready for the sample trays of pupils' work that were to be submitted for inspection.

> 'Not because it represents who you are, but you think that if my performance fails, this will be my proof, this is my evidence of my good practice. To show that I can get the kids working. It's my back-up.'
>
> (Aileen)

Carol (Reception) does not like accommodating since,

> 'It's almost like telling us to change our personalities . . . to say to some-body: "You can't do that any more" (after 24 years' teaching) is completely and utterly demoralizing . . . it's so alien to the way we work. [However, she] has to get to grips with it for my own sanity . . . otherwise there's a kind of inadequacy in it. Even if I don't like it, I've actually got to kind of deal with it in some way and prove that I can do it.'
>
> (Carol)

Working the system

Like the 'survivors', these are adept at working the system. Carol is 'creative' with her plans. She 'writes the plans out, fills in the outcomes later, and changes the plans if she alters her direction'. She has always been a 'compromiser'. Aileen similarly is creative in her accommodation. After a traumatic inspection for her she nevertheless puts it behind her after a few days.

> 'If you dwell on problems you get depressed. The resistance to the pressure is not to let it get you down and to move on and forget it. I accept that the system has won but I have to get on and work it.'
>
> (Aileen)

Bronwyn went along with what she thought the inspectors wanted to see during Ofsted week.

> 'I manoeuvred the geography into a lesson I knew I would be happy with, and I manoeuvred the science to an activity with which I was comfortable but would be good to stretch them as well. So I manoeuvred most lessons so that the lessons showed the differentiation going on . . . I took a group and moved them on to some more stretchy stuff and I also had a young group in the corner and I used lots of things with them so I was stage managing it so they could see that we were using all the different aids that we had. They didn't know that I was shaking in my boots. I have this tremendous ability to appear so confident nobody knows that really.'
>
> (Bronwyn)

Her scepticism is created by these contradictions, by the differing realities that are contrived, and the shame she feels for her part in that process. 'I've never had such brilliantly planned lessons in my life. It's absolutely pathetic.'

Arrested professional development

Bronwyn says 'I've lost my impetus, I've lost my oomph.' She spoke of incentives they used to receive, such as one twenty-day block maths course, which

> 'was wonderful. We were given new ideas, we were lectured to by modern people who were on the ball, with whom we bounced ideas. We got the latest ideas, we had the whole four weeks in which to think about what we could do. I came back afterwards and I was so bursting with ideas. I wanted to do this and I wanted to do that. I felt really refreshed and in charge of it all. Now I haven't been on a course for three years apart from my half-a-term, half-a-day ones and my once-a-term update on maths. I keep applying for them but of course there's no money, and I'm bogged down.'
>
> (Bronwyn)

These courses, she feels, have been replaced by courses based on Ofsted criteria focusing on how to cope with an Ofsted inspection. 'That's so negative, that's so threatening. People won't learn from that.' Carol found that attending some courses,

> 'everything's been taken out of my hands, any ideas that I have or anything that's mine has gone from me. You've got to fit into this kind of structure, haven't you?'

This was compounded by her experience of training for a literacy project, sponsored by the Government and launched as a pilot study in the autumn of 1996:

'It was like an evangelical experience in the way it was put over. It wasn't alien to some of our practices but it was a bit like fascism, everyone has to do exactly the same thing, there is a manual and we weren't allowed to ask questions as the training went along, though they did attend to some of the questions later. It was all run to a formula and even the trainers seemed constrained.'

(Carol)

Bronwyn is also aware that there often is not time for the whole school to reflect upon policies:

'So I've got all these prepared papers and I was going to give this thing at the staff meeting on music. They're all done, all the homework is done, but that was about six months ago I prepared it and we haven't done it yet. It's nobody's fault, we just keep chasing our tails all the time or something else takes priority. You've got to be really quite pushy for something like that to get done.'

(Bronwyn)

Carol is irritated that she spent 'part of the summer working with the deputy head on a listening and talking scheme of work, but we don't seem to have had time to write it up'.

Diminished individuality

Bronwyn values individuality. Her school is a small one and she was dismayed that its Ofsted report was presented in such a way that individuals were subsumed by it and only a bland overall representation constructed.

'Every teacher you interview or discuss things with is different, every person's different. But how frightening if everyone was a clone. Are they trying to make us all clones so that in the end we're all the same and we all teach the same? I have visited schools and everyone's supposed to teach maths the same way, but the classroom isn't the same. Are they supposed to display the same way? I find it quite scary.'

(Bronwyn)

Like Elizabeth, the 'ambivalent enhancer', she wrote the maths policy for her school, but unlike Elizabeth, felt it suppressed rather than enhanced her individuality:

'It's cloning us again. I've written the maths policy the same way as everybody else has done, but it's not couched in the way that I speak or I think or I believe. I wouldn't put anything down that I didn't actually believe, but it's couched in such a way that it's not come from me. I'm not allowed to be "me" even in my maths policy statement.'

(Elizabeth)

Aileen is caught in a tension between team and individual. An inspection criticized some aspects of her department, although she was assured that her own practice was fine:

> 'The department morale is low at the moment. It is difficult for me, for I feel close to the department team but the more public this criticism becomes I know that colleagues of mine in the area know that I'm in this department and I will be tarred with the same brush. It's depressing. I'd rather not dwell on it.'
>
> (Aileen)

She feels that the concept of the 'team' which she supports also has its problems because of the pressure it puts on teachers to conform. This leads, in her case, to feelings of guilt or inadequacy:

> 'Because they keep on talking about the team being only as good as the weakest link, I keep thinking, "I'm the weak link here, I'm going to let the others down" and obviously people are beginning to feel "Oh gosh, I'm going to spoil it for the school!" So you lose confidence, you don't perform as well, so the whole thing kind of escalates.'
>
> (Aileen)

She knows 'that after 25 years of teaching it is now their agenda,' but that any criticism of her practice reflects upon herself as a person. She cannot distance herself, unlike some other conformists:

> 'I try my best. Because you are a good teacher, because for all those years you've aimed to be good, you've tried to do your very best and then to be told, "No, well you're not good here, you're not good there – it's a blow," it's got your pride as well hasn't it? You can't separate teaching and you. You put so much into it, you can't switch off from it, you can't take a step back. In order to be good, you've got to be wholehearted and the children have got to see that you really care and you are committed and you want them to do well and you care about them . . . it's all or nothing.'
>
> (Aileen)

The bland evaluations of a local inspection are laughable, even to her son:

> 'It was funny last night. My son said, "How did you get on?" And I said, "Oh, *satisfactory*," and he said, "What! mum, you try ever so hard and you work every night, and you work every Sunday, and dad's got to make the Sunday lunch because you're doing school work, and that's *satisfactory*? Oh, Mum, *satisfactory*, after all these years!".'
>
> (Aileen)

Moderators for the SATs come to check up on how she is administering them.

'In other words, "You're all sort of crap and I'm going to make sure I catch you" . . . It's an invasion of you and what you've done and what you're doing or assessing.'

(Aileen)

Aileen comments on the inspectors' awarding of grades to teachers:.

'Once you give a mark you're summing someone up. You reduce everyone to a number. You're reducing years of experience to a number.'

The assault on values

Bronwyn expresses the basic tension in the teacher manager's role for one who feels strongly about class teaching,

'It is all very well making me into a managerial role and making me in charge of this and that, but where am I going to find the time to do this wonderful job as well as teach? . . . You run the maths in the school, run the computers in the school, help with the music in the school, and PS "Can you be a damn good class teacher as well?" And that's an impossibility unless I became a technician and just handed out the stuff. That's called "cold teaching". You have a day off to do your maths each week, a day off to do your computers each week, a day off to do your music teaching, which means that you'd be around the whole school more than you'd actually be back in the classroom.'

(Bronwyn)

She sees teaching as an art, and assessing art cannot solely be done by the use of quantifiable criteria:

'How can you give them marks out of ten? I got a ten out of ten maths lesson. But that's because I knew what they were looking for; they were looking for differentiation. It was a real con. Differentiation, pace, explanations and then to move them on if they'd done it right because I knew what I was doing. It just seems so sad that they just come in but they don't know what's going on in my head – they couldn't judge that I was choosing Fred Bloggs because "I knew he knew how to do this concept," they can't see that.'

(Bronwyn)

Carol feels that all her values and experience count for nothing when the history of her work and development is not taken into account, 'as though we've just been messing about and having a good time and not trying to teach the kids to read':

'I certainly feel that having taught for twenty-two years, all of a sudden our practices are being called into question. I'm very good at deciding

what needs doing at the time. I don't like to stick to what I am supposed to be doing. I'm quite happy to write them out, but basically
what I do at the end of the week is see what I haven't done and I do
it then, rather than planning everything tightly and thinking all the
time, "I've got to do this and this".'

(Carol)

The teachers' concern about their pedagogic values is compounded by challenges to their professional values concerning teacher collaboration and new
developments in managerial monitoring. Carol is keen to continue a collaborative way of working that involves all the staff in her small school in the
development of the curriculum. When she last introduced a major change in
language policy – developmental writing,

'the reason it got off the ground was something to do with the fact that
the people weren't coerced into doing things, and people didn't feel
threatened by it. They weren't made to feel bad about what they were
doing . . . It was a slow, gradual process . . . We've got to hold dear to
that fact that forcing people into situations, being made to do things,
doesn't work.'

(Carol)

She does not want to engage in the sort of subject monitoring that is advo-
cated currently – the observation by subject 'managers' of colleagues' work. She
would prefer a more collaborative approach where teachers share experience
and learn together:

'I would like to start with Veronica (Year 4) and go in and see what she
is doing and first of all learn things for myself and then discuss her
work with her. I would see monitoring as finding out so the information could be shared with all of us.'

(Carol)

The drift to technification is prefigured in Bronwyn's reflection: 'I think
perhaps I'm caring too much and perhaps we should take the job as it is. It's
just a job.'

Non-compliant teachers (four teachers)

These are teachers who, for one reason or another, find difficulty in coping with the change in role. They experience a high degree of role tension.
There is no enhancement, however critical; no accommodation, however
sceptical. The result is struggle and conflict. They are at times reluctant, indis-
posed and antipathetic towards the teacher manager role. Naomi, Victoria
and Clare decided to maintain their way of working and to confront parts of

the system in one way or another. They feel so strongly that survival is not an issue for them – they are prepared to risk being dismissed. Naomi is a respected upper junior teacher at The Suburban School (Morghouse); Victoria teaches in The Small Inner-City School (Trafflon) and is a bilingual teacher who was brought up abroad and obtained teaching and MA qualifications in her first country. Clare works part-time in the same school as Victoria, teaching the rest of her week in another school. These non-compliers exhibit defiance, withdrawal and reclamation of their own lives.

Defiance

All three teachers have asserted that they will not be dominated by paperwork. Naomi (Year 6) who has responsibility for dance asserts:

> 'I'm not doing it, so they are going to come in and ask me for my file and I'll say, "I haven't got one," are they going to sack me? I've got these things but they aren't filled in properly, so they can have those, I've got my file which I write lots of things in, not in the format they like or want. I haven't got the record-keeping they want. People do it, I don't, I'm naughty.'

> (Naomi)

They all feel that they want to focus on teaching. Victoria (Year 3) observes that, 'I spent too much time *functioning* last year and not listening to the children. I want to teach the children not work from records.' They all refuse to observe the detailed planning approaches currently required. Clare had her own way of confronting the issue.

> 'The paperwork doesn't affect me now. I did it for Ofsted, then afterwards I went to the head and said, "I won't do it. If you make me I'll leave." I'm still here, because the head knows I plan well in my way and I'm a good teacher.'

Victoria's way was slightly more covert,

> 'I didn't have the plans that "kill you" in school when a local inspector asked for them. If they catch me I'll stop working and become a supply teacher.'

Withdrawal

These teachers were prepared to 'withdraw' if put to the test. Three weeks before the inspection at Naomi's school, her mother died and she took some time off school to grieve and make funeral preparations. She needed more than the school allowed, and 'the pressure to come back had been immense and although I did come back the grief hit me. I was threatened by the management with withdrawal of salary if I didn't return which I thought was cruel given I was a single parent with no savings. I was looked on as a piece of machinery. The school was run like a system.'

(Naomi)

However, she was defiant and eventually the school management agreed they had been a little hasty, and she came back in her own time.

Clare put the shutters down on her feelings about the inspection. She feels bitterness and anger over the way her school was portrayed in terms of SAT results and feels this was very unfair for they were dealing with very deprived children, but she can deal with it. 'I made myself recover. I have coped with it by blanking it out. If I discuss it with anyone I get very upset.' In terms of curriculum management, she has also withdrawn. New approaches to curriculum responsibility mean that post-holders now construct and select policies themselves or from courses and get them ratified by the staff rather than building policies in a whole-school approach (Webb and Vulliamy 1996). When her post-holder proposed a new language scheme, she

'nearly came to blows with her, one of my friends. I was the head of a literary project and I was not involved. I could see she didn't know as much as me. But I wouldn't volunteer now for I am not appreciated because I am part-time and it's not the way policies are drawn up anymore. We used to do them altogether.'

(Clare)

Victoria has withdrawn from 'pretending that I'm covering the curriculum because I was not covering it. I couldn't really stop and teach when I thought it was necessary.'

Reclamation

Naomi has reclaimed herself by prioritizing grieving time for her mother over an Ofsted inspection. 'The Ofsted inspection had no meaning for me. I wanted to talk about my mother. There are three things in life – birth, love and death. Ofsted doesn't figure in any of them.' In a discussion about death, she observed: 'I don't mind dying but I don't want to be nothing.' She has been training as a counsellor: 'Teaching is not my whole life. I'm trying to get out.' Once she had thought teaching was her life but she is still able to reclaim her life when it appears to be taken away from her. Clare's husband had been declared redundant from teaching in a college and the stress of the job and the redundancy had meant for Clare that 'I have to hold the family together; he is in no fit state to do it'.

Victoria has reclaimed her life with her own children.

> 'I have had to go back to see things from their point of view. While I
> was working so hard and having to get up so early and working so late
> I thought that they were making my life more difficult deliberately.
> Now I know I have to appreciate them more and listen to them more.
> It was mad. I was trying to get through listening to the children read
> in my class and not hearing my own children.'

She is also reclaiming her methods of teaching, 'taking time when I think
they don't understand and making sure they become confident rather than
just covering the curriculum'.

Diminished teachers (seven teachers)

These are experienced teachers who have either become damaged by the
changes, or have chosen to leave. The leavers have given up resisting to avoid
becoming damaged. The 'sinkers' are often exhausted, ill, confused, disturbed and worried. They are struggling to survive.

Leavers (four teachers)

Frank, Tania and Helen are our leavers. Frank had been deputy head of
The Village School (Cottingly) for over ten years. He had a number of other
responsibilities – class teacher, language consultant, INSET coordinator,
appraisal manager and teacher governor. He had been at the school for over
twenty years, where he taught in the upper juniors. He decided reluctantly
to retire in July 1996, at the age of 63, in spite of the fact that he still felt at
the height of his teaching capabilities and would have liked more pension-
able years. Tania had taught mainly infants in The Small Inner-City School
(Tafflon) for twelve years. She had taken up teaching when she came to
England from Cyprus in the 1960s. She was 60 when she retired, though she
had intended to carry on until she was 63. Helen, who was in her second
year of teaching in The Village School, like Frank and Tania left almost
exactly one year after their inspections. These teachers felt devalued and
disillusioned.

Devalued

By contrast with the reinforcement felt by enhancers and some conformists,
Frank (Year 5) felt the opposite. Many of the parents' questionnaires sent out
by Ofsted were returned to the school unsealed, and naturally the teachers
looked at some of them. There was a high proportion of ticks against the
'moderately well' boxes. Frank took no comfort from this:

> 'It sounds as if you only half do it, doesn't it? If they'd [i.e. Ofsted] just left it, "do you agree" and it was "yes" or "no", it would have been better. "Moderately" to me is the kiss of death, it's like "fair work".'

Similarly, the inspection report itself was so bland that Frank didn't feel that the teachers had been appreciated at all.

> 'It all comes over as faint praise. We were told unofficially that it's one of the best reports he'd seen but that doesn't come over . . . The staff are not mentioned much . . . Good teachers were not rewarded. So there is a little bit of bitterness for me really. I felt quite cross about it.'
>
> (Frank)

Tania (Year 1) was also an enthusiastic teacher, who had also tried to accommodate innovations. She had the post of responsibility for maths and regarded herself as a music specialist. However, her music lesson and maths were criticized in the report. Added to this, certain complimentary comments, which she felt should have come to her, were made about the work of other post-holders. 'They inferred that my science work was the result of the post-holders' ideas. I objected to that because they were my ideas.' Like the 'disturbed conformists', her individuality was subsumed under the managerial view that all expertise comes from the 'subject manager' (Webb and Vulliamy 1996). She felt she had done her best to conform and it was not appreciated: 'They said nothing positive to me about my work and my teaching.' Furthermore, it was not understood. The criticism of the music lesson was that some children did not have instruments, but she argued that they were taking part in the story around which the music was being created.

> 'They didn't ask me what I was doing. I could have done singing in rounds – this was applauded elsewhere in the school – but I thought this lesson in musical composition was appropriate. Another music advisor had been recently to my class and said the music was impressive and progressive.'
>
> (Tania)

Tania argued that evaluation carried out without any conversation about teacher intention obscures a full appreciation of teachers' work.

> 'I'm in favour of inspections but not ones like this. They condemn by omission and don't know their subjects. The maths person knew nothing about this national maths project I'm involved in. Who says they're experts?'

The criticisms made of her work and coordination, the art, music and maths, left her feeling angry and bewildered at this sudden loss of worth. 'If I had been doing it all badly, then surely someone would have said something over the last twelve years I have been here?'

Helen (Year 1) was wrestling with the tension between developing her individual style as a teacher and having to conform to recent management practices introduced in her school, and she was constantly thinking 'I can't relax if I feel all the time that someone's checking up on me'. She was experiencing a loss of worth in spite of only just beginning her career.

> 'When I was training they'd say, "If a child brings something in, it might be something brilliant, let the whole class join in with it." You can't really do that now because you're constantly planning in such detail that I think, "I'm not getting through what I've planned".'
>
> (Helen)

Her local inspector described her

> 'as "good enough for a newly qualified teacher". It was a horrible comment. I'd like to feel what I was doing was right.'
>
> (Helen)

This hurt her a lot, for she was 'doing what I'm told. I'm constantly thinking all the time about how to do it right.' She teaches in a small room with over thirty children and she recounts how the inspector commented on the noise level in her room in an early visit. The same inspector then suggested she reorganize the distribution of her colouring pencils differently, and in spite of her arguing with the head 'that I wanted to encourage independence,' she felt she was forced to change her practice. She was caught between trying to hear all her children read regularly and the need according to her inspector 'to move around the room more'. She was worried that her children did not have enough play in their curriculum, but: 'The small room and the pressures to get through her plans prevents me doing so much of that. Will the inspectors expect to see more?' She 'emphasized all the right health and safety aspects' to a PE lesson her school coordinator was watching and 'tried to be perfect'. She felt that: 'We're always having to prove ourselves.'

These tensions made her feel more 'condemned' and 'guilty for not getting it all done. She felt 'guilty for not completing my work and worse for the fact that there is no relief.' She worried about whether comments in the Ofsted report could be laid at her door: 'How will I feel afterwards. Can I face the parents? Am I good enough. Will they remove their children from my class if I'm criticized.' She harked back to her teaching practice where she felt that tutors had 'supported her and talked to her about her practice. They don't do that now. If I could talk to them I wouldn't mind.' She felt that the Ofsted process made her interrogate herself much more and made her much more self-critical: 'I have not had any years of teaching to get my confidence.'

Disillusionment

Frank became disillusioned by excessive paperwork and loss of control:

> 'I love the contact with the children and when I say paperwork, I'm not talking about marking or preparation. It is the interference, not from the head, but from the Government and outside bodies . . . So much of the pleasure is going from it . . . We are so busy assessing children that we're forgetting to teach them.'
>
> (Frank)

By contrast with those who felt their teaching enhanced and control increased, Frank felt the opposite. He loved teaching, and English and drama, often via history, are his abiding interests. His preferred mode of teaching was 'going with the flow' (Woods and Jeffrey 1996a).

> 'I very much create on the hoof. Sometimes I'm going for a drama lesson and children say what are we going to do and I say, "Ha!" . . . and then it'll come, an idea. I do hate all this detailed planning . . . Ofsted want lesson plans. Now that would irritate me dreadfully, because then you're teaching in a false way. It's a personality thing . . . teachers do get inspired . . . That to me is a very important freedom for the teacher – to do what you want when you want and for good reasons.'

He was dismayed at the diminution of risk-taking and creativity in teaching, and the squeezing of teaching opportunities within a much tighter curriculum: 'There used to be time to talk. I can remember lunchtimes, you'd have a game of chess, which I thought was terribly important.'

The new managerial operations were anathema to him. He had been drawn into the increased budgeting and financial responsibilities of local management of schools but was not 'confident in myself doing loads of figures and estimates and all this business. But I'm confident in my own ability to teach.' Like Bronwyn, he disagreed with the trend towards subject coordinators monitoring other teachers, particularly in primary schools. He regarded this as the head's role, because: 'You've got to live and work with these people.' He didn't mind the role of 'teacher's friend', which he took with probationary teachers at one time, but thought it

> 'wrong for you as a teacher to criticize other teachers' work . . . How would that affect the atmosphere in the staffroom? You're going behind a colleague's back. . . . It's very cold, the whole thing . . . The whole way it's going is very, very depressing. This isn't what I came into the profession for at all.'
>
> (Frank)

For Frank, it was not a job he would want to do if he was starting again: 'If I could go back as it was, yes. But knowing all these aspects now, no, I wouldn't go into teaching now.'

Three months after the publication of her inspection report, Tania developed high blood pressure and took sick leave for over two months. 'She looked the picture of a victim. You know how much she prided herself on her appearance, well, she looks a shadow of herself . . . She's having a breakdown,' commented her deputy head. Tania, however, recovered with medical assistance and she did return to work: 'I like the job.' However, two months later she decided to retire:

> 'I'm better and off the medication but it has made me think about myself. It took a long time to recover and so I've decided to retire. I would have liked to have gone on to 63 but things happen.'
>
> (Tania)

She was disillusioned with what she saw as the contradictions and inequities of the new process of accountability. 'My husband and the headteacher told me to forget the comments but I couldn't.'

Helen was disillusioned with the stress she was put under: 'I can't do any more. I've had it up to here.' On the impossibility of teaching creatively: 'I'm always getting at them to be quiet or concentrate.' And on the impossibility of being perfect: 'It never ends. I've tried to beat it but I can't.' She also didn't 'want to let the school down'. After the inspection she was 'drained' by the Ofsted methods: 'They didn't look at any of my files, they made a criticism of science in the school that wasn't accurate and they said my children were not enthusiastic which was not true.' She resolved to 'have the summer for herself and her housework.' She worked the next term during which she suffered from heavy colds and pregnancy reactions, but since having her baby, had not yet returned to teaching some 18 months later.

Sinkers (three teachers)

These are successful, experienced teachers who have become damaged. They are often exhausted, worried and debilitated. We focus on Veronica and Esther, who have both taught for over twenty years. Veronica works in The Small Inner-City School (Trafflon) and has responsibility for technology, and Esther teaches in The Estate School (Lowstate) and has responsibility for music and art. At the time of the research, they were showing pronounced symptoms of stress, notably physical illness, feelings of worthlessness, and confusion.

Physical illness
Weekends are just 'nightmarish' for Veronica currently:

> 'On Saturdays all I seem to do is just fall asleep. I go to do something and I feel sick with tiredness . . . I was out like a light. I think it's my

mental way of surviving, my brain's telling my body to shut off. I think it's worry more than anything and I've started nosebleeds again ... I find it very difficult to eat and I gag ... it just won't go down.'

(Veronica)

Veronica (Year 4) recounts: 'I've come out in rashes and spots. It's like hell, it's stupid little things really, hundreds and hundreds of them, tiny, just started coming up yesterday and patches of eczema.' Two weeks after Esther's (Year 1) Ofsted inspection, she had large cold sores on her mouth, swollen glands, sore throat and an inflamed nose. 'I knew I'd be ill if I got run down.' Esther notes in her diary,

> Bed at 11. Read till 11.55. Awake at 1.20, 2.20, 3.30, 4.08, 4.40, 5.15, 6.05. Gave up and got up at 6.15 to write this and have a cup of tea.

Worthlessness

Veronica feels now

> 'the same way as I did when I came here six years ago. I felt quite worthless as a teacher then and I feel quite worthless now. Whatever I'm doing it's not right, I can't make it fit, whatever I'm supposed to do I can't, it's not good enough. Toni went over my paperwork with me and she was very nice about it, very positive but I can't do that, my head won't work that way, I can't break it down, maybe I've just got a block about it.'

In Esther's case, it is meaninglessness.

> 'Keep making lists, this is the way to cope with it. Oh dear, I don't know what I'm doing here to tell you the truth.'

Even the computer is no help. 'It always tells me I haven't got enough memory to do whatever it is that I'm supposed to be doing.' Nothing works when you're drowning.

Confusion

Esther talks of a

> 'black hole in my classroom that things disappear into as soon as I leave them! I photocopy some sheets or something, come back in here and I set them out and I go out to the get the children and bring them in and I do the register and I say: "Now here are your worksheets" and I can't find them! ... Totally disappeared – it's incredible.'

Veronica tells how she

> 'Forgot to take the National Curriculum booklet home at the weekend to actually write down at the side of this week's plans exactly where they fit in, and it wrecked my weekend. My other half did some ranting on

Saturday morning, about my reaction to forgetting them. "They're just ordinary people and if you know what you're doing is right and you believe in what you're doing it'll be OK." I said to him, "You don't understand," as I sat there in floods of tears, but I don't know. I can't do it, I can't do it, I can't do it. Do you know what worries me more than anything? I don't lose my rag very often, but like most people, once you flip, you flip and I do go absolutely bananas.'

When Veronica tried to conform to the demands for forecasts of her teaching plans, it results in wasted time:

'I've looked at it and I've thought, "What the hell is that doing there, that's this week's stuff!" And I flick through it and it's totally muddled. I've got half of last week's stuff in it and half of this week's! I must have just turned the page over accidentally. I thought "I just don't believe I've done that." '

Loss of self
These teachers found themselves acting in ways alien to what they considered to be their real selves.

'Some of my kids who didn't know any sounds at the beginning of term have now got the majority of those sounds and they're so proud of themselves. I should be over the moon about that but I'm thinking, "Shut up kid, we've got to get through this because we've got so much to fit in." '

(Veronica)

Domestic life is affected in the same way:

'My mother's been staying for about ten days. By half way through Sunday I was ready to kill her. I just wanted her out of my house. I love my mother dearly. She doesn't irritate me, she really is a lovely lady, ever so gentle. I just wanted her out so that I could get on with the paperwork because I knew I had to get it done by Monday morning and how do you say that to somebody who's elderly, lives on her own, and loves coming up?'

(Veronica)

When her mother rang to say how much she had enjoyed her visit, Veronica

'could have cried buckets. I felt terrible because the time I spent with her, one half of me was with her and the other half was thinking, "How am I going to get these records in?" '

(Veronica)

These teachers are not simply incompetents who cannot manage the changes. There is a complexity of factors at work, which we examine in Chapter 7 where we consider the general issue of teacher stress. We include these cases in the analysis.

CONCLUSION

Looking across the types, we could divide the responses into positive and negative features. Prominent among the positive features are a welcome for the order and framework of sound planning, new opportunities for self-development, an increase in ownership and control of one's teaching, the ability to 'engage' with others and greater expertise. The negative features are a mirror image of these: bureaucratic and work overload, diminished selves, loss of ownership and control, distance rather than engagement, and an atrophying of skills. Both strands are represented among our sample, and with some teachers the positive outweigh the negative. But the balance on the whole strongly favours the negative, as is clear from both the numbers and the qualitative testimony. This means a preponderance of stress and coping, avoidance and survival strategies in teaching, as contrasted with the creative teaching for which English primary schools were once internationally renowned. They have indeed become more like secondary schools in that respect, where wrestling with unhelpful circumstances with inadequate resources has been a traditional feature for some time (Woods 1979).

Some teachers are feeling enhanced by the reforms, however, so why not others? It could, of course, be a matter of values, as is clearly the case with one example we shall examine in Chapter 5. Osborn *et al.* (1996: 150) also found some evidence to show that 'teachers who had perceived themselves as strongly child-centred, creative and spontaneous in their approach were those who often felt they had the most to lose under the National Curriculum, and were, as a consequence, less positive about it'. Values are a factor, but by no means the only one. Osborn *et al.* (1996: 150–2) consider a number of institutional and individual factors among teachers in their research which enabled them to 'take control of the changes . . . and to selectively modify and adapt them'. They point to school ethos and strategy for change, neighbourhood factors (such as yielded by inner-city schools in working-class areas with high degrees of special need, contrasted with schools in affluent middle-class areas), leadership and collaboration. Above all, however, they feel the sheer pace of change to be the major factor, and that if only teachers had been 'given an opportunity to take ownership of the innovations, "mediation" and creative response to the changes might have been the predominant response' (ibid.: 152). This, however, only begs the question of why they were not allowed to do so.

It could be claimed that a measure of deprofessionalization has set in. Deprofessionalization involves the loss or distillation of skills, routinization of work, the loss of conceptual, as opposed to operational, responsibilities, the

replacement of holism by compartmentalization, work and bureaucratic overload, the filling and overfilling of time and space, loss of time for reflection
and for recovery from stress, the weakening of control and autonomy, and, in
general, a move from professional to technician status (Apple 1986; Densmore
1987; Apple and Jungck 1992). There is clearly some of this here among a
majority of the teachers, who have experienced new degrees of role tension
and constraint.

Inevitably, there is a large psychological component accompanied by emotional trauma involved in such radical change. This trauma is not just a way
of 'letting off steam', but serves the main social purposes of deprofessionalization. The teachers' responses show what it feels like to be deprofessionalized
(see Jeffrey and Woods 1996).

Role tension, of course, is functional for the technification of teaching,
if that indeed is the aim. It is only likely to be a problem for professional
teachers, not for technicians who will meet the role obligations others have
set for them whatever they may be. It is functional, since the higher the tension, the higher the pressure to resolve it, by accepting the changes, or by
leaving. The general push towards standardization is assisted by management
systems which police for conformity to prespecified models like the 'good
teacher', a 'one best way' solution to all education's ills. This appears to be
eroding individuality, as one would perhaps expect. In pedagogy, we have
seen how this discourages risk-taking and innovation, which, arguably, are
associated with excellence in teaching. So, are the changes, overseen by Ofsted,
encouraging mediocrity rather than excellence? What are the implications
for school improvement? What are the children learning about society when
they see teachers engaged in some of the 'compliance games' reported here?

CHAPTER 4

Making the new headteacher role

INTRODUCTION

Before the 1980s, the main function of headteachers was seen as 'leading professionals' (Davies 1987; Dunning 1993; McHugh and McMullan 1995), promoting the school's educational development through their own example. They were considered teachers rather than administrators or managers (Coulson 1980: 93), reflected in the fact that they were called 'headteachers'. There was a strong moral and ethical component to their leadership (Grace 1996: 142). They were essentially autonomous regarding the policy and practices within their school, and appeared to carry out the role in isolation (Pollard *et al.* 1994). Restructuring, however, has brought a radical change in the head's role. As noted in Chapter 1, the Government saw the heads as key 'change agents' in their schools. In the era of new public-sector management, 'it is principals who are at the sharp end of change' (Lauder 1996). But if they were to be effective in this capacity, they also had to change themselves.

New primary headship, in a managerialist era, goes considerably beyond moral and educational leadership (Grace 1995). Heads have responsibility for such items as budgetary planning and administration, marketing, financial and personnel management, staff development and appraisal. They preside over fundamental redefinitions of the relationship between parents and schools, and between teachers and teachers. At the same time, the head has lost none of the old responsibilities. In consequence, Dunning (1993: 81) sees the role of the head as having expanded considerably:

> In schools of all sizes it [the headteacher's role] is now a multifarious role, involving the constituent elements of leadership of professional development and curriculum: management of organisational structures, resources, public relations and finance; as well as the disparate respon-

sibilities of being a general administrator, planner, initiator, evaluator, assessor, appraiser, team builder, problem solver, decision-maker, and pastoral figurehead; and even this list is not exhaustive.

Most writers, while agreeing with this, see the head's role as having changed markedly in *emphasis*. It has commonly been represented as shifting from 'leading professional' to 'chief executive' (Hellawell 1990; Ball 1990; Bowe and Ball 1992) or 'educational leader' to 'business administrator' (Menter *et al.* 1995b) or from 'moral purpose' to 'commodification' (Grace 1996: 156). Hellawell (1990: 407) suspected, however, that rather more heads were trying to keep to traditional practices than openly admitted doing so in a valiant attempt to meet the requirements of the multifarious role identified by Dunning, and to uphold the values and moral purpose in their practice.

This is a classic recipe for the generation of tension. Acker (1990a), for instance, shows how a head, in order to 'manage the drama' of primary school life, must necessarily adopt a fragmented role to deal with the complexity and chaos of the institution and its social processes. So diverse and demanding were the tasks of Acker's head that she was 'pulled one way then another between them' (ibid.: 250). Blease and Lever (1992) also stressed the 'intensity of the role, the lack of time for adequate reflection about issues, the multiplicity of their function (Hayes 1993: 2). Webb and Vulliamy (1996: 117) neatly illustrate the tension for heads. Whatever action they take stands to be criticized. Thus heads have been censured for using LMS to 'validate flight from the curriculum' (Haigh 1993), while teaching heads have been criticized for using their teaching commitments as a coping strategy against managerial pressures (Hellawell 1990). Not surprisingly, they conclude that, since their role has become 'so diverse, expansive and responsive, although heads work to long term goals, there is a sense that "getting on top of it all" in the short term was impossible' (ibid.: 138). Grace (1996: 155) concludes that 'moral, ethical and professional value dilemmas in school leadership have probably never been as sharp and complex as they are now'.

The impact of the new roles on headteachers has been as diverse as the roles themselves. Pollard *et al.* (1994) anticipated that heads' responses to the changes would lie along a continuum ranging from compliance through mediation to resistance. The heads of their research, however, clustered around compliance and mediation with no modes of resistance being apparent. Grace (1996) notes a limited form of headteacher resistance where heads are openly critical of the Government's policy. While finding some heads not coping, Webb and Vulliamy (1996) also describe headteachers who were either 'celebrating' (in Grace's terms; Grace 1996) the introduction of the post-Education Reform Act model or 'welcomed it because it drew upon their particular interests, strengths or latent skills, providing especially for those who had been in post for some time, a new phase to their career (Webb and Vulliamy 1996: 140–1). Certain heads were found who

'relished the transformation of the headteacher role from leading professional to that of chief executive' (ibid.: 141). A large number of others who
were reluctant, or who found it impossible to adapt, have taken early retirement (see Chapter 6).

In this chapter, we examine the adaptations of three heads (Chris, James
and Raymond) to the new demands being made upon them. Only one of
them is meeting the new challenges with enthusiasm and confidence, but all
are retaining their individuality and values, and handling new demands in
their own manner. They have distinctive styles, therefore. All are considered,
by a variety of evaluators including pupils, parents, governors, fellow teachers
and school inspectors, to be 'good' heads. In fact, all three took over their
schools when these institutions were having problems, and have 'turned them
round', taking their schools to new heights. Their cases show how the individual can, in certain circumstances, steer a personal course through what
may appear to be times of constraint. They show the possibilities for creative
leadership in both meeting new requirements and preserving one's cher-
ished values. They are *making*, rather than *taking*, the new role (Turner 1962;
Plummer 1975). We discuss each head in turn, but to facilitate comparison,
we structure the discussion around key aspects of the new headteacher role.
These are as follows:

1 Promoting and guarding the school ethos or 'institutional bias'. Pollard
   (1985) has described the headteacher's power to create the school 'ethos'
   or 'institutional bias'. The teachers in his research, however, had some
   power to influence the head or subvert his intentions. The resulting 'institutional bias' was thus a 'negotiated order', with the head being the most
   powerful reality definer (Riseborough 1981). Institutional bias, or school
   ethos, has been identified as the most important item in school effectiveness (Rutter *et al.* 1979; Mortimore *et al.* 1988). It is to do with the values
   upon which a school is run, and how they are implemented. This may be
   in many symbolic ways that have become part of everyday life, and it is this
   that gives a school a distinctive character. The head stands at the centre
   of this, preserving and promoting the school 'way' (Pollard 1985; Acker
   1990a; Nias *et al.* 1989).
2 Gatekeeping. The head stands at the intersection between school and the
   outside world. External policy is filtered through the head. However pre-
   scriptive, it has to be implemented in individual schools in distinctive ways
   in harmony with their own ethos. Similarly, the school is represented to
   the outside world by the head. The head is also parents', and others', point
   of access to the school. The head used to have a traditional function of
   'protecting the school from the interference of parents and other outsiders, creating a community "sufficient unto itself"' (Coulson 1976: 101).
   Here, parents were seen as 'problems'. This had already moved on in the
   1970s to more of a 'harmonizing' school and home role, and one more

open to outside influences (ibid.), with parents as 'partners'. The central-ization of education and the marketization of schools in the 1980s and 1990s brought altogether a new relationship with parents – as 'consumers' (Webb and Vulliamy 1996: 122).

3 Managing. As we have seen in Chapter 1, the role of the head as business manager has received much emphasis in the restructuring of schools, and is the one requiring most change in existing heads. But there is also a more general emphasis upon management, as opposed to teaching. Peters and Waterman (1982), American management gurus, talk of the successful manager as a 'values shaper' – linking with (1) above.

4 Professional leadership. The head is still expected, if not necessarily to teach, to provide a lead in curriculum, pedagogy and classroom organiza-tion in the school. The head's curriculum leadership in this respect is still considered a key factor in effective schools (Webb and Vulliamy 1996: 132). Indeed, as a result of the changes, this part of the role has expanded considerably (Ofsted 1994). As for teaching, the DES Discussion Paper (Alexander *et al.* 1992: 48) urged that 'all headteachers should teach' and should 'lead by example'.

5 Cultural leadership. D.H. Hargreaves (1994) has argued that teacher cul-ture is undergoing a transformation, primarily from one distinguished by individualism and classroom autonomy to one marked by collaboration and teamwork. Teachers must work together to see the changes through, whether working with them or resisting them. The head is integral to this structure, but the style of participation can vary from a 'strong steer' to 'collegial support'.

THE COMPOSITE HEAD

Chris began her teaching career in the 1970s, in a school which she described as being almost 100 per cent bilingual. After a short time off for child-rearing, and a number of posts in various schools, she became head in 1990 of a lower school of some 200 pupils, catering for the age range 3–9. Up to 90 per cent of the children come from families who originate from the Punjab area of India and Pakistan. There are eight full-time teachers, two half-time teachers and one full-time bilingual non-teaching assistant. The school, like several of Chris's previous schools, was one with a number of educational and social challenges.

The previous head had done little about the implementation of the National Curriculum ('no records, no policy documents'). Chris had therefore come into a school which had an established culture developed in a vastly different world. She needed to build up relationships and confidence between herself and her colleagues in order to accomplish change. Previous models of head-ship were of little avail. She had to fashion her own.

Many informal discussions were held with Chris over a period of a year between 1995 and 1996. She was observed in action several times, and three semistructured interviews were held with her in the course of the year. Teachers in the school also volunteered information about her from time to time.

School ethos: a caring community

Chris's views are very much child-centred, which is in part backed up by her choice to continue teaching half-time, and also in the way she feels that resources are best deployed in the school. She believed in 'our children' having 'somewhere pleasant to work in', and felt she 'had to plough all the money back into the kids'. There is a prominent caring attitude in the way Chris talks about the pupils – 'kids', 'our children' – and her feelings of defending their rights as she sees them. The school boasts an outdoor swimming pool, a very spacious and well-equipped library, a new technology room, carpeted areas in every classroom and Archimedes computers in every classroom.

Basic to Chris's view is the need to treat the pupils in her school as individuals, and she measures the success of her school partly on this ability to make persons. Their attitude was the key to success, and she wanted them to 'feel comfortable' and to 'go home feeling good about themselves'. She was keen for the school not to add more stress to their lives, but that

'we're here to support and to be part of their lives and that relationships are good. For a lot of them, we are the most stable people in the community, we're here every day, and we can hopefully deal with things in the same way every day.'

She has the same views towards her staff, wanting

'them to be happy, to come in with enthusiasm and joy, and to take risks with children that will put a spark in them . . . [You can only do this] if you feel safe and secure and happy, and if children feel safe and happy with you, they are going to respond on a level which says we are independent learners because we're trusted, we're cared for, we're respected.'

The school offers consistency and stability, especially for some of the children whose families are often split up for long periods of time as parents and siblings make journeys back to Pakistan or India, though this is not discouraged by staff, who understand the importance of these visits for the development of the children's cultural identity. Care is often seen as a central aspect of much that typifies primary education (Acker 1995; Hargreaves and Tucker 1991), and yet, must be set within perspective, where care is valued alongside educational development. For Chris, like Nias's (1989: 41) teachers, 'caring was not a soft option'.

Gatekeeping: status builder and community worker

With the previous head, the school was almost an island, strongly insulated. But in the new era, schools need to be more outgoing, and to raise their profiles and status within the educational community. They also need help from outside in implementing the many reforms. To this end, Chris has opened the school to educational outsiders, local colleges, local education anthority advisors, professional groups and a variety of visitors. The school has been used to host special INSET days to which teachers from around the borough have been invited. An opera group spent a week working with particular classes. In addition to student teachers on teaching practice, the school has also had dance students and physiotherapy students carrying out special projects. There are close contacts with neighbouring schools.

Chris screens incomers for suitability. She is confident of allowing outsiders into the school as she has a great belief in the talent of her teachers, though invitations in most instances are given only after consultation with staff. Where visitors are 'foisted' onto the school, such as a group of Section 11 teachers whose visit was arranged by the local education authority, Chris was more inclined to take care of the visitors herself rather than have them disturb other classes.

Chris wants to develop closer links between the school, parents and the wider community. The children make frequent trips into the community, for example to the local church, Mosque and Sikh temple, to the local museum, to an old people's group meeting in the local community centre where they sing songs and talk with the members of the group. The close links with the local community include the local police, and in particular the cadets who raised money to pay for coaches to take the whole school to the cinema, and who regularly 'drop in' to the school for a chat and a cup of tea. Chris sees parents as 'partners' (compared with the previous head's 'problems' disposition). A number of initiatives have been mounted, such as a parents' reading group. Developments have been slow, since parents are very reserved, but there has been a growth in the number of parents attending more scheduled events such as sports days, special assemblies and parents' evenings. Chris herself spends a great deal of time on home visits, not only to families where perhaps children are having problems at school, but also to families of new entrants. She tries to visit most families through the year.

Managing: the professional mother

Chris's management style has parallels with what Griffith and Smith (1991: 24) call the 'mothering discourse', whereby there is an 'expectation that mothers [teachers] will love, care, and sacrifice'. The 'mother made conscious' (Steedman 1985) aspect for Chris, as noted earlier, extends to creating a homely environment in the school, and providing stability for the children. Chris actually likened herself to a mother figure when talking about the relationship she has with the staff:

> 'I always say, "Well, I am your mum," and other times I say, "I'm not your mum, you do it." It's like a standing joke . . . There is a need for tender loving care, and a great need for it to be very, very . . . I'm trying to think of the word . . . "constant".'

She likens the school to the family:

> 'It's like your home, isn't it? If your mum and dad are unhappy . . . so who do you get right first? Maybe you get it right by doing it all together; or maybe by me being your mum, being exactly the same every day, treating the same thing with the same kind of approach, the same to the children as to the staff. That's my job to be here in school, that's my job to help you do that . . .'

She talks about the supportive nature of her own family, her view of the importance of looking after the health of her children, and that 'they are very nice, caring, kind, supportive people which has always mattered more than their sense of achievement through school'. Similarly, Chris's interest in the children at her school goes beyond academic achievement and she is strongly committed to their overall health and welfare. As a mother would be, she is also concerned about the children's development over an extended period of time, not purely for the year she might be their class teacher.

> 'They have a right to a sound, good, education but that is wider than literacy and numeracy . . . They also have the right to the wider side of education, the medical side, physiotherapist, and all agencies that are around . . . caring isn't enough.'

Yet the 'mother made conscious' applies not only to Chris's belief system in how children and staff should be treated. Chris talks about herself as a 'reacting person':

> 'I can't leave anything alone, I have to do it as it happens, I will take it all home and have a go at it and give it back. The pace is fast, it has to be, otherwise we don't [get done]. You have to manage change according to what you have within you. I know how to manage change, but I don't [do it well]. It comes at us fast and furiously, it happens every day.'

Taking a reactive role is how parents deal with incidents and crises at home, as a great many decisions cannot be planned ahead. Additionally, as with the role of the housewife, Chris points to the multitask nature of her role as headteacher, much of which she feels is peripheral to her main job:

'We deal with budgets, we deal with maintenance, we deal with personnel, we deal with contracts, we deal with maternity allowances, we deal
with the playground, we deal with drains, we deal with phones that don't
work, we deal with . . . whereas before all this it was up to the council.'

Unsurprisingly, perhaps, Chris was not happy with some aspects of the new
managerial role, which seem to attract ' "macho" methods of educational
management' (Cunningham 1994: 103) in some schools. Al-Khalifa (1989)
feels that the term 'management' itself is very much associated with masculine traits such as analytical detachment, strong task direction, 'hard-nosed
toughness', and also physical strength and size as a desirable attribute, which
indicates the ability to control. Women, she feels, were reluctant to apply
the term 'manager' to themselves (as did Chris), and saw this abstention as
a positive statement about self-worth and values (see also Hill 1994b; Grace
1995). 'For many of these women, their experience and skills as education-
alists and as heads were felt to be positive and valued by them but denied
or not legitimized by current ideas and practices within the school context'
(Al-Khalifa 1989: 90). Al-Khalifa (1989: 89) found that the women managers
she researched specifically rejected those elements of the role of management
they saw as masculine – 'aggressive competitive behaviours, an emphasis on
control rather than negotiation and collaboration and the pursuit of competition rather than shared problem solving'. It is not known how far these
attitudes towards management are still being sustained by women heads,
though Grace's (1996) women heads took teamwork to be a normal process
(i.e. not created by management), and were less upfront about competition
in their discourse. Certainly, they seem reflected in Chris's strategies.

Professional leadership: total commitment

Hill (1994a) illustrates the 'all-embracing nature of the primary head's role'
from the DES Conditions of Employment of Head Teachers (Department of
Education and Science 1992b: 66), which 'charts an awesome set of responsibilities and duties'. Hill asserts, however, that 'we know that the most effective heads do not attempt to heroically do it all themselves' (ibid.), and many
primary heads consequently have lost contact with children and staff (McHugh
and McMullan 1995). Chris, however, has a compulsion to try to 'do it all'.
There is a pragmatic element in her universalism, particularly in marrying
what in other circumstances might be discordant features of the old and the
new, as in 'leading professional' and 'managerialist' discourses. Chris talked
about how poorly resourced and funded the school was, which meant that she
needed to work half time as a classroom teacher in addition to her responsibilities as headteacher in order to save money – and a teacher. However,
her reasons for remaining a class teacher are much wider than this. Basically,

Chris's compulsion for universalism derived from her need to express her self through teaching (Nias 1989). She also felt that she needed to establish her teaching credentials with her staff if she were to achieve change in the school. This role is tied up with her conception of self:

> 'I like teaching. I've learned more than anything that basically I am a teacher. I'm not a manager or accountant, a maintenance woman . . . I'm basically a teacher . . . and I really wouldn't want to give it up. I think it's been effective in some of the changes that we've been able to do, certainly some of the projects that we did in the early days. I don't think people would have been happy to do them if you weren't doing them yourself and managing with changes, and I think you lose touch really quickly.'

Despite taking on a large amount of classroom teaching, Chris still has a kind of omni-awareness, involving first-hand insight into all aspects of school life, a physical presence in all areas, and experience of other roles within the institution as well. In doing so, Chris is sustaining a long-standing feature of the primary head's role. As Coulson (1976: 102) notes, primary heads 'perceive a need to involve themselves personally in every aspect of school life' (see also Donaldson 1970; Cook and Mack, 1972).

> 'I can close my eyes and visualize every class and have some idea of what's going on, and I know where the kids are, and I know what they're doing, what kind of teaching and relationship they've got. That is very important to me. I think the teachers, when I go in to do supply and do things, I'm very trusted [*laugh*].'

Chris's readiness to do supply work for other members of staff has been noted on several occasions – when other teachers have had hospital appointments, or courses to attend, moving house, illness. On one occasion, a new teacher, taking the place of someone on secondment, was having serious problems with her class who were generally recognized as difficult. Chris arranged to exchange her own reception class with the new teacher, thus providing welcome relief. Amongst other things, this helps to satisfy her need for contact with the children, a need she shares with many other primary teachers (Campbell and Neill 1994a; Pollard *et al.* 1994):

> 'I really like it when we're talking about the children, and I have as much to say about them as the teacher because I do know them. I have more to say about the families because I do know them. I have taught most of the children in the school at one time or another, and when I go and see them, they respond to me very warmly, not just as the head.'

Communicating and contact is of the essence, not only with the teachers but also with the children, as she passes news and messages directly to the children rather than via teachers. She also makes full use of daily assemblies in order to keep abreast of any developments within school. Her involvement in what goes on around the school could almost be said to be omnipresent. She has even been observed serving school dinners when one of the dinner staff was absent. This illustrates Blease and Lever's (1992) point about the comparatively low-level nature of some of the tasks heads perform. The idea of being constrained to working in her office, to taking purely the 'chief executive role', is not one which Chris contemplates:

> 'If I came out of teaching, I would actually timetable something so I would take a class anyway. So I don't think I'd ever just end up in here [referring to her office].'

As Dunning (1993) points out, critics of the teaching head question how far the class may receive adequate teaching provision when their teacher is being interrupted by callers, messages and minor crises. Chris is not spared such interruptions when she is teaching. But Chris tends to deal with these matters quickly, and when dealing with children from other classes, has actually involved her own class in discussion with the pupil visitor. On one occasion, for example, when Chris was part way through a story with her reception class, Faisal, a boy from another class, came in to show Chris some photographs of his family. Rather than asking Faisal to come back later, Chris showed the children the pictures and involved both Faisal and the children in a discussion about them. This was an opportunity for talk with a purpose and genuine interest in this particular child's family photos which had been specially taken by a local studio photographer, to take to Pakistan. Once over, Chris returned to the story. There seemed heightened rather than reduced interest. It was an incidence of truly 'going with the flow' (Woods and Jeffrey 1996), and of 'orchestration' (Woods 1990), that is, pulling together potentially discordant elements of interaction into an harmonious whole.

Cultural leadership: controlled collaboration

Collaboration is at the heart of Chris's approach to cultural leadership. In practice, through force of circumstances, it is 'pure collaboration' only in some respects, 'controlled' in others. The former is described by a classroom teacher with regard to planning:

> 'It's very much a team effort. It's probably because we're all quite vociferous really. We argue in the true sense of the word, not in falling out. We work through and think things through together. And people are incredibly open. If something has worked and they are really pleased with something, everybody knows about it, just as much as they do when they've had a terrible day, and everything they've done's fallen to bits. And if somebody does something good, or has a good idea,

> nobody would dream of keeping it to themselves. It develops at differ-
> ent levels and people take it and make it their own, but in terms of
> sharing stuff, I've not yet been into another school like it . . .'

At the level of policy formation, however, from the way Chris describes the
process, collaboration is a little more controlled.

> 'I suppose I do a fair bit of it then pass it on to the coordinators. Then
> we talk that through, and only when we feel that we know what we are
> asking, in terms of changes, do we present it to the rest of the staff, not
> as, "Oh this is it," but "This is manageable," and we can talk it through
> properly. Then, when there are questions that we are asked, we can
> actually answer. We do work very closely together because of the very
> good relationships we have.'

Here, Chris exemplifies the omnipresent aspect of her leadership role, that
of needing to be involved in all the stages of development. Chris's managerial approach appears, at first, as 'top-down', in that she will often begin the
process of change, and is involved in all aspects of change. She sees it as her
responsibility, for good or ill, but she wants as much participation as possible:

> 'I feel we talk it through. I think everybody has their say, everybody, and
> when I walk away, that this is what we're going to do. But how am I
> going to get from there to their thinking the decision was theirs? Most
> of the time I've managed to do that but it still leaves me feeling I'm
> seen as taking full responsibility.'

Chris is, however, happy to delegate responsibility. In practice, as there are
only six full-time teaching staff sharing curriculum responsibility, some of the
teachers coordinate for more than one curricular area, and Chris is often
included in developing policy as part of the senior management team.

The composite head

Chris tends to adapt her role to the needs of a particular situation, and will
therefore become the chief executive or the leading professional when circumstances require. She will comply with, redefine or resist policy directives
depending on what changes she thinks are necessary, and whilst maintaining a collaborative culture in the school, she will make the final decision
when necessary. She has become a 'composite' head, in that her role is made
up of many different aspects which work at different levels, and which can
be attuned to different situations. In this, and in the apparent conflicts and
contradictions of her role, she would appear to be making the kind of adjustment required in the postmodern age – flexible, adaptive, creative, opportun-
istic, collaborative, with a drive towards improvement and self-development
(A. Hargreaves 1994a).

How does Chris do it? One way is by taking 'time out' to do the administration. In this way, the bureaucracy does not impinge on her teaching – 'only' her family life. However, this runs the risk of removing one tension by creating another. Grace (1995: 185) remarks that while women heads were able to 'balance their family and professional responsibilities in the 1960s and 1970s, the education reforms of the 1980s and 1990s have, through a process of intensification, brought this social balance to the point of crisis' (see also Evetts 1989). Several of her teachers remarked on how hard Chris works after school, often not going home until eight o'clock in the evening. Even then, she would frequently take work home with her. Chris makes clear that this is a difficult mode of working:

> 'It is hard . . . especially because I've also got a family, and sometimes you're doing it in between doing your ironing – it's almost like a break. But then again it could be poor management of my time during the day. I actually can't work in school, because it's not quiet enough for that, you're here for other reasons because I'm not a paper pusher in school, so you have to work around it. But it is hard.'

Sheer industry is Chris's main trademark, and is needed for the universalism she feels she needs to practise. Whilst productive in many ways, it carries its dangers, both for her and her colleagues. A classroom teacher comments:

> 'She is such a workaholic that if you don't keep up with her you feel somehow or other you're just a bit below par and you kill yourself . . . She's got incredibly high energy levels . . . She actually works far too hard than is good for her, and I'm sure her health will tell some time . . . It raises the old stress levels.'
>
> (Chris's colleague)

Webb and Vulliamy (1996: 135) found that headteachers in schools with between 100 and 200 pupils who had a class commitment, 'were finding it an increasing struggle to maintain the quality of their teaching'. This illustrates the measure of Chris's achievement, but 'it is hard'. There are tensions between school and family life, between authority and collaboration, and between the effects of intensification and devotion to child-centredness. She says herself that she is 'very aware of not doing things well', but adds 'that might be something to do with Catholic guilt'. This may provide a clue to her motivation, for she may be caught in another tension – that between 'persecutory' and 'depressive' guilt (Davies 1989). Persecutory guilt arises from failing to meet specified requirements, or doing something forbidden (Hargreaves and Tucker 1991). Depressive guilt, which has its roots in childhood, is one borne out of situations in which 'individuals feel they have ignored, betrayed or failed to protect the people or values that symbolise their good internal objective' (Davies 1989). Teachers like Chris who have care as a prominent concern are very prone to depressive guilt. For her, this form of guilt is the greater for feeling responsible for a whole school, pupils, teachers, policy and practice. It may be the source of her resistance to those parts of the Government's policy that she feels are inappropriate to the needs both of the staff and of the children in her school.

THE ENTREPRENEURIAL HEAD

We have already met James and his school Meadowfields in Chapter 2. Meadowfields was considered to be at the forefront of implementing the changes and James was regarded as a good exemplar of the new headship. He clearly enjoyed headship in the new managerialist era and felt quite comfortable with the new role.

Data on James come from observational fieldnotes, informal conversations and interviews over an 18-month period during 1995–1996. He was seen formally and informally in a range of contexts including his office, staff meetings, parents' meetings, staffroom and around the school.

School ethos: working together – the 'Meadowfields way'

> The school strives to develop the maintenance of close links with our parents to strengthen our shared responsibility for our children's education in a caring, cheerful and industrious atmosphere.
>> (School Development Plan Vision Statement 1993–1994)

Often when James was addressing the staff in meetings and on inservice training days, he would use the phrase 'the Meadowfields way'. He explains:

> 'We do care as colleagues for the children and each other in a professional way, and I think that my belief that we have a shared responsibility in bringing up the children means that we expect parents to be involved in what we're doing in the school, and therefore that their involvement and the intensity of that involvement means that we're opening ourselves . . . I'm not the kind of person that can pretend things are happy. I'd rather say it and thrash it out. I think things should be discussed, and when decisions are made sometimes it's not to everybody's liking but we vote for it as a group, we all accept that the majority rules. So if "the Meadowfields way" is being that, being me in some ways, I hope I'm working at it, and I hope the school is one where we do work with people and we do our best for people. It's about working together, not just in here as teaching but outside as well. That's my way, and if it means it's welcoming and it's open and it's honest, then I hope that is "the Meadowfields way".'

Evident here are themes of collaboration, working together, informal relationships, caring, community/parental involvement, openness and a concern for a wider professional community. Like Nias's (1993) heads of collaborative, whole-school cultures, James articulates a belief in the value of the individual and in the primacy of human relationships in education. The school was an expression of James's self – 'the Meadowfields way is being me in some ways' (cf. Southworth 1993). James 'actively sought to promote these explicitly shared beliefs in the work of colleagues' (Nias *et al.* 1992). Indeed, one aspect of his vision was the belief that values be shared by the staff group and in this he appears to have been successful. A teacher commenting on 'the Meadowfields way' said:

> 'I think it's all those things you can't put your finger on. It is the informal staff, the way you can share and you can admit weaknesses and not get a lot of criticism for it. But you will get constructive criticism. There is a sort of working together, we are all on the same side. We are all working for the good of the children. It is about creating a happy sort of relaxed atmosphere, where the work is going on, but it is done, hopefully, in a relaxed, fun way. It is a welcoming place. I suppose you get so used to so many people coming in that you do sort of look up and say "Hi, come on in". If you do fit in as a Meadowfields' person, it is having a sense of humour.'
>
> (newly qualified teacher – Reception Year 1)

Gatekeeping: vigorous promotion and defence

James promoted his vision vigorously both inside and outside the school, more so than Chris. He saw parents more as 'consumers' than 'problems' or 'partners'. He felt that schools were now constantly in the 'public eye' and stressed the importance of the school projecting a favourable image. He was afraid of parents going to the local press following incidents at the school. He was aware of bad press coverage of schools and used cuttings as a focus for staff meetings. This was not a stimulus for critical discussion but simply to say: 'This is what people think about schools and we have to take it seriously.' He would invite the press into the school to report on innovations, such as home/school links, parents and others helping in classrooms, and nativity plays.

The school was open to the community, parents, researchers, teachers from other schools and international visitors. On one occasion, a senior teacher objected to the impending visit of twenty American students because she thought it would disturb the Year 6 children who would be involved in taking their Standard Assessment Tasks (SATs). James dismissed this objection saying that testing was a feature of English education in the 1990s and that overseas visitors should be made aware of this fact. Further practical expression of the vision was seen in his celebration of aspects of the Education Reform Act which supported it. This was particularly so with parental involve-ment in the school.

> 'If parents have a better understanding of what we're trying to do, then we've got greater support . . . We get them to our surgeries and we show them all our year plans and things. So there's a huge involvement there.'

He busied himself in a great deal of work outside the school. He was prominent in the county's primary headteachers' group, and represented them in the media on topical issues such as an Ofsted report on the length of the school week. He would give talks to the heads' group and at heads' conferences about management/leadership issues, for example on how to handle school inspections.

As for policies coming into the school, much of James's work was devoted to ensuring that both he and the teachers complied with the Government's policies regarding management, curriculum and assessment. However, unlike the heads of Pollard *et al.* (1994), he led the way in resistance where he thought this was necessary. Coercion and lack of consultation over many of the changes which had taken place had caused resentment. Prominent among things resisted were the assessment and testing arrangements. Assessment had proved to be the sticking point for teachers nationally and resulted in the 1993 boycott of national tests. James had exerted pressure on certain members of staff to participate in carrying out the SATs at Key Stage 1. The school also participated in the Key Stage 2 non-compulsory pilot tests. However, he claimed that: 'You can only change things from within.' He wanted to know what the tests were like and their impact on teachers and children before mounting an objection. On completion of the Year 6 pilot tests, he requested and was granted a visit from a senior officer of the Schools' Examination and Assessment Council (SEAC). This visit gave James and those teachers who had been involved in testing an opportunity to voice their criticisms of the tests.

In the first year that schools were required to give parents an annual report on their children's progress, which took a nationally standardized format and showed progress in terms of attainment levels in subjects, James refused to do it on the grounds that it was a further unnecessary burden on his teachers, protecting his staff, like many of the heads in Webb and Vulliamy's (1996) research. His teachers had spent a great deal of time and effort in producing a comprehensive profile of each pupil's achievement. This was the basis for an ongoing record of achievement, documenting progress, and a focus for formative assessment involving dialogue with pupils and parents. Told by a senior assistant education officer at a heads' meeting that he was 'breaking the law', he said: 'I don't think I am, because we've already put a phenomenal amount of money, time and effort into doing this and we shared it with the parents, it was all part of *our* reporting system.'

James resisted official moves to deregulate the local education market. Whereas official policies of open enrolment and LMS had placed the local schools in competition with each other, the local heads' group had reached an agreement whereby they would unofficially regulate the education market in the town. However, one member of the group, the head of a neighbouring school to Meadowfields, set up a nursery unit without discussing this with James or the group. Since Meadowfields did not have a nursery, James considered that the action of this head was unprofessional and would give her school an unfair competitive advantage. James resigned from the heads' group in protest.

Managing: the new business manager

James is a paradigm example of the head in the new role of business manager. Being a manager has become part of his professional *and* personal identity. He plays golf and attends dinner parties with friends who are executives at a nearby car-manufacturing plant. These friends are a positive reference group external to the school (Nias 1989). They help him reflect on his position handling the school budget. They tell him that in the private sector managers would know budget details well in advance of financial planning and not have the kind of vague information which James has in LMS as a basis for budgeting and development planning. It is perhaps significant that before taking up teaching, he was a trainee accountant in the engineering industry. He also did vacation work as a manager in a national chain grocery store.

When introducing a researcher to the staff he said: 'Alan is coming into school to shadow me for a couple of weeks to study effective management – just like Marks & Spencer.' James was proud when the Government inspector leading the school inspection praised him for the efficient way he had assembled a wealth of pre-inspection documentation. She asked: 'Have you been on a management course?'

The local authority regarded him as being at the 'leading edge' of new headship/managerialism, and he spent a year on secondment acting as a 'troubleshooter' to help headteachers in the authority implement new management structures following the introduction of the Education Reform Act and LMS. He considered that training for management should be high on the agenda for deputies and heads of primary schools. He had recommended courses run by the Industrial Society, such as 'Effective Training for You and Your Staff', to the local authority headteachers' association. He felt that 'many of the courses can be tailored precisely to your requirements, whatever form suits your school'.

James drew upon his previous management experience in commercial contexts when talking to the staff about the importance of their managing resources prudently. He hoped to treat his staff as 'professionals', and did not consider he operated a 'top-down model' in management, but

> 'when things get tight and people get panicky about it, it's important to turn lights out and turn the heating down during the day when it's not needed. Photocopying is staggering – very expensive. If you could exercise good housekeeping . . . When I was working for Dunnants they used to have an annual bonus if profits were up. There was a sign next to the light switch in the loos saying SHUT THE LIGHT OFF YOU'RE LOSING OUR BONUS! It's coming here – it's burning someone's job if you think about it.'

James saw himself as a new-style manager and this separated and distanced him from the other teachers – and from our other two heads.

Professional leadership: educational exemplar and monitor

Though expanding in the managerial role, James had not abandoned his role as educational leader (Hughes 1973). He could still do their job, if his teachers could not do his. Being a good primary teacher was still very much part of his identity:

> 'I've got some good teachers here, but I've never seen anybody yet who I couldn't throw my hat in the ring with. And give me a couple of weeks to throw off the dust and I'd be in on a regular basis. I could be as electric in my relationships with kids, my planning and my effective way of managing my displays, my reporting.'

Head as exemplar

Although not timetabled like Chris, James would still teach in order to re-lease teachers to conduct SATs or work collaboratively with colleagues. Since physical education was his specialism, he usually took the opportunity for teaching large groups of children (for example, two classes of Year 2 children while their teachers carried out a reading test) in areas which were open to the gaze of the other staff in the school. This was usually the main hall or playground. The public nature of this teaching acted as an exemplar to the other teachers and, as with Chris, maintained his credibility as a primary teacher. He was particularly keen to promote learning in out-of-school contexts such as residential visits to field centres. As well as encouraging the teachers to organize this type of experience, he also led a party of Year 6 children each summer abroad.

James would use assemblies, not for curriculum development as Nias's (1993) heads had done, but, again, to maintain credibility and provide an exemplar for his staff in the areas of class control and staff–pupil relationships. These are issues high on teachers' agendas:

> 'I often get the jibes: "You can't handle them, and it's a while since you taught them." But I still teach PE and still do certain things at certain times. I've taken assembly or got a group of children together. People know I can control a group of children. In those terms that's important, that I can walk in and the kids will respond to my reactions. If I say, "Thank you," then they're quiet, and if I say, "Come on, let's have a laugh!", they'll laugh.'

James projected charisma. In a parents' evening, he was the protagonist in a dramatic performance to introduce a new prereading scheme to the parents. The infant department who adopted the scheme wanted to use the evening for curriculum development, in that children, teachers and parents would be involved in the launch of the scheme and learning something of its aims, structure and content. James led the presentation which involved five infant teachers, two classroom assistants and all of the Reception and Year 1 children. The children were dressed as characters in the phonetic scheme, such as 'Annie Apple'. James would humorously introduce each character, make its sound, and then join letters up to make words. He was the star of the show, and his performance and pedagogy was witnessed by a hall packed full of parents.

James involves himself in planning with the teachers and leads INSET sessions on aspects of curriculum development. In the early stages of the implementation of the National Curriculum he played a central role in decoding policy and helping the teachers to implement it. For instance, he helped two Year 6 teachers to negotiate their way through an unrealistic number of Attainment Targets (ATs) which they were attempting to incorporate in their topic.

Head as monitor

One of the most constraining aspects of policy which impinges on new headship is the requirement that, in the interests of quality assurance, headteachers review and monitor the work of teachers, a part of the role emphasized by Ofsted (1994). Monitoring is such a significant aspect of the role of new headship that James now sometimes refers to himself as the 'inspector in residence'. James uses formal and informal methods in his monitoring. He would tour the school, noting teachers' pedagogy and classroom management, and

> 'would interfere a lot, because there were things going on I didn't like. I'd say, "Can I see your plans first? Can I have your evaluation of that?" If I saw fifteen kids standing in line while an old dear sat at the desk at the front, and I could see Fred at the back saying, "You go in front of me, you go in front of me . . . !," and he's spending the day there, I used to question that, because I'd rather see Fred doing some art in class, or standing on his head in a corner, or contemplating his navel rather than just standing in a line pathetically doing nothing.'

James keeps his finger on the pulse of the school, trying to piece seasonal ups and downs into a larger picture of school development. He checks the pupils' work, in books and classroom displays:

> 'I usually will see the books from the year groups, probably twice a term. Not on a formal basis. I tend to say, "Can I have a look at a cross-section of the books, like maths and the English ones?" I tend to look through the books a lot . . . I make it my business to see. I'd formally see the books during the year and if I felt that things weren't going right, I'd say . . . And there'll be evidence on the wall showing what's been done. So I'll be able to calculate whether they've [the teachers] been having an input into it.'

James takes informal opportunities to observe teaching when it is occurring in an open area. For instance, the corridor to his office is separated from the main hall by a glass door and large window, and both are covered by a net curtain. At one staff meeting, he was talking to the teachers about the disjuncture between their planning and the actual lesson. It was immediately obvious to the staff that in order for him to make this claim he must have observed their PE lessons in the hall. One of the teachers sitting in front of the researcher at the meeting turned to her colleague sitting next to her and said, 'Oh you've noticed the twitching curtain as well have you?' This hidden surveillance contrasts with the open omnipresence of Chris, and suggests that 'the Meadowfields way' is *his* way, and that the 'working together' works under his auspices.

Formal systems exist for review and monitoring. The senior management team (SMT) have teachers' lesson plans submitted to them and they note 'gaps' in curriculum coverage and notify James. Sometimes the subject coordinators note gaps when they teach classes other than their own.

> 'I am aware of a lot of things that are going on through the management group meetings, that's where I get the information from. But quite often it will come out – somebody like the music coordinator will come to me and say, "Look, the infants are doing terrific music, from

the work I've been doing, but there's nothing going on in Year 6 or Year 5, and I'm worried about it." So I will then say to Year 5 and 6, "How much music have you done within your plans?" '

In two staff meetings we attended, James told the teachers that he had discovered unsatisfactory planning in PE, music and maths.

James and the SMT were responsible for school development planning and much of it was concerned with monitoring and review (see Troman 1996b). As we saw in Chapter 2, James created the role of the floating 'key' teacher for the deputy head in order that he could get first-hand information on teachers' adherence to school and national policy and spot disjuncture between policy and practice.

Cultural leadership: micropolitical director

We have already discussed this topic extensively in Chapter 2. James's cultural leadership was marked by strong direction, and by the cultivated use of micropolitical action. Like many other heads (Pollard *et al.* 1994; Webb and Vulliamy 1996; Grace 1996), this was his response to the dilemma caused by the need to promote a culture of collaboration to implement the reforms, while at the same time giving the lead in pushing the reforms through in his school. We call this a dilemma in his case, since there was no sign of tension, and it was resolvable by rational thought. The contradictions in his case were perhaps only apparent. For example, James might have believed that 'It's not a top-down model here,' as reported earlier; and in some ways it was not. In others, perhaps the more significant, it was. James knew what he wanted, and as long as others agreed with him, democratic processes could be observed. In this sense, a collaborative culture was a strategy for him, not a matter of principle. If it did not work, and difficulties, or delay, arose, then other strategies, less democratic would be brought to bear. But these would always be subtly interwoven into the fabric of interstaff relationships, to maintain the appearance of 'the Meadowfields way'.

The entrepreneurial head

An entrepreneur is a manager, often occupying an intermediary position between producer and consumer, who uses initiative to increase profits for his organization. Heads are key middle persons between the Government's reforms and classrooms. James is keen to use the reforms for the profit of his school. He is very confident and self-conscious in his new role. He is not taken over by the managerialist ideology, not uncritical of the reforms. He is not simply conforming to the Government's policy, but is his own man, given strong legitimation by the changes.

In consequence, whereas Chris's role is full of conflicts and tensions, James's is bristling with single-minded confidence. There are contradictions and inconsistencies in Chris's role; James's is more organic:

> 'Somebody says to you, "Can you drive this bus?" and you say, "Yes, I've passed my test" so he says, "Right, OK, you're the bus driver, I'll sit and you can drive the bus and that's it." If somebody then said to you, "Right, you're driving the bus, taking the fares and bringing it into the depot and putting it in the garage at night", you'd say, "Hang on a minute, how many jobs have I got here?" That's what is happening through the changes and the opportunities they have given. They have made us an accountant and it's made us a social services worker. It's given the opportunity to change from outside agencies and advisors running courses to you doing it. It's given you so many huge things to do that I think that this job has changed from the expectations of what a headteacher is about to something absolutely and totally different. I think I feel comfortable about coping with most of it.'

There may well be a gender element here, which disadvantages heads like Chris, but gives strength to those like James. Riley (1994: 90–1), for example, reports on a 'new image of educational leadership emerging in the UK. Leaders are tough, abrasive, financial entrepreneurs, managing the new competitive educational markets. Managing educational organizations is increasingly seen as 'men's business'. The major thrust is in management. His teaching has been tailored to meet managerial requirements. He has adopted a more business, managerial discourse. He controls, monitors, directs in a way that would be quite foreign to Chris. He sees his school as being harmonious with his vision, and where there is discord, he brings his managerial skills into play to restore the balance.

There is no less an air of industry about his work, but it is fuelled by confidence rather than guilt. There is little sign of tension or constraint in James's role performance. Rather, new choices open out before him, and a whole new range of dilemmas appear. Transforming these is what being a new head is all about. He once described a deputy head as being no good as a 'trouble-shooter' (someone who identifies the source of trouble and deals with it, i.e. transforms dilemmas) – clearly a role he saw himself as being good at.

THE REFLECTIVE REALIST

Raymond began teaching in 1970. He had a year teaching a nurture group with young children before settling into junior teaching. He became a headteacher in the 1980s and was head-hunted by the local education authority in 1988 to carry out a difficult amalgamation of two schools into his current 600 pupil primary school in the middle of a large working-class estate in

London. He was very keen to teach in such an area for he wanted to give working-class children opportunities through education. The majority ethnic grouping in the school is African, with a significant Vietnamese and Afro-Caribbean population along with a minority of white pupils. The school received a good Ofsted report in February 1995. The data on Raymond have been collected over nearly two years between 1995 and 1996 by observational fieldnotes and by taped interviews with both Raymond and other teachers.

School ethos: people centredness

Raymond put children before the curriculum and had great faith in his teachers. People and the relationships among them were the most important element in his philosophy. He has no preconceived agenda beyond helping the pupils and teachers:

> 'I don't think I have ideas which are just mine, and I just want to do it. I don't have . . . some kind of vision.'

He saw his values as under attack in the changes. In the early days of the National Curriculum he was part of an ILEA subcommittee developing the use of the National Curriculum in schools, while holding on to his own values of activity-centred learning. He now feels that change has accelerated and that the content of some of the subjects has come to dominate the process. He argues that many management tools use an instrumentalist approach and he would like more of a continuing debate about 'what education is for'.

When he arrived at the school he found that the pupils 'didn't really want to be there nor did many of the teachers'. He had a high turnover of staff. He felt that 'neither the children nor the staff had very high self-esteem or confidence'. His approach was, first, to give the pupils an academic edge and he focused on literacy skills. The improvement in reading standards was noted in the Ofsted report (1995: 13) which records that,

> standards of achievement in English are average in relation to national expectations and often good in relation to pupils' abilities at both Key Stages. The development of literacy skills is given a high priority and an appropriate amount of time is spent on the subject.

Secondly, he resolved to raise the self-esteem of the pupils. To this end he has taken seriously the research on positive role models for his predominantly ethnic intake and ensured over eight years that nearly 70 per cent of the staff are from the ethnic minorities. One of his two deputies, also, is of Afro-Carribean origin. This has helped ensure a specific commitment from the staff towards sustained achievement for its ethnic minority, inner-city school population. Many of the staff talk about how they have chosen to work in 'an area like this'. Many of the teachers are known to the pupils by their forenames. Teachers are often to be seen with their arm around pupils' shoulders, and it is not uncommon for pupils to be seen in the staffroom talking to teachers or using the photocopier for their teachers. In the playground, aggressiveness is now rare. Raymond also gave a high priority to music, an area he judged of particular importance for his pupils. One of his first actions was to employ a full-time, and other part-time, music specialists, and acquire a stock of musical equipment . He felt that this would encourage 'pupils' public performance'. The school now boasts a large steel band, and a brass and woodwind orchestra that has played with the London Philharmonic. One observer reported that they 'played very well', and that 'you could see their chests come out when they were interviewed [by a television personality]'.

Raymond encourages all positive performances outside the school by pupils, not only for pupils', but also for teachers' self-esteem. He believes that the teachers also feel a pride in what the children achieve and consequently feel good about the school and themselves. The Ofsted report (No. 155) states:

> The school ethos is based on sound principles, concerned with fostering an ethos where pupils feel valued, respected, and gain a sense of pride.

Gatekeeping: reluctant image constructor

Raymond has a more limited activity outside his school than James but he is possibly more active than Chris. He has an 'open-door policy' for those he counts as members of the school population, which means that when he is in school he sees any parent, child, teacher who wishes to see him at short notice. He deals with family problems and pupils who need 'time out' from the classroom. He is also on the lookout for how his school can be helped by outside forces. He allowed the local education authority to invite a Department for Education and Employment representative to the school after his good Ofsted report, and agreed to meet the Secretary of State for the Environment who was doing a tour of the local community. However, he does not portray this as kudos for him or the school but as a pragmatic event which could enhance the school's resources or standing.

At the same time, the 'open door' is not unguarded. He critiques the opportunism of the local education authority and the visitors and some of their values. He has publicly regretted some decisions, such as the invitation to a journalist from a national newspaper who used the visit to 'peddle their own ideas' and wrote what the staff thought was a biased report. He also now regrets letting inspectors do some monitoring in a manner damaging to the school, and he has resolved to gain more control in the future. He protects school personnel from potentially harmful material from outside, by debunking it, ridiculing it and using humour. This has the effect of consolidating unity on the inside. Of one group, he said: 'I ridiculed their organization and kept them out of the classrooms as much as I could by sending them off to watch the steel band and recounted these tactics to the staff . . . I don't ignore the outside, I keep it in its place. I see it for what it is and deal with it.' This is not just done spontaneously:

> 'I would never bring a critical article from one of the tabloids into the staffroom before I had intellectually worked out why it was stupid. With the language survey from Ofsted I got all the arguments together before I commented.'

Raymond uses the term 'filtering'. He has wrapped a cloak of defence around the school, albeit a permeable one to let in assistance. He manages the finances to ensure plentiful support for teaching staff in terms of people and resources. Like the others, he 'shields' his teachers from problems as far as he can: 'You keep it from other people and do it yourself and take all the stress . . . and not talking to other people about your worries.' He encourages a climate in the school which is 'critical of the outside', particularly if others are trying to dominate the school:

> 'We satirize people as we go on, and critique everything . . . It's kind of keeping it in its place but it is done in a humorous debunking way, like trying to see it for what it is but also having to deal with it.'

Raymond constructed 'fronts' (Goffman 1959) to meet the gaze of the outside world. The school was carefully constructed, for example, for the Ofsted inspection:

> 'If you're actually going to be watched then you're going to organize in ways where you're definitely going to be in control. So you wouldn't do any risky lessons, anything particularly innovative, would you? . . . They definitely missed a lot of good, inventive, innovative teaching that would have been done normally. It's a shame the whole thing is a kind of contrivance isn't it?'

Like other headteachers, Raymond has been drawn into a concern for appearances. 'The inspection only coincided with the development of our schemes of work, but we made sure they were presented well.' However, immediately after the report was published, the local education authority played it up in the local press and Raymond felt he was treated like a 'pariah' by some of the local headteachers for 'we had made it more difficult for them to live up to our report when they have their Ofsted'. This situation damaged him, for he valued some of his headteacher colleagues as people. A year later, after repairing some of these relations, he was saddened to see 'good people in difficult situations being blamed for getting a poor Ofsted report. I agreed with them about the injustice of the situation but could only be supportive on a personal level'.

Raymond may be finding that one of his principal roles is that of image constructor for competitive, rather than educational, reasons. He has been forced to compete with colleagues for pupils, a role he is reluctant to take up. He employed a consultant to construct a press release and produce a brochure.

> 'I'm not ashamed of the brochure now. We are competing with other schools for pupils. If I don't do it, others will. Because of the current way that education is set up it's in a school's interest, whether they like it or not, to have a good report. It is a boundary role full of tensions.'

Managing: process management

One reform Raymond has found useful is LMS, for this has given the school its own budget, and allowed him and the school to develop their own ideas. LMS has 'cut the bureaucracy a bit'. A great number of other innovations such as appraisal, national assessment, target-setting, achievement levels he sees as 'managerialist tools', which have little to do with education. Raymond is not, therefore, a manager in the James 'upfront, leading manager' style. He prefers a process management style. This involves a belief in the transitory nature of organization, and using a distanced managerialism as empowerment for teachers.

Transitoriness and experimentation

Raymond does not see an organization as one in which systems dominate to the exclusion of people. He builds on 'the experience of the difficulties of past organizational structures, and at the same time expects the structures to be redefined by the people who have to work them'. It is a kind of humanistic managerialism, as contrasted with hierarchical or mechanistic ones.

He is keen to support teachers' ideas – 'If someone comes with an idea then they can run with it.' A computer room and a science room have been equipped because of the enthusiasm of two members of staff, and he has retrained a support worker to act as science and technology technician. She, again, is enthusiastic and she shares some teaching with the teachers. He has not used the inspection report as a stick to develop particular programmes: 'I can't think of any issue I have used it for.' He argues that the National Curriculum, testing, and the Ofsted process 'make it constraining for teachers to be creative. It is bad for their lives and for the children'. So, Raymond is keen to encourage teachers as individuals within supportive frameworks and also keen to encourage experimentation. How does he create this climate of opportunity?

Distanced managerialism as empowerment

Raymond has accepted that he cannot be an expert in everything – unlike James (who did delegate to the SMT, but held the financial reins and retained upfront educational leadership) – and neither does he expect to have an omnipresence like Chris. He has given up his curriculum expertise and control and does not impose pedagogic control over teachers. In this way he creates the climate for development. He is keener on ideas and dialogue being developed rather than school development plans: 'We should stop producing development plans and just get on.' The visions are not his alone: 'I consult and discuss and talk and then make a decision.' The introduction of the SEN (Special Educational Needs) code of practice was one such example where there was 'lots of talk to the deputies and the SENCO [Special Educational Needs Coordinator] teachers before we tried the idea'.

In this way 'ideas arise from the situation itself'. He believes that his talking, asking advice and listening are powerful means to achieve understanding and provide guidance for action. This makes him part of the decision-making process but it distances the hierarchical tinge of his role. 'To some people, I'm the spider at the centre of the web, and to others I'm at the top of the pyramid, but each depends on the person and the situation.' He is uneasy about doing curriculum monitoring himself and feels that subject coordinators should be supporting teachers, not monitoring them. 'I don't accept that monitoring and assessment necessarily raises achievement.' His 'management by wandering about' not only keeps him 'in touch with the grassroots and the children', but is his curriculum monitoring. He is able 'to let go' as well, for he has been on a term's secondment, which he sees 'as a break to reflect on my work and life'. He is confident that his deputy heads will manage very well, albeit in their own way – he sees this as an opportunity for *them* to develop.

Professional leadership: educational enabler

Raymond no longer engages in classroom teaching himself. His leadership is expressed through striving to create the best conditions for his teachers so that they can operate to the best of their ability. He considers this a full-time job. He occasionally lectures to students at the local university, attends local headteacher meetings and belongs to a small group of primary heads who are studying primary practices in other countries, but he gives most of his time to the school: 'I don't want to become one of those heads who roam across the country building a career outside the school.'

Raymond believes that relationships are the cornerstone of his values. When he taught, he 'thought of the pupils as people to be treated with respect'. In the same way, he argues that it is difficult to advise teachers how to perform in relation to children: 'You just do it.' When he was a teacher, he developed relationships through the curriculum and at the same time used them to develop pupils' learning, but,

> 'now I'm a headteacher I've been more distanced from the curriculum and I must rely on my teachers to develop it now. I now develop relationships through school groups and through giving time to individuals. What really matters is classroom experiences so you have to value the teacher.'

He is keen to encourage individual teacher methods 'to keep the teacher operations flexible':

> 'I think this school works towards there trying to be some consistency, but on the other hand it acknowledges a teacher's own experience, autobiography, training and all the rest of it. They're not all going to be the same. They're not all going to be teaching in exactly the same way . . . There's certainly no drive to make teachers clones of each other.'

Raymond's looser connection with the curriculum compared with James's and Chris's has resulted in considerable power to his teachers. He has instituted 'phase groups' in his school which consist of four departments covering the age ranges from 3 to 11. They meet fortnightly, alternating with staff meetings. They were initiated 'to work as a support group rather than as a curriculum-planning group'. But he also has curriculum teams, where teachers volunteer for membership, and one or two lead members of the team are paid above scale monies. The posts are permanent but the subject headings are flexible according to the needs of the school, and staff could be asked to take up other areas. The leaders report back to Raymond from time to time. He slots himself into teams where he thinks they may need some support or help, but the driving force is the team members themselves.

Raymond sees the phases as only a stage in a perpetually changing organization, change which is based more on his experience rather than on outside managerial proposals emanating from the literature or courses. 'I see my past in the present organization.' Experience has also taught him that there is a transitoriness about systems and that experimentation is a key to generative change. He does not imagine, for example, that his phase groups will work like clockwork:

> 'They are successful for some of the people for some of the time and I have to accept that . . . In some years there may be difficult relations between a phase coordinator and an individual teacher. I would not take sides, the difficulties may have to be lived with.'

Raymond does not monitor his staff, like James. He operates through trust and encouragement. He is sensitive to pressures on staff. He cancelled all staff meetings, except fortnightly phase-planning meetings, in the term prior to his Ofsted inspection, and he used up two INSET days just prior to the inspection as 'home preparation'. The days just happened to be the Thursday and Friday when the staff were due back to school after a Christmas holiday. He is also sensitive to individual staff's lives as he showed during their Ofsted inspection.

> 'I tried to play it down as much as possible. I gave the staff a day-to-day briefing on what was happening, and tried to be humorous about it, especially about the people we knew were going to be inspecting us. I just tried to take the whole sting out of it . . . I told them what I thought about it and what it meant for us, and that as far as I was concerned we were doing what could be expected of us, and that we were a good school anyway.'

Cultural leadership: collaborative culture

Collaboration is also Raymond's preferred mode, but, curiously, and rather like Chris's, both bottom-up and top-down. He wants to empower his teachers, and is always seeking ways to do so. But it doesn't always work like that:

> 'It always seems to me to be a bit daft to talk about collegiality where you've got a hierarchical system of management, which you have in schools. You consult people, discuss things with people, talk about things with people, and then you make the decision.'

Raymond has developed a 'critical fun' culture to run alongside the professional one. This is not for hedonistic pleasure:

> 'There is an underlying deadly seriousness about the professional side of the fun we have, which is basically about debunking authority. This is in turn about debunking myself. Maybe there is an element around humanizing authority.'

At the end of every half-term, there are drinks and food made available in the staffroom which is full of comfortable and attractive furniture. At Christmas, the whole school staff including support workers, kitchen staff and cleaners attend a Christmas party in the school. The hall is decorated for the event and various groups of staff construct performances and sketches alongside dances, karaoke and quizzes. Raymond's part in these events is to let his hair down and take as full a part as anyone. 'I want to be seen as the same as them as far as possible.'

Raymond has regular morning meetings with all the staff at 8.50 a.m., at which notices are given out. However, he also uses this opportunity to crack a joke, tease someone, and generally get a smile from everyone before they leave together for their classrooms. The staffroom is in constant use until about 5.30 p.m. and it is not unusual to hear cries of raucous laughter coming from one group or another at any time. 'I'd rather they had a laugh than spent all their time doing the paperwork.' The development of this sociability culture ameliorates to some extent the intensification of a teacher's life and enables them to balance the bureaucracy.

Raymond employs a high profile in the culture of the school, but a reflective and orchestrating role to enable a dynamism to take place. In this latter role he is often seen as a quiet man who listens a lot. Unlike James, who leads from the front in vigorous style, Raymond orchestrates like a composer behind the scenes, letting the players perform the composition in their own way. The Ofsted report recorded that:

> The headteacher provides the school with clear and effective leadership which is both supportive and demanding. He is highly valued by pupils, parent, governors and staff. They are appreciative of his work.

The reflective realist

Raymond is a reflective realist who, albeit unconsciously, works in the spaces between the entrepreneurial and the composite head. He structures the organization like James, but with looser connections which may fray from time to time. He is keen to encourage some autonomy in these structures and within teachers' classrooms. He is not looking for the 'one best way' to run the organization but believes in a dynamic approach where ideas and experiments are creative for the organization.

Raymond would not consider himself a leading manager, like James, nor a classroom teacher like Chris. He does not try to do everything, like Chris, and is happy to delegate. He works through his teachers, and his main managerial emphasis is on the development of each individual teacher, as well as on systems. He encourages individuality in their practice. At the same time, what matters is the cooperative relationship with others, not the competitive element that attends so much of the Government's educational policy. However, when competition threatens to work against the interests of this school, as when another head tried to poach some of his pupils, the realist comes out in him and he responds in kind, marketing his school. He rails against the 'effective schools' movement, because he feels the quest to find key factors is useless, and not a reflection of real life in schools, since circumstances and people affect situations differentially over time. Unlike James, he is not effusive or publicly dominant, but low key in his style, familiar, informal and quietly humorous. He prefers the personal touch, and to listen, engage and experiment. He is not tied to visions, objectives or outcomes, but responds to any outside pressures in a pragmatic manner, being guided by how far they ensure a good education for his pupils. This is his yardstick for reflecting on, and critiquing, educational policy. He sees this – reflecting on issues, and fostering a climate of debate in the school about what is best for the children – as a central part of his role.

As with Chris, Raymond's choice of role is tension prone. He has talked of feeling ashamed that he felt annoyed with some staff whose practice was criticized by inspectors prior to Ofsted. During the Ofsted experience, he 'barked' at children which 'was not like me at all'. He feels that headteachers and their schools

> 'feel more and more on the edge, only just managing, only just coping, needing more and more energy. The school and I are only one day, or one thing, person, event, or mistake, or a bit of bad press over SATs or anything away from tipping over the edge.'

Raymond's local education authority were keen to encourage heads to take secondment as part of their retention policies. He was one of the first to apply and agreed to look critically at the problems of 'value-added in assessment' for the authority. However, within the first few weeks of the secondment, his reflections threw up other disturbing reactions to his work.

> 'I suddenly realized the fast pace of decision-making I'm involved in and the need to react quickly to events. There's been a massive reduction in stress since I started this secondment and I've realized that I've been stressed for so long I didn't recognize the symptoms. There's a vicious circle.'

It was an uphill battle against macro forces which seemed intent to 'cause stress in order to control'. He had gone away with his 'cluster' group of heads, and there was 'frantic behaviour':

> ' "Have you got a policy on this? Have you got a bit of paper which tells you about this?" You could see good people that were in ridiculous situations.'

The 'reflection' is more natural to him than the 'realism' – the acts he carries out through political necessity though against his inner convictions. The two in conjunction are a recipe for tension. Raymond, like Chris, lives 'on the edge'.

CONCLUSION

Table 4.1 summarizes the differences among the three heads in performing the five major functions of the new headteacher role as identified earlier.

Table 4.1 Styles of headship

Teacher	Promoting school ethos	Gatekeeping	Managing	Professional leadership	Cultural leadership
Chris: the composite head	Caring	Status builder and community worker	Professional mother	Total commitment	Controlled collaboration
James: the entrepreneurial head	Working together	Vigorous promotion and defence	The new business manager	Educational exemplar and monitor	Micropolitical director
Raymond: the reflective realist	People-centred	Reluctant image constructor	Process management	Educational enabler	Collaborative culture

One important difference among our three heads that we should empha-size is between size and type of school. This key difference between the three heads is undoubtedly one important factor behind their different styles. For example, Chris would probably have found it impossible to teach half-time in one of the others' schools. Also, hers was a lower school, with a nursery unit attached, and it is often claimed that early years' teaching has special char-acteristics (David *et al.* 1992). Webb and Vulliamy (1996: 132) point out that changes in role are very different for heads of large and small primary schools. The larger the school, the more the change. It was harder to be a *direct* cur-riculum leader in a large school,' which needed a more complex manage-ment structure, with delegation of leadership functions to deputies and even members of the senior management team. Teaching heads of small schools followed more traditional leadership styles, and they tended to be 'doers' rather than writers of policy documents (Webb and Vulliamy 1996: 133). Chris's school is not large, nor, at two hundred, is it small. It is in-between. This, then, is another reason why her role is likely to be tension-ridden. She would like to hold to a traditional model, but the management responsibil-ities do bear on her.

Raymond's and James's schools contrast with Chris's, and with each other. James's 'Meadowfields' lies on the fringe of a small and prosperous South Midlands market town. The catchment area is predominantly mono-ethnic and there are few indicators of material and social disadvantage. James has been making major changes involving restructuring and reculturing since the mid-1980s (see Chapter 2). Raymond's is an inner-city, multi-ethnic school in a predominantly working-class area with a high degree of socio-economic disadvantage. Chris and Raymond both chose to work in their type of school freely since it suited their own personal values. James also seems well suited. It is doubtful whether any of them could have followed the same formula with such success in one of the others' schools. There are, of course, other important factors, notably those of a personal nature – values, experience, career, personality – and we have brought out something of these in the chapter.

Though we have concentrated on how the heads differ, there are a number of ways in which they are alike. They are all successful, 'turning-round' heads. They have all accommodated the changes, though they are all critical of some of them. They all contribute to aspects of the new role in some way or other, fostering external relations, protecting their staff, delegating, encouraging collaboration, selling their schools with image management. Also, while we have drawn attention to prominent features in each of their role performances, this is not to say that some of these features were necessarily absent from the others.

However, it is the collective sum of the role performances that is important, yielding distinctive styles of leadership. We could characterize Chris's leadership as matriarchal, James's as patriarchal and Raymond's as liberal. Chris and Raymond subscribe to what Grace (1995: 186–7) describes as the 'sharing–consultative model' of educational leadership, while James leans towards the 'masculine–strong leadership' model. It could be argued that this type of head is reasserting patriarchical and male power, temporarily interrupted by the progress of women and democratic educational leadership in the different cultural and ideological conditions of the 1960s and 1970s. As Grace (ibid.) points out, the changed conditions of the 1980s and 1990s have jeopardized that progress. However, it should be noted that both Chris and James derive a great deal of self kudos out of their new positions, as omnipotent mother on the one hand and managing director on the other.

Is there still any pure form of a 'collaborative culture'? Raymond comes closest to it, with his cultivated ethos of sociability and satire, and mode of delegation. Even he admits to having to take decisions unilaterally on occasions. Both Chris and James feature a measure of contrivance, but here we might distinguish between 'forced' and 'selected' contrivance. Raymond and Chris could claim to be driven, at times, into more direction than they would have wished. Such is the nature of tensions and constraints. James chose the micropolitical manoeuvering of his cultural direction as a deliberate strategy to resolve what was, for him, a dilemmatic situation. It was a reluctant feature of Chris's and Raymond's approaches; a celebratory one of James's. This is not to say that they were unskilled micropoliticians – there is a sense in which all teaching now is inevitably politicized. But they reserved their skills in this department mainly for dealing with the outside world, rather than for handling staff within their schools.

Smulyan (1996: 186) points out that

> the current literature on effective school principals focuses on the traits, roles and skills which characterize good leaders. These attempts to

encapsulate or propose static models for the dynamic process of leadership . . . run into problems; this research still lacks a sense of what leadership looks and feels like in action.

She also observes that claims that effective heads are democratic, or women
heads are more collaborative than directive 'oversimplify a complicated process' (ibid.: 187). It is the same with the implementation of policy. There is
no linear application of policy into practice, but a complicated process involving school and/or heads' values (ethos), the heads' gatekeeping and chosen
style of leadership. We have tried in this chapter to illustrate some of the
complexities as they are lived out in the leadership of three successful, but very
different, heads. This shows that there is more to success than any simple
listing of factors, and that there is more than one route to that success. The
one outstanding quality all three heads possess is a fiercely independent
spirit, accompanied by the will to succeed and commitment to their cause.
This equally puts those who fight against the grain – like Chris and Raymond
– at risk, and we have seen how both have experienced stress. While James
is firmly and confidently in the new 'leading manager' head mould, they continue 'on the edge'. But there are signs of hope. Raymond is gaining succour
from his reflective secondment, and as we shall see in Chapter 5, Chris was
to receive new-found confidence from what was seen as an unlikely source –
an Ofsted inspection at her school.

The catharsis of inspection: normalizing, confirming and reconstructing self

INTRODUCTION

The Education (Schools) Act 1992 introduced significant changes to the methods of external inspection of all maintained schools in England and Wales. Amongst the welter of reforms since 1988, the institution of the Office for Standards in Education (Ofsted) was arguably the biggest strike for change yet. Schools were to be inspected fully every four years according to stringent criteria. Hitherto, there had been scope in the system for the kinds of adaptations discussed in previous chapters. The Ofsted inspections, however, are meant to have a more direct effect on the policy and practices of schools, and to 'police' the changes that should have been made. The declared purpose of Ofsted is 'to improve standards of achievement and quality of education through regular independent inspection, public reporting and informed advice' (Ofsted 1994). The task of the inspection teams is to 'collect a range of evidence, match the evidence against a statutory set of criteria, arrive at judgements and make those judgements known to the public' (Clegg and Billington 1994: 2). Schools are required to devise 'action plans' on the basis of the inspectors' report, and to carry them out within a specified period. It is a linear model – inspect, report, plan, change, improve. But if it works like this for inspectors, it does not do so for teachers. Inspections can hold different meanings for different teachers, and can have variable and contradictory effects.

We take three teachers from our researches, two of them in the same school, to illustrate this variable response. We have already met Chris in Chapter 4. We were interested in how her adaptations to role as expounded there stood up to the test of an Ofsted inspection. For purposes of comparison, we consider a classroom teacher in Chris's school, Theresa, who teaches a Year 2 class and is the science and technology coordinator in the school. At the time of the research, she had worked at the school for twelve years. The third teacher is Shula who is in her late thirties. She has taught for approximately thirteen years and has been at her current school as deputy head for seven years. The school is a large inner-city school with over 600 children. At the time of this research, she was teaching Year 4.

Our analysis suggests that the three teachers experienced intensification of work as a result of the inspection, but in markedly different ways; that they constructed distinctly different realities of the inspection process, as well as enjoying vastly different outcomes. The comparison illustrates widely differing effects of Ofsted, the traumatic impact of inspection on teachers' self and identity, non-linear aspects of the change process, and variable consequences for professionalism and educational improvement.

We shall consider the three teachers' different experiences of intensification, the different realities of the inspection they constructed, and the different implications for their definition of self and role.

INTENSIFICATION

As noted in Chapter 1, intensification manifests itself among professionals, like teachers, in an increase in routinization and bureaucracy, in accountability and assessment, and a decrease in time for reflection, sociability and reskilling (Apple 1986). The consequence, it is argued, is deskilling and deprofessionalization. This is certainly a point that has been made about teachers in recent years (Kelly 1990), but as A. Hargreaves (1994a) has pointed out, the intensification theory is rather deterministic. We know from implementation theory (Bowe and Ball 1992; Vulliamy and Webb 1993) that teachers do have some room for manoeuvre in the implementation of the Government's policy, even when it is laid down in an uncompromising manner. However, Ofsted appears all-pervasive. Since warning of an inspection can be given up to a year in advance, and the results require action, the process is much longer and more complex than it might appear. This may be a major constraint for many teachers, therefore, an intensification of intensification, with even more increased bureaucracy, accountability, assessment and surveillance; and a decrease in control and choice, and in time for reflection, sociability and reskilling. But is this the case? The first part of the answer focuses on the extent to which the inspection led to intensification and the teachers' experiences of it. We found widely varying experiences among our three teachers, from 'modified intensification' (Theresa), to 'extensification' (Chris), to 'aggravated intensification' (Shula). We shall consider each in turn.

Modified intensification

Theresa experienced intensification, but not in any straightforward way. Her views changed somewhat over time, and she recognized benefits as well as costs in the increased work involved, though the costs predominated in the end. Throughout each of the interviews, Theresa spoke of the amount of work that went into preparing for the inspection. She felt that there was too much planning needed.

> 'People have wanted extra things, and we've had a good sort. We had a mound of orders and things to do to make sure we got all the resources in . . . It was just things that we maybe would have left a bit.'
>
> (Theresa)

Theresa was commenting here prior to the inspection. In some ways she justifies the paperwork. These are things which would have been done at some point, but the timetable for work had been brought forward. There is a sense that the extra paperwork which is requested by the Ofsted Inspectors is done purely on the grounds that it is necessary for the school. The week after the inspection, she was much more critical:

> 'All that work, what is the point? . . . I spent hours and hours and hours filling in stuff . . . It cost a lot of money, it took a lot of our extra time!'
>
> (Theresa; post-inspection interview: 1 week)

This may have been more an expression of pent-up emotions built up during the inspection, but it was a view largely sustained, though with an acknowledgement of some positive achievement by the school, a term after the inspection:

> 'We all really got cracking and finished off all the things that we'd started. All the policies were bang up to date . . . but that was only at the expense of coming in and working till 8 o'clock and working nearly every day of the holidays and you just can't do that normally. I spent ages with the science equipment. It was something I wanted to do – it was to re-box it and colour-code it and label it and everything. We're reaping the benefit of it, but you just couldn't keep going at that pace normally. Things have to take their priority. So there are advantages that have come out from that but only because we've worked ourselves

to a completely unreasonable amount – more than should be expected of anybody really. There was intense planning which isn't necessary normally, it all works fine without it.'

(Theresa; post-Ofsted: 1 term)

Clearly, as A. Hargreaves (1994a) has demonstrated, intensification and its effects are not straightforward concepts. Theresa recognized the benefits of 'a good sort' – a kind of periodic 'spring clean' – but in the end, it 'all works fine' without that kind of intense planning, which can obtrude on her view of the real purpose of teaching.

Extensification

By contrast with Theresa, Chris felt empowered as a result of the inspection. It removed a great deal of the self-doubt recorded in Chapter 4. Though going through similar intensification processes as Theresa – indeed even more so, as head – she interpreted them differently. For Chris, in fact, the experience was more one of 'extensification', involving intensive work certainly, but endorsing, expanding and renewing the self in its effects, and enhancing her sense of professionalism. Intensification constrains and pulls the individual down. Extensification, by contrast, expands and uplifts. The concentration of work, the filling of time and space, even to the extent of take-up of leisure time, the additional paperwork – all was in the service of the school as Chris defined it. There were great gains to be made. This will become clear from considering her view of the preparation for the inspection.

Chris's view about the paperwork also changed before and after the inspection, but far more dramatically than Theresa's. For Chris, as a headteacher, part of her everyday job had been to deal with paperwork, which she often marginalized, as it seemed to interfere with what she felt were more important aspects of job. Chris tended to deal with paperwork outside normal school hours (see Chapter 4). As the inspection loomed, inevitably there was an abundance of paperwork generated for the week, though Chris insisted:

'This has been done for the school, for the teachers, not for the inspectors. Most of it was under way already, though the teachers have put a great deal of extra time into the work.'

(Chris; pre-Ofsted interview)

Like Theresa, therefore, Chris strategically redefined the purpose of the paperwork. However, during the period prior to the inspection, Chris was increasingly under pressure to complete the paperwork for the inspection. When, uncharacteristically, she took sick leave in the autumn term, many of the teachers put her illness down to stress. Yet, despite the intensity of the workload, Chris commented after the inspection that it had been worth all the planning:

> 'They [the inspectors] said how we'd made the inspection very easy for them through the paperwork, because all the evidence they saw quite quickly, paperwork explained exactly what we were doing, where we were looking to go. That was great . . . and the feedback he [the registered inspector] gave me was great, because you could go back to people and say, "It's all going really well".'
>
> (Chris; post-Ofsted interview: 2 weeks)

For Chris, therefore, unlike Theresa, the paperwork was a necessary method of showing the inspectors how the school operated. Consequently, though there are some features of intensification, in the main it was not experienced as such by Chris. She did not, in retrospect, see the extra paperwork as threatening to her professionality or as putting at risk the educational purposes of her school as she saw them, but as an opportunity to show all the good things about the school.

The planning of the inspection week itself was of vital importance to Chris because it was a showcase week. At stake was the life of the school. Given the shortness of their visit, detailed documentation was essential if the inspectors were to gain a true insight into the qualities of teaching and learning:

> 'You do need to take it on and plan it, and show, because if you don't, what they don't see they will comment on. I know that's not fair, but . . . they make all their judgements on the school's history, and the school's future in four days.'
>
> (Chris; post-Ofsted interview: 1 week)

Chris's responsibility was to the school's future, and not to her own teaching practices, as was the case with Theresa. She thus put the experience within a positive frame. There was a lot of extra work, even trauma, some of which was unpleasant, but on the whole it was positive trauma (D.H. Hargreaves 1983), working to the advantage of the school and the individual. In this respect, the inspection worked as a kind of critical event for the school, with all the gains that that implies (Woods 1993). Chris's construction of the 'intensification' caused by the inspection was to recast it as a 'celebration' in retrospect, an opportunity to display the school at its best. It might also be remembered that having the opportunity to show the school at its best, at least on paper, did allow Chris a degree of negotiability to interpret and re-interpret the school for the inspection team within her school's social context. There was less opportunity for Theresa to achieve the same sense of negotiability on a personal classroom level, which again may account for her feelings towards the paperwork. It had little if any value to an individual classroom teacher, but was of value to the school overall.

Aggravated intensification

Shula experienced intensification more acutely and comprehensively than
Theresa, through a vastly increased workload, a diminution of power and
control, dehumanization, a technification of work and the marginalization of
her personal values.

The preparation for the forthcoming Ofsted inspection started nearly a
year prior to the event. Ofsted coordinating meetings were attended at the
local teacher's centre. Like Theresa, Shula actually considered these beneficial, though her views were soon to change. Policies were brought up to date,
and huge folders were prepared by all the teaching staff. These were kept
as the oracle to be used to answer questions about the school, its policies and
operations. Ofsted's influence became all-pervasive, and Shula noted that
'all people are doing is living until Ofsted'. Because of the huge workload
involved, some normal features of school life, such as class trips, disappeared.
Shula considered it dehumanizing in that 'you've got eight people inspecting
you who don't actually know you particularly well as an individual'. She felt
that 'it removes people's sense of worth in what they know they can do'. It
exacerbated tension, because:

> 'you do not know when the door's going to open and an inspector's
> going to come in . . . how long he's going to be there . . . the nature of
> the things that he's writing down . . .'
>
> (Shula)

There is a shift from seeing oneself through one's own perspectives and
seeing oneself through Ofsted eyes – a technification of self:

> 'People are looking at themselves and thinking, "God, what are they
> going to say? Am I doing that right? Well I know that area of my
> practice isn't correct, but this is good".'
>
> (Shula)

Here was something else to nag at teachers' conscientiousness (Campbell
et al. 1991b). They felt constrained to

> 'put themselves through hoops because they don't want to let their year
> group down, and feel that, "Oh God, maybe it was me because he came
> in on that day and little so and so was doing whatever . . ." '
>
> (Shula)

Shula has seen her values marginalized during this period of Ofsted
preparation:

> 'My ideal would be bringing in all the things that I am able to enjoy
> around us and bringing that joy and my "kind of being alive" and all

that into the classroom and children to do that as well. It's about being able to take an idea and seeing what you can do with it, and help them to go with it. I don't do that anymore. My life is about Attainment Targets and programmes of study basically.'

(Shula)

Pedagogic change, the question of self and the dehumanizing process are encapsulated in Shula's worries and concerns two weeks before the inspection. With one week to go, she was contending with 'multiple jigsaws', she felt no job satisfaction, and her nerves were frazzled. She was too tired to reflect and meditate – her way of relaxing – and her main motive force was fear. In order to 'maintain a unified person I have to see the inspectors as bogies'. One week prior to the inspection she was 'depressed at seeing all her teaching life typed onto seven pieces of paper' – her plans for the week. Her phase group had relinquished flexibility and tightened everything up and altered plans to satisfy the inspection team. She had given the group a list of do's and don'ts, but was 'trying not to chivvy her team for fear of pushing them too far'.

REALITIES

An inspection report implicitly claims to describe a school as it really is.
(Wilcox and Gray 1994: 250)

A criticism often made of the Ofsted mode of inspection is that it represents only a snapshot of the school, and not necessarily a faithful one (Jeffrey and Woods 1995). Teachers also might construct a particular image of the school for inspectorial purposes, but which may not be truly representative of their customary reality. Schools may be becoming adept at strategic responses of this kind as they adapt to the post-modern world where they face a number of contradictory demands (A. Hargreaves 1994a). This may be yet another instance of the flexibility discussed in Chapter 2 that produced 'moving' or 'manipulative mosaics' in school organization. Here we have 'moving', and possibly 'manipulative realities'! Within schools, teachers may also have different stakes in the inspection, depending on their positions, careers, aspirations, commitment, values. Some may have more to gain, or lose, than others. The question we are interested in here is, what kinds of realities of inspections do teachers within a school construct? Might they be different? If so, what are the bases on which they are made? What are the implications for the school as a whole? Our teachers constructed widely different realities. For Theresa, it was an artificial performance. For Chris, by contrast, it was essential reality, while Shula experienced anomie – a pronounced disruption of reality.

Artificial performance

There was a strong sense before the inspection in Theresa's school that nothing was going to change simply to fit in with some idea of what the inspectors might be looking for. Life would go on as normal. As time grew closer to the inspection, things began to change. The basic paper signs on each of the teachers' doors to indicate which class it was, often made by the children, were suddenly replaced with uniform red plastic plaques. New displays were mounted and, as Theresa pointed out before the inspection:

> 'Everything that you've got in the classroom has got to be spot on perfect. Like with the children's folders, all the drawers, I've been labelling them, relabelling them so everything was tidy – and the displays of course. We're supposed to have something to represent all the curriculum areas. Getting the classroom well organized, so the children work well in here and they know where everything is.'
>
> (Theresa; pre-Ofsted interview)

However,

> 'It's such an artificial situation that you feel that you've got to perform . . . I agonized over every lesson, because I think: "Right, I've got to show this, I've got to show this, I've got to show this," so I'll get it all packed into that week and we've got to be perfect, because so many people have said to me: "If they don't see it, it's not happening" . . . Oh gosh, I wouldn't run a lesson like that usually would I? . . . And I wasn't relaxed. I'd got: stage 1, step 2, step 3, do this, do that, go there, do this, and it was like – regimented.
>
> (Theresa; post-Ofsted interview: 1 term)

For Theresa, she and her colleagues had the skills to put on whatever performance was demanded – to manipulate the reality:

> 'If we'd have cottoned on to what it was they'd wanted, we could've performed in any situation. I can be formal, I can be completely laid back. You have to actually catch on to what it is they want . . . And then perform it.'
>
> (Theresa; post-Ofsted: 1 week)

The prominent feature of Theresa's teaching during the week was 'playing safe'. Despite her feelings of not wanting to change too much, some alterations were noticed during the week of the inspection, particularly with regard to her customary practice of allowing children the opportunity of free-choice activity once they had finished their work. When asked about this in the week after the inspection she said she 'didn't let them go and play' even though she believes 'the time that they're playing is really valuable. But I just didn't want to have to justify it'.

She liked to be flexible over what got done, and when, but

> '[in the Ofsted] you couldn't change, you had to stick to everything. Everything was planned to the last minute. When people did change at all they got caught out, and then when people arrived to see something, there's nothing to see. It was really very hard.'
>
> (Theresa)

Timing things so punctiliously is not like real teaching for Theresa. Even the timing of the inspection as a whole had an effect on the school's 'real' term. The inspection took place in the first week of the spring term. With the new term, new foci of curriculum subjects are introduced throughout the school. The main focus for this term was Electricity. This created a constraint for Theresa and indeed the whole of the staff, in that in order to show the school at its best, many of the teachers were put in the position of having to cut down on introductory work and launch straight into investigative work. For example, in science and technology

> 'I had to throw them into those activities just to show off . . . whereas . . . I always start off very slow on the science and technology, because you do need time to find out where they are . . . and yes we got a good report, but it was artificial. We had every resource in the school.'
>
> (Theresa)

Similarly with art, she would have done what she did normally, but 'it would be spread out', and introduced more gradually, 'without the diving into the making. But if they didn't see that, then it doesn't go down on our report'.

Despite the feelings of deprofessionalization during the inspection week, the effects on Theresa were temporary, as she appeared to return to her normal classroom practices straight after the inspection with little difficulty. As many of the teachers commented immediately after the inspectors had left, all that they wanted to do was to 'get back to normal', and Theresa seemed to achieve this quite quickly.

Essential reality

For Chris, the inspection was not artificial, not a performance. On the contrary, it was very real, a kind of essential truth, rarely captured, but sparked into life here by Ofsted. When the school first had notification of the inspection, Chris had commented that the inspection week would be planned 'like a wedding'. The metaphor encapsulates her view of the event. It would be a trial certainly, but ultimately it was to be a happy occasion, providing cause for celebration. The celebration was to be in honour of all the school stood for receiving the stamp of approval, which carried with it widespread and long-term legitimacy. It represented a 'coming of age' for the school – and

for Chris. If a union was involved, it was between school and external authority, with the inspectors as witnesses. As with any wedding day, too, a great
deal of preparation went into the making of a perfect day. Chris, like the
'mother of the bride' (sustaining the 'matriarchal' analogy from Chapter 4),
spent a great deal of her time in planning for perfection. She did a list of
all the lessons, and various aspects of them, and the staff took that, and all
planned lessons in detail for the whole week together. She 'would have been
foolish not to plan in detail', since the inspectors otherwise might have
missed something. She would spend the same amount of time on it again,
though 'people thought, "She's mad, she's working too hard"' (post-Ofsted
interview: 1 term).

For Chris, in consequence, the 'performance' was one of the school at its
very best, an excellence that went to the heart of the institution, and that was
not just a veneer for the occasion:

> 'You couldn't plan the quality teaching, quality learning, or the quality
> of resources and teamwork and all of those that they put down. And
> I don't think it's possible to do a [show for someone and not have the
> talent], but on the other hand I think it's very important for a school
> to show its strengths.'
>
> (Chris; post-Ofsted interview: 1 week)

Theresa's view of the reality of the situation is limited to her own practice. Chris's view, as head, encompasses an overall consideration of the whole
school, and she looks at the whole picture. For Chris, regardless of how carefully planned the week was, there were certain unknown (or perhaps known)
factors which could not be planned for. The abilities of her staff to teach and
the behaviour of the children could not be incorporated and detailed in any
lesson plans. Chris in fact commented on one particular incident that highlighted how the inspectors saw the reality of the school. During one teacher's
PE lesson, an inspector was in the lesson observing, and two children were
misbehaving. The teacher stopped the lesson when Chris came into the hall,
and explained to her why the lesson had been suspended. Chris then repri-
manded the children, in front of the inspector, for their bad behaviour. The
class teacher (Anne) was worried that this would be seen negatively by the
inspectors, but as Chris told her:

> 'I think you've done us all an amazing favour. Just forget it, because
> nobody cares, not about them [the inspectors]. Stuff like that, you just
> do. We're here day after day, and I have good days when I'm teaching
> and I have bad days, and I will be here tomorrow and tomorrow teach-
> ing here all the time, not somebody drafted in for four days to make
> judgements about [things]. It was that kind of aspect, "Yes, they've
> come in to see us," but there are things that go on here that enable us
> to get as far along the line as we have, and there's no way of pretending

that we never get cross, that we never need to tell children off, that's just a nonsense.'

> (Chris; post-Ofsted interview: 1 term)

The incident had shown an aspect of 'normality' in what was an 'abnormal' week, and something that Chris felt was important for the inspectors to see. In fact, in the final report, the inspectors commented:

> Any bad behaviour is dealt with quickly and sensitively with minimal disruption to the good working environment.
>
> (Inspection Report: para 5.2: 50)

However, Chris admitted that not all of the creativity that the teachers usually brought to their teaching was allowed to flourish. She gave history as an example. The previous term they had done 'an enormous history topic' planned into very specific hours, but, though they had been happy with it, the inspectors would need to see some *good* history going on, so 'we were *less* imaginative with it'. But she did not see that as a problem:

> 'None of the things that we'd actually been working on or the way we'd been working changed. So that was quite a positive thing.'
>
> (Chris; post-Ofsted interview: 1 week)

Anomie

Anomie is a state of breakdown in normal behaviour, a situation in which 'the rules and standards by which an individual is accustomed to live are rendered irrelevant by changing circumstances' (Worsley 1977: 484).

Like Theresa, Shula feels the focus on one week reduces education to something artificial. But for her, the artificiality of the inspection could not so easily be set aside. It cut deep into her being as a teacher:

> 'It's immoral. That's the word to describe a process that can put you through so much stress and strain that you are no longer talking about yourself as a rounded person. We're like cardboard cut-outs, we're two-dimensional people. We are people, we leave our houses, we come in, we teach, after the kids go home we put up displays, we talk at INSET meetings, we go home, we sit and we write stuff out again and that is the whole of our lives. The two days we are not in school, we are so tuned into school that you still don't actually, really switch off . . . So I want to start going back to being a three-dimensional person . . . They have actually chipped away at what is a very important part of me . . . The only way I can think of it is that you became a machine and you have no other emotions or feelings other than that associated with school.'
>
> (Shula)

Here is a very clear expression of the threatened technification of work and of the self. The week of the inspection confirmed this drift:

'I actually find it offensive because they're not valuing you . . . There must have been points where people have been performing well and just some kind of recognition of that would give people the impetus to go back with a good feeling . . . it is demoralizing . . . Now, if you're not being told anything at all then you search for the meaning. "He raised his eyebrow at that particular point. What was I doing? What were the kids doing? What does that mean?" It's unfair, it is. They're doing all the things that we would not do to children.

(Shula)

On the Monday following the inspection, Shula gave a remarkably evocative account of her feelings:

'I feel I should be just glad it's all over but instead there's this kind of anti-climax really, a non-event almost. It came and went so quickly that I'm thinking, "I've spent a year getting ready for this, this momentous occasion that's going to totally take over my life," and it's come and it's gone and we've heard, "Yes, it was very good," and that's it. I keep thinking, "Yes, all right, it's over and whoopee!" But there's no sense of joy, there's no sense of achievement. There's no sense saying "Wow! I've gained something from this" . . . It's been a nothing. It's been an unreal week, like a surrealist painting or walking into something that isn't quite real, and at the end of it you can't remember what was real. I was there but it wasn't real anyway so how do I hold on to it? What do I hold on to? You don't come away holding on to anything. It's like seeing those surrealist paintings and you get your mind right into it but there's nothing to hold on to. I just can't get over it. I keep thinking. I keep waiting to feel something, in fact I'm *dying* to feel something. It seems to be OK to function for a week, to prove God knows what in this unreal world, but now we're back in the real world. It's as if we are saying that the premise [by] which we do everything in the real world is wrong anyway because it wasn't the real world. Last week wasn't the real world. Up until the previous Friday this was the real world, this was our reality. In fact what they've done is mess with our world. It's exactly what I'm saying about a surreal painting. They've messed with our reality and maybe in trying to step back into our reality we're horrified that it can be shaken so easily. It's horrible because I don't like feeling nothing, I like to feel something. I should feel something.'

(Shula)

For Theresa, the inspection was a charade, but she did not get caught up in it, nor did she lose her own sense of reality. For Shula, however, Ofsted invaded and upset her own private domain. She gives a superb expression of a reflective teacher wrestling with the onset of anomie. What Goffman (1972) calls the 'interaction order' has broken down for Shula. The 'face work' that used to maintain the 'expressive order' which sustained normality no longer works. She feels both guilt and shame, as in statements like

> 'It's quite frightening because the actual inspection week turned everything upside down that you'd ever done before, and you resent the fact that you've actually gone along with the process. Why didn't I just say, "Stuff you and your bloody timetable"? Why didn't I say that? Why did I say, "Oh all right, I'll do a timetable"?'
>
> (Shula)

Anomie is associated particularly with periods of rapid change, so it is not surprising that some teachers experience it during the current restructuring of the educational system. Shula had coped with, and accommodated, most of the changes, but the inspection appeared to discount the rules and standards that have guided her teaching hitherto, and to redefine quality and invert her values.

OUTCOMES

> For many teachers the school represents perhaps the most intimate focus of their professional identity and esteem.
>
> (Wilcox and Gray 1994: 250)

> . . . to adopt the identity of 'teacher' was simply to 'be yourself' in the classroom.
>
> (Nias 1989: 182)

> Inspections can be regarded as potential learning experiences for those involved.
>
> (Wilcox and Gray 1994: 257)

We have noted earlier a degree of negotiability in the implementation of policy. How far is this affected by an Ofsted inspection? Is there a sense in which, like the Education Reform Act 1988, a school inspection offers 'a micro-political resource for teachers . . . to interpret, re-interpret and apply in their particular social contexts' (Ball and Bowe 1992: 100). How far does it offer them opportunities for enrichment, and an expansion of skills and knowledge, for enskilling and for extending their professionalism? How far does it foreclose on such opportunities? How far was this the case among our teachers, and what are the implications for schools and inspections? Again, we note a variable response, from 'normalizing', through 'confirming', to 'reconstructing' the self.

Normalization of the self

In the week after the inspection, Theresa returned immediately to her usual classroom practice. The strict timetable had gone, there were no more lesson plans for reference, 'choosing' time was restored, the atmosphere was re-laxed and it seemed that the inspection had merely been a temporary inter-ruption to Theresa's normal practice. Asked what she was doing one afternoon, she replied

> 'We're going to do the silhouettes today. And the rest of them, I'm going to let them carry on [the work the children had started in the morning]. I think for some reason they're going to take longer than I planned to. I think they were quite good at that, but because of the Ofsted I've undertimed it a bit.'

> (Theresa)

When Theresa was asked in the week after the inspection if she was pleased with the result, her reply was an unenthusiastic 'Yes'. She 'did not get a real sense of achievement . . . like if you've passed your exam or your driving test'. By the end of the term, she 'was pleased with the report, but it was so wordy and doesn't really make that much difference'. She just felt relief: 'OK, that's it, done, we can just get on with it [i.e. life as normal].'

The report had not 'told them anything they did not know', and Theresa felt the whole inspection had been 'a waste of time and money'. She was able to see the value of a good inspection report for both herself and the school, and felt 'pretty sure now that if I went for a deputy headship I could get one . . . But I don't do it for that'. As Theresa is not interested in promotion, the elevated status of the school within the area had little impact on her, and she is quite dismissive of the inspection, feeling that the school could manipulate its own distinctive autonomy:

> 'If they'd have said something that we didn't agree with, we would have paid lip-service to it, but I don't think we would have done it really, because we're that sort of place, aren't we?'

> (Theresa)

Theresa's strong identification of herself as a classroom teacher had remained intact. The week of the inspection had been a 'fake' week, and as such was easily put behind her. It may have been easier for Theresa to return to her usual teaching practices because of her responsibility for testing her class the following term in the Standard Assessment Tasks (SATs). As the report had had little impact on her personally, or affected the running of the school in any major way, she was able then to concentrate on preparations for the SATs, and 'just get on with it'. Interestingly, unless specifically asked by the researcher, Theresa rarely talked about the inspection, though conversation often centred around the subject of SATs or general discussion about the children and their work. By contrast, conversation with Chris often seemed to return to inspection. For her, the experience had had much more import.

Confirmation of self

Chris felt that the inspection enhanced both her own and her teachers' professionalism. Her initial reaction to the inspectors' report was one of elation. It removed all her self-doubt, gave her confidence, recharged her inspiration:

> 'I'm thrilled! I can't tell you what a sense of relief it was to know we're all going in the right direction [and] for the first time to feel I can do my job. To lose all those agonies. I am doing my job . . . First time ever, I feel I can manage it . . . I feel we're moving in the right direction, and we're quite a long way down the road, but we'll keep going down the road. That's worth twenty thousand of anybody's money!'
>
> (Chris; post-Ofsted interview: 1 week)

The inspection had been a defining event in Chris's transition from her old post of deputy head in a previous school, to the head of her present school. The six years of her headship prior to the inspection had been characterized by the uncertainty, insecurity and anxiety typical of the transitional phase of status passages (Van Genep 1960; Turner 1969; Glaser and Strauss 1971). She was so concerned about her ability as a headteacher prior to the inspection she often commented that if anything was found wrong with the school she would take the blame herself. There was 'no way that she would ever say it was due to the lack of expertise of teachers in the school'. After the inspection, she said she would have 'found it very difficult to have carried on working if the inspection report had been poor'.

Once Chris received the report from the inspectors, however, her attitude towards her own abilities changed significantly. The inspection report signalled her reincorporation into the new role:

> 'I feel I'm really good for here which is great. I love it here, and when we got the okay it was one of the best days I've had. We all had cakes. I was *so* relieved. I swanned around and didn't do any work. It's the only day I've ever done that! It was one of the most wonderful! . . . I'll always remember that day . . . It's nice to feel comfortable with the job, and it's the first time I feel confident about what I do . . . it's also the first time I feel *respected* . . . and respect that I've actually *earned*. And that's really, really good.'
>
> (Chris)

The school also had achieved a new status – not surprisingly perhaps since it was so closely tied up with Chris's role as head. The inspectors, none of whom had ever been in the school before, had asked for some of the school's paperwork to take away as exemplars. Chris and her colleagues 'were so pleased to see the back of them they would have given them anything', and she 'just felt as they walked away, "Yes!"' The report gave them 'new confidence' and Chris felt that the school would now 'leap forward at a real rate'.

Notwithstanding her elation at the result, there were certain aspects of the inspection which invoked Chris's anger and disgust. In particular, she disapproved of the bureaucratic, dehumanized way in which the inspection was conducted and the report produced. The Registered Inspector (RGI) who led the inspection team, for example, was distinctly cool and restrained. He had referred to the paperwork, for example, as 'extensive', whereas a local inspector had found it 'exemplary', and had even asked if he could use it for training purposes. He had told Chris that the parents were 'very pleased with the school'. However, he managed to make the parents' response sound negative rather than positive. After the inspection, his verbal report to the governors, according to Chris, was so

> '*flat* and deadpan. He just delivered it as if the school was closing, and I couldn't believe it! . . . It was almost as if he was bored by it. He's obviously on to the next one . . . And of course for us it's still very much hot news . . . we're just so thrilled with it, and then to get that! I actually feel, "God! I must have misheard him!" . . . I don't know how you work in education and not say "Course, it's really good!" [*said with feeling, laughs*].'
>
> (Chris)

The plaudits that she received as head were

> 'quite nice, but I really could have smacked him in the gob on Monday. "You can keep that, but just give a bit more to the people who are actually here day after day after day, doing their job and getting tremendous results," and I was *just*, disappointed about it.'
>
> (Chris; post-Ofsted interview: 1 week)

The style of the written report was also disappointing:

> 'I just keep saying to people that the actual report is really boring and it won't feel that it's us . . . It was bland reading, but that is the language of reports and of Ofsted.'
>
> (Chris; post-Ofsted interview: 1 term)

The managerialist discourse of the inspection is impacting here against the general discourse of primary education. These inspections are auditive rather than appreciative, an objective accounting against a standard template, rather than an attempt to grasp the ethos of a school – its major motive force. But primary teachers invest a great deal of their emotional selves in their jobs (Lortie 1975; Nias 1989; Woods 1990; A. Hargreaves and Tucker 1991; Acker

1995). For Chris, there is a strong need for teachers' emotional investment and this paramount feature of their teaching to be recognized by the inspectors. Their bland, emotionless response suggested that that element was unappreciated, which, in turn, drew from Chris an emotional response. Lortie (1975: 121) pointed to the 'craft pride' of teachers which is apparent when teachers 'succeed in reaching work goals that are important to them'. One of these work goals described by Lortie was a pride in an impressive public display or performance which results in public and community recognition. Lortie also found that most of the sources of pride were located in the classroom for the teachers. For Chris, as head of the school, craft pride extends beyond the boundaries of the classroom to include the whole of the school and local community, and is something she wants that wider community to share. The nature of the feedback process from the inspectors obstructed this.

Reconstruction of self

In marked contrast to Chris and Theresa, Shula's inspection was devastating, almost totally deconstructing the world on which her teaching was based. Out of the ruins, however, and through her own efforts, a new Shula was eventually reconstructed. Two months after the inspection she felt it was 'like a bad dream that comes back to haunt you every now and again', but she was busy on the task of personal reconstruction:

> 'I find myself thinking, "What's my purpose? What's my role? What am I going to do?" It goes right down to where you see yourself in the scheme of things and what's important. I've never, ever, ever, had something that's really made me question something so big all at once . . . It's this terrible lost and empty feeling of not holding on to anything anymore which is scary.'
>
> (Shula)

Mills (1959) argues that a crisis in personal values emerges when people become conscious of the conflict between wider, macro influences and their own lives. Shula is struggling with that crisis. We hear in her words an individual getting to grips with anomie, seeking, perhaps, through the expression of it a way of coming to terms with it which will provide a platform for a redefinition of self. For her, it has raised deeply moral issues not only about herself, but about what kinds of people are being constructed through her teaching:

> 'I may be thinking that I'm challenging these children to think for themselves but am I really? Am I just really constructing for them what the status quo wants me to do? Am I really helping these children to challenge what it is important about their lives, and to expose the wider

issues of society and the world? Am I giving them false hope by challenging racial bigotry and promoting equal opportunities? . . . Am I being
fair to these children?'

(Shula)

However, some nine months after the inspection, Shula had returned to her
educational roots of active learning and pupil engagement:

'Someone said to me today, "God! there's so much going on!" and I
said, "This is what I like, this was me six years ago," everything buzzing,
going, and happening. Ships being painted, embroidery going, and it's
all happening. It is really wonderful. It looks chaotic but it's all happening and the kids are buzzing because they're going: "Oh, I haven't
done that, I haven't done that yet, Miss! I want to do that!"'

(Shula)

For Shula, however, unlike Chris, this was not a result of Ofsted's legitimizing
her work, rather the opposite. For in mounting such a wholesale challenge
to her self, Ofsted provided a catalyst for reconstruction.

'I was in turmoil because I wasn't expressing myself in any way that I
felt was creative because my definitions had gone . . . It wasn't my choice,
it was outside influences. The Ofsted really shook me and it might well
have been a good thing. It made me start to kick back and say: "No way,
no way, I'm not sitting back and taking this. I'm a person, and part of
the way I teach and what I do it's got to work with my kids".'

(Shula)

She was challenging Ofsted's importance, personalizing her work, reasserting herself and reconstructing not only herself but her pedagogy.

'I said to myself "Come on Shula, Ofsted and the Government didn't
define you in the beginning. They didn't set up my hobbies, interests
and they didn't define me as a creative person, did they?" I'm a
teacher as far as they go and that's it – DES number – that's it, end of
story. So it's about what I bring to it and how I approach what I do and
how I see, how I feel children learn . . . I don't know what the final
picture's going to look like, but what I will say is that it's the excitement
of rediscovering or reconstructing myself. I might be able to give you
a picture in six months or two years, but at the moment I'm having real
fun doing the reconstructing.'

(Shula)

Shula has broken out of the boundaries imposed by the National Curriculum
and Ofsted:

'All the time you are being told, "This is your place, this is where you
stay." It's been a long process of five or six years. Now slowly I've begun

Table 5.1 Changes in a teacher's practice following a school inspection

Prior to Ofsted	After Ofsted
Steadily implementing the National Curriculum by subject	Fitting National Curriculum targets to her curriculum
Standardizing planning in her department	Encouraging more flexible planning
Doing more class teaching than formerly	Planning topics, but leaving teachers to develop their own interests
Preparing work for groups rather than individuals	Allowing individuals more time on task
Not using children's interests as a basis for the curriculum	Allowing children's interests more of a place in curriculum choices
Following a timetable fairly closely	Developing a more flexible timetable
Encouraging specialist curriculum coordinators to prepare work	Encouraging more dynamic interchange

to kind of accept it, but every now and again I'd have a little break-out, whereas now the excitement is to get in there and get involved with the kids. I will get across what I need to do, but I'm going to do it in my way because I will enjoy it and therefore my kids will enjoy it. Sometimes you have to accept there are boring bits, but we can do our boring bits really quickly. We talk and we discuss, we whizz through and do what we need to do, and we can do the other things.'

(Shula)

The Ofsted process, therefore, was a major catalyst for Shula, a critical moment, that in the end promoted self-redefinition in ways unforeseen. She rediscovered herself at a point when the oppressive weight of the changes might have led to internalized adjustment without her realizing it.

How some of Shula's practices changed as a result of the inspection, in ways that could not have been predicted, are shown in Table 5.1.

CONCLUSION: THE PROCESS OF CHANGE

Ofsted plans on a strictly linear basis. The principle is to carry out an inspection as systematically and formally as possible, according to a standard formula, make recommendations, require an action plan and due procedures within a

Table 5.2 Responses to an Ofsted inspection

	Intensification	*Realities*	*Outcomes*
Theresa	Modified	Artificial	Normalization
Chris	Extensification	Essential	Confirmation
Shula	Aggravated	Anomie	Reconstruction

specified time period, and thus bring about school improvement. Even from the three cases examined here, it is clear that change for individuals is rather more complicated. It has different meanings for different people, and takes different forms. (These are summarized in Table 5.2.)

Meaning differed among our three teachers depending on how much status and control the teachers had within the school system, and on their different professional identities. The fact that Chris was a head, and Theresa and Shula classroom teachers, was no doubt an important factor. Their different situations, Theresa and Chris in a lower school in a small Midlands town, and Shula in a large, London primary (the latter, arguably, under more pressures from the changes), are no doubt another influence. For Theresa, the class teacher, as with many of Jeffrey and Woods's (1996) teachers, there was a feeling that the inspection process held little personal relevance, despite her own personal investment in terms of time and responsibility in the preparation and planning for the inspection. As a class teacher, Theresa is a member of a team, or a collectivity (Cohen 1976). As such, she takes on a corporate identity. For Theresa, the corporate identity of the school appears to be more important than the individual identity regarding the result of the inspection, and therefore the outcome of inspection has less meaning to her personal self. Part of this is evident in the way Theresa often refers to the collective rather than the individual when talking about the inspection outcome:

> 'It wasn't as bad in a lot of ways as I thought it would be but only because *we* came out well. If there had been criticisms of things that *we* thought were quite good, then *we* would have been most upset about it and there's nothing you can do about it really.'
>
> (Theresa; post-Ofsted interview: 1 term. Our emphasis)

Shortly after this inspection, a new format was introduced into the regulations whereby heads were to be informed of individual teachers' performances. Had this been in place at the time of the inspection, Theresa might have seen things differently. Career aspirations might have been another inducement, but Theresa was content in her role of classroom teacher. This totally governed her perspective, therefore.

Chris, as headteacher, is responsible for the creation of the corporate identity, and therefore needed to invest a greater amount of her personal identity in order for the collective to work. Had there been criticisms of the school, this would in turn have been a direct criticism of Chris. In this way, she had much more to lose had the inspection report been a poor one. Theresa, however, because she views herself as part of the collective, would have had mutual support from colleagues in the event of a poor report, and any blame could have been dispersed among them. For Chris, though no doubt the staff would have shown support, the blame would have been more personally felt, such that she would have resigned had the inspection shown the school to be failing. By the same token, Chris had much more to gain from a good inspection. The corporate identity was safe, hence the feelings of vindication and validation regarding her practice and management. There was little individual merit for Theresa in this, for the good report was to be shared equally among her colleagues. For Chris, the collectivity was her self – they were one and the same. Theresa's self was subsumed within the collectivity.

The Ofsted inspection in the long run provided a positive, confirmatory experience for Chris, whereas for Theresa there was certainly a lack of this sense of achievement. For Theresa, there was a sense of unreality and abnormality about the inspection. For Chris, by contrast, it was essential reality, a celebration of the 'marriage' of the school and official policy by mutual consent (as opposed to a 'shot-gun wedding'), and of her substantial self to the new composite role she had fashioned (see Chapter 4).

Both experienced intensification to some degree, but our study supports others that suggest that deskilling and deprofessionalization are not inevitable consequences. Theresa was left with skills intact, while Chris felt positively empowered. An interesting question, however, is whether Chris has enhanced her professionalism, or whether she has been taken over by managerialism, captured by the agenda set by Ofsted. Is she joining a 'dependency culture', whereby she depends on external experts to validate her role performance? She had always been very confident of herself as a teacher. Had she received any negative assessment on those grounds, she would have rejected it. But she was unsure about her acquittal of new managerial responsibilities. It was the assurances given in this area that gave her most satisfaction.

A key question is whether her teaching and headship as she sees it have been enhanced as a consequence, and whether the managerialist aspects were unconnected to teaching – a kind of 'disjunctive bureaucracy'. For Theresa and Shula, much of the paperwork was disarticulated from their educational work. Will that now be continued into the future for Chris, increasingly taking over the work of the school? A number of factors suggest that it will not. Firstly, an important question in professionalization–deprofessionalization arguments is how teachers themselves feel about the nature of their work and the changes that have occurred (A. Hargreaves, 1994a). Does it make them more or less able to effect change themselves? In Chris's case, there is no doubting the feeling of empowerment. A great constraint has been removed from her, enabling her to go on to loftier heights of achievement. She has manifestly gained in 'professional confidence' (Helsby 1995: 324; and see Chapter 1). For the first time ever, she feels comfortable with her job, and 'respected' – respect she has 'earned'. Secondly, it might be claimed that Chris had become a slave to paperwork, but, for her, the paperwork was not disarticulated from the mainstream work of the school. On the contrary, Chris claimed that it was done for the school and not for the inspectors, and gave the school an opportunity to show how good it was. It was not a front, but hard truth. Thirdly, in her critique of the discourse, she has demonstrated the ability to 'become critical' (Carr and Kemmis 1986). She has not been taken over by the Ofsted culture. Her critical powers are intact, perhaps keener with her new-found confidence. She has taken what she needs from the experience, and is arguably more in control of her own destiny than formerly. Fourthly, Chris's 'compositeness' (Chapter 4) was still intact, indeed reinforced, since areas of unease had been removed. Some heads have been criticized under the new regime for continuing to teach, and not being managerial enough (see, for example, Woods 1995: Chapter 6). Chris has fashioned a mode of adaptation which meets both official scrutiny and her own principles. Fifthly, the school imposed its own reality on the proceedings and retained a large measure of control. This was evident in the meticulous planning, and in the way Chris and her colleagues moved to 'embrace' the inspectors. This is another instance of 'teachers being as professionally resourceful as ever' (Brimblecombe *et al.* 1995: 60).

It may be, also, that the inspectors did not feel entirely constrained by the explicit criteria of their brief, but exercised some 'professional judgement . . . guided and focused by their own insider knowledge and belief about schools, and by their own professional values' (Nixon and Rudduck 1993: 144). Certainly there seem wide differences in approach among inspection teams, with some more collegial than others (Brimblecombe *et al.* 1995: 55). On the other hand, if that were the case, this team may only have achieved 'managed participation' – a 'severely restricted autonomy and control over decision-making *vis-à-vis* both the nature of the inspection and the well-being of the schools, the teachers and the curriculum' – which is little more than 'an extension of the state's ideological powers of surveillance and control' (Evans and Penney 1994: 532). By the same token, Chris's euphoria may be licensed euphoria, and a kind of 'managed self-development' – that permitted within the boundaries of state control. This would be a more subtle form of control, a kind of 'no hands', 'steering at a distance' (ibid.: 529) form, where people are persuaded to conform with enthusiasm through the illusion of space wherein they appear to have room for discretion. We only raise that possibility as a precaution, and as a note for further study. Certainly Chris does not condone the inspection process as it stands, and would prefer a system based on encouragement and support rather than one that identifies failure. In some ways, her personal enhancement was a side product of that process, one that she had herself engineered. Given the points made above, Chris's record as an independent thinker, her strongly established beliefs and values, and her strategic expertise in adapting to difficult situations as described in Chapter 4, it would seem safe to conclude that she is retaining a strong measure of control in her own school. The personal cost, however, is a high one, and possibly beyond many teachers.

If Chris experienced 'positive trauma' (D.H. Hargreaves 1983) as a result of the inspection, Shula experienced 'negative trauma'. But it was to have a positive result in the end. Unlike Chris, prior to the event Shula had appeared to be drifting into managerialism (see Table 5.1). The inspection was a push too far. In scrambling any sense of reality, it required her to take stock and reconstruct, going back to first principles. So she also, after a deeply disturbing and emotional experience, appears to be emerging stronger. Prominent among the resources she brings to bear is a highly distinctive discourse. It contains strong rhetoric and powerful metaphors in the effort to sustain self and identity. This is the 'constructed network of symbolic connection' (Moore 1996: 41), the literary devices used to help convey, and in this case construct, meaning. The deep emotional charge firing the symbolic expression adds mood, morale and feeling to the discourse. Within the content is articulated a change in her conception of the rules governing the fulfilling of roles. Before Ofsted, Shula seemed to be following standardized, non-negotiable, external rules that were applicable to all schools. After Ofsted, it is as if she has been shaken out of this mindset. In her statements, she seems to be celebrating a new-found negotiating ability, and is formulating rules as they apply to her particular self and situation at the same time as she expresses them. In this she is developing a discourse, fashioning a new role for herself as she simultaneously tries to make sense of it after the 'non-sense' of the inspection (Graddol 1994).

In contrast, Theresa and Chris felt no need to change the rules. Theresa was relieved when the school eventually returned to 'normal'. Chris's conception of the inspection as a wedding illustrates her view. Ceremonies like weddings stand apart from everyday life (Goffman 1983). They are strongly and formally rule-governed, with people in appropriate role positions enacting their duties as required. Once completed, life returns to 'normal'. Chris's career continues on an upward path, with the massive endorsement from the inspectors of her managerial practices. Shula, as she speaks, is engaging in major reconstruction of her self through a radical interrogation of *everyday* rules as they affect her practice and situation. That she should experience such pain and Chris such elation in seeking to fashion new professional selves from a similar experience is, perhaps, not so surprising, given the general 'turmoil and stress' attending the radical changes in schools which have produced the whole range of emotions (D.H. Hargreaves 1994: 424).

We have seen in this chapter variable experiences of school inspections, which demonstrate that what one teacher experiences as constraint, another might find as opportunity; what may be experienced initially as constraint is not permanently so, but, through self-determination, reflexivity, commitment and support, can be turned into new, unforeseen opportunity; and that Ofsted as a change agent has to work through these interpretive processes. Ofsted makes no allowances for this, operating in linear, one-dimensional fashion, ministering primarily to managerial practices, and consequently is unable to cope with personal and emotional factors. The inspection can be worthwhile to some like Chris, futile to others like Theresa, and an abomination to others like Shula. There is no straight path to educational improvement. Teachers have to accommodate the changes in their own ways. Failure to do this results in stress and burn-out. We examine this issue in the following chapter.

CHAPTER 6

A price of change: teacher stress and burn-out

INTRODUCTION

The years of change have been accompanied by a rapid rise in the incidence of stress and burn-out: 5980 teachers retired on grounds of ill health in 1995–1996 (Government statistics, quoted in the *Times Educational Supplement* 13 December 1996), compared with 5549 in 1993–1994, 2551 in 1987–1988 and fewer than 1400 in 1979 (Macleod and Meikle 1994). The number of teachers taking early retirement for whatever reason has risen by 68 per cent over the past decade, jumping by 50 per cent in 1988 – the year of the Education Reform Act – and climbing to a total of 17 798 in 1995, even though the Teachers' Pension Agency latterly tightened up the interpretation of the rules. Furthermore, there are those who remain in teaching but earnestly wish to leave. In a survey of 430 schools in ten local authority areas, Smithers (1989) revealed a deeply discontented profession, with one in three teachers feeling 'trapped' and wishing to 'escape'. The late 1980s and early 1990s saw the phenomenon of 'escape committees' – groups set up, officially with union sponsorship, or unofficially, to help teachers 'escape' the profession. Travers and Cooper (1996: 106) report that 66.4 per cent of their sample of teachers had actively considered leaving the profession in the previous five years. The situation is even worse for headteachers. The National Association of Headteachers says four out of five heads are opting for early retirement and that its officers are dealing with enquiries from members who feel burned out in their forties (Fisher 1995). Moreover, there is evidence that teachers in some respects have been worse off than other professions at risk (Travers and Cooper 1993). Furthermore, the real extent of the problem may be concealed. One report, echoing some experiences reported in this book, states that the strains of the job were causing heart attacks and strokes, but also (O'Leary 1996: 35),

> Panic attacks, sleeplessness, broken relationships, excessive drinking and smoking, loss of confidence and breakdown are not reportable industrial illnesses. But they are as devastating to the teacher as broken arms, amputations and poisoning are to other workers.

The increase dates from the Education Reform Act of 1988, heralding, as outlined in Chapter 1, a major restructuring of schools and teachers' work. This is not just a mere correlation. Travers and Cooper (1996: 117), for example, found that the highest stressors among their sample of teachers currently all emerge from government policy, and 'are connected to change, its pace and implementation' (ibid.: 121). We have suggested that, in some respects, this is an illustration of intensification. This may now be the nature of the world we live in, to which we have to adapt accordingly. Casey (1995) interprets the effects on teachers as the product of the change in the structure of the world economy from Fordist work forms (which allowed some autonomy and alternative identities) to post-Fordist work forms (of which marketization and managerialism are a part), where workers live in a state of ambivalence about their work. Indeed, there are indications that even among teachers publicly expressing enhanced professionalism, privately they may have more reservations, setting up a stressful ambivalence (Menter *et al.* 1995a). Casey (1995: 194–6) argues that 'the self negotiates a private psychic settlement with the corporate colonizing power . . . the integrity of living one's life according to the calling of one's occupation is now denied'.

An alternative explanation, or even one that could be subsumed within that of Casey's, making the effects even more pronounced in the shorter term, might see the changes as a passing phase of a long-term event. Status passages (Glaser and Strauss 1971) have their own stress producing aspects. Van Gennep (1960) conceived of three main stages of status passages – separation, transition and reincorporation. The legislation of the later 1980s and early 1990s sought to 'separate' the education system from that of the Education Act 1944 and of the hugely influential Plowden Report of 1967, and to establish a new, restructured system, as outlined in Chapter 1. The system may still be in the 'transitional' phase, one that Turner (1969) argues is typically characterized by 'marginality' or 'liminality'. There can be much confusion; fear of the unknown; nostalgic hangings-on to the past; much experimentation, some leading to false trails. There is a sense of rapid, uncontrollable change, in itself a major stress-inducer, involving 'change-on-change beyond the control of most teachers' (Cox *et al.* 1988), leading to 'innovation fatigue'. In status passages attended by politics, as in education, there will be an aura of conflict and struggle. In short, the transition phase can induce anomie (see Chapter 5). A teacher of some thirty years' experience provides an example of personal experience of anomie, echoing others we have heard earlier (Hawes 1995):

> 'One of the main reasons I threw in the towel [i.e. resigned] was that the job was no longer the one for which I had trained and which I had enjoyed. When the praise changes almost overnight to criticism, when you are told that what you are doing and *know* works is all wrong, but are not told how or why or even given any hints as to how you should improve, demoralization swiftly follows. I was no longer convinced, as I had been up to about 1985, that I knew what I was doing, that I was doing it well, and that the children were benefiting.'

How long does it take to adjust to a new system – if, indeed, it is a phase, and not more permanent? There is some evidence (for example, Osborn 1995) that teachers are gradually adjusting to the changes (and so becoming 'reincorporated'?), but as noted in Chapter 1, and supported throughout this book, there appear to be contrary tendencies occurring at the same time leading to diminished professionalism on the one hand, but enhanced on the other. What, then, promotes one course rather than the other? Why do some emerge from the changes intact, and even empowered in some cases, while others are driven under? There is a complex mix of factors at work. Drawing on our various researches, and other studies, we examine some of the micro factors operating at personal level and meso factors operating at institutional level, which operate within the macro forces of intensification and marketization, and which are associated with stress. We view tension and constraint as the seedbed of stress, when (Woods 1989: 84):

> a teacher's personal interests, commitment or resources not only get out of line with one or more of the other factors, but actually pull against them. The classic case is having too much work, plus a strong moral imperative to do it, and not enough time and energy within which to do it. A variant on this basic theme is being pressed to do more work, given fewer resources with which to do it, and then receiving no reward or recognition, and worse, perhaps censure, when it is nonetheless accomplished. In all of these instances there are elements grating against each other.

As a teacher told Gerald Haigh (1995a: 3):

> You have to believe, in this business, that you are making things better and moving things on. If that particular spark is not there – if something happens that makes you think things are going the opposite way – it can be a very destroying occupation.

In the UK, in the 1990s, there have been many things 'going the opposite way' in teaching, setting up an unprecedented number of tensions, which for many teachers have been irresolvable. In the remainder of the chapter we consider how the macro forces of intensification and Government policy combine with personal and situational factors to produce an increase in teacher stress and burn-out.

PERSONAL FACTORS

We are not concerned here with the psychological factors associated with type of personality (see Travers and Cooper 1996), but more with micro-sociological factors, the most prominent of which are commitment, career and role, status, values and personal life.

Commitment

Not all teachers are equally committed to teaching, nor in the same way. Vocational, professional, instrumental and political forms of commitment have been identified (Sikes *et al.* 1985). Teachers may have some or all of these to varying degrees. We would argue that teachers at most risk of stress are those with strong feelings of vocation, those who care strongly about their work and their students (see also Rudow 1995). For these, the personal 'self' is inextricably bound up with the teacher role. They cannot switch off at the end of the school day to another life and another persona. Teaching is an essential part of their identity (Nias 1989). So much is this the case, that if suddenly deprived of opportunities to exercise their preferred mode of teaching they may experience a form of 'grieving for a lost self' (Nias 1991). Such teachers may be very self-determined, and experts at self-renewal, but for highly committed teachers, selves can be easily 'ruined' (Woods 1995). This is because they 'cannot help but get their sense of personal worth mixed up with their professional competence' (Haigh 1995: 3). Coping strategies and personal adjustment that involves simply falling into line with external prescription are not on their agendas. They do not put on 'performances' for external approval, even though they might be rewarded. Thus, Terrie was caught out when asked a 'trick' question at an inspection:

> 'It makes me cross. I just took at face value what they were saying . . . Like an idiot, I should have fallen in straight away, she was trying to trick me. It wasn't till I repeated the conversation, that everybody else was say-ing apparently it wasn't the answer I was supposed to give . . . I'm not devious enough. I kept saying to the headteacher, "I can't play these games. I don't know what smart-arse answers I'm supposed to give!"'
>
> (Terrie)

They continue to strive after perfection following their own self-imposed demands in circumstances where others are making contrary demands

(Osborn and Broadfoot 1992). Consequently, they are easily 'damaged' (Radnor, in Haigh 1995a: 3–4). A teacher comments:

> 'You lay yourself bare. You are not thinking of protecting yourself, because that's counterproductive – every fibre is going for the progress of the child, and that makes you vulnerable so that the slightest flick hurts so much.'

Haigh (ibid.) quotes another example of a teacher who was the subject of a parental complaint, which was later shown to be unjustified. What was important was 'the devastating effect it had on him, not just as a teacher, but as a person with a private life and a set of emotions' (ibid.: 3). The teacher said, afterwards:

> 'I now doubt my ability right across the board. I dread each day. I'm left with a legacy of low self-esteem. They've stolen a period of my life, and I feel terribly hurt by that.'

Another skilled, successful teacher would welcome a little more praise for things well done, and less blame for things that lie outside teachers' control (Richardson 1995: 67):

> 'Stress is not merely the effect of working hard. Many people, myself included, have worked many hours a day for many years. Stress is caused by feeling bad about oneself and constantly being made aware of one's inadequacy even though one is actually quite good at the job.'

For teachers who stretch themselves to the limit as a matter of course, work overload can be especially crippling, like two of our 'sinkers' from Chapter 3:

> 'the problem is I try to do too much, because what I think is right is what I know is working. That's when I worry myself sick or feel guilty because that's what I had planned on paper.'
>
> (Terrie)

> 'I always plan to do too much, we all do. I've always said that's a failing because then you're left frantic because it comes near the end of term and you've got all these plans for doing this and this and this and you've only got half-way through them. Once you've put it down of course you've got to do it, well you feel obliged to. You feel, "Why have I not managed this?"'
>
> (Esther)

Evans *et al.* (1994: 169) distinguish between 'sane' and 'over-conscientious' teachers, according to how far they 'allowed' themselves to be overcome by pressures deriving from the National Curriculum. This, however, fails to recognize the press on primary teachers to be 'conscientious' – a virtue in an earlier age, which has now become something of a fault as far as coping with the National Curriculum is concerned (Campbell *et al.* 1991b), though Evans *et al.* (1994: 174) do note that stress affected *all* their teachers, and

> arose from a deep sense of frustration at not being able to complete their work to the standard they thought they ought to do.

The 'over-conscientious', of course, may be among the more highly judged teachers. There is some evidence that such teachers are particularly vulnerable to stress (Smilansky 1984). It is not the case, therefore, that weaker, less-effective teachers are being selected out of the system, which some might argue to be a price worth paying for the disruptions caused in the profession.

Role and career

We have discussed in Chapters 1, 3 and 4 changes in the teacher role and the growth of role tensions. As noted, the character of the primary role for many teachers has been indistinguishable from self. Nias (1995: 2) remarks,

> For such teachers, the personal and occupational self may be so closely related that, in their own terms, they 'become' teachers: The persons they perceive themselves to be go to work, and the teachers they feel that they are come home, often to occupy their sleeping as well as their waking hours.

The reconstruction of the teacher role, therefore, strikes to the heart. This, in turn, has had implications for teacher careers.

Teaching used to be a secure job – a job for life. That used to be one of its attractions, a benefit to set against the relatively poor material rewards. This is no longer the case. There has been what one ex-teacher describes as an 'explosion of insecurity'. A series of budget reductions in recent years has led to a large number of redeployments and redundancies (and a concomitant growth in class size and use of teaching assistants) to add to the early retirements. Just as selves can be ruined, careers can be 'spoiled' (Goffman 1968). There is – or used to be – a career structure, with a notional idea of progression for aspiring teachers. For many, this provides a framework for their working lives. It becomes part of their present and future selves. At any particular time, the career structure presents opportunities for some, frustration for others. A generation ago, a teacher might expect to progress through various positions of responsibility to, perhaps, a middle or senior management post. There were never enough of these posts to go around among the aspirants, and 'mid-life crises' around the age of forty were not uncommon (Sikes *et al.* 1985). Now, however, these posts, which used to attract hundreds of applicants, are not wanted. Re-advertisements are running at a high level (Smithers 1989). Dean (1996) reports a particularly dire situation in London where job losses among heads are reaching record levels, and where one commentator expects '40 per cent of primary headships failing to get filled'. The top of the career structure has evidently become blocked off even for many of those who formerly might have expected advancement. One deputy head comments (Hooper 1996: 2),

> 'I'm in a trap. I enjoy the time I spend at work and am well paid but I've been in the job too long. Tunnels once led from it to exciting horizons but most of them have been blocked or collapsed...The main tunnel left leads to headship. Why don't I take it? Because I can't find a model of a happy primary headteacher. They are all stressed, overworked and overburdened.'

Bell (1995: 11) comments that:

> some teachers now feel that they are so bruised by constant changes which have to be implemented at a speed, allowing no time for reflection, that they have probably lost their sensitivity to the processes of re-creation. A worrying number make it clear they no longer wish to be promoted.

This is not so much a matter of salaries as conditions. As Fisher (1995: 12) reports:

> Many teachers are less than anxious to leave their classroom to occupy a power vacuum. Deputies who might once have considered themselves automatic promotion prospects withdraw from the fray. They say they're put off by money as well as stress. 'The difference in salary wouldn't keep me in the paracetamol I'd need,' says one deputy who will avoid the headaches of ambition. 'Why should I take on all that aggravation for 10% more money?... I've looked at a lot of heads and I don't want to end up like them.'

Those in such positions become subject to feelings of inappropriateness and/or inadequacy as the nature and demands of the job have changed. Such problems of role ambiguity and conflict are well known factors in the production of stress (Travers and Cooper 1996: 46–8). The headteacher's role in particular has changed radically from that of 'leading professional' to one of 'chief executive' in the 'scientific corporate management' structures that are being introduced in the increasing drive for efficiency, with their implications for depersonalization, top-down management structures, and division of labour between heads and their staffs (Ball 1990). We saw examples in Chapter 4 of how two heads were struggling to maintain their values within the system. One headteacher who had retired early told us that he felt the role was becoming depersonalized, and he feared for his own self-development which was a necessary part of his teaching (Woods 1995: 153):

> 'It had gone beyond the point where it was being used to challenge the person further within the context of their own personal development,

and was making demands on them that would ultimately have a clone-
like effect, a stereotyping effect, that I felt I needed to resist quite
strongly.'

Also, as Evetts (1994) has shown, by no means all teachers, especially women,
are aspiring in this particular way. Nias (1989: 76), for example, has pointed
to the virtue of lateral careers for some of the women teachers in her sample,
and has urged that a more flexible definition of careers be available to men
also, 'whose morale and enthusiasm might also be revived by the opportunity
sometimes to move sideways (or out) as well as up'. At the moment, however,
for many teachers the sense of the 'normal career' still holds, and men in
particular may feel it difficult to adjust to the new situation.

Even so, where others are guided more by considerations of maximizing
the intrinsic rewards of teaching, here, too, for some, the future has become
blocked off as those kinds of opportunities have declined. The natural forces
of the 'market' dictate that schools recruit as cheaply as they can. Dean
(1996) reports that many primary heads are having difficulty in finding the
right quality of applicant at a price they can afford. Thus, more experienced
teachers are hampered in any quest for new positions because of their cost
to schools, now managing their own budgets and confronted, because of
economic pressures, by the prospect of having to make some of their existing staff redundant. The former staff experience what has become known as
'occupational locking-in' (Travers and Cooper 1996: 56); while the redundant staff are, for the most part, unwilling leavers. If times are hard, some
consolation might be found in the hope of future prospects. Where those are
curtailed, the difficulties are the greater. To the question of 'what am I doing?'
is added that of 'where am I going?', compounding the sense of anomie.

Those most at risk in these respects are those in mid- to late mid-career.
They have been socialized into those kinds of expectations. It is too early for
them to retire, and it is difficult for them to move to other jobs or professions (Smithers 1989). They are stuck. Further, the prospect of early retirement is receding further and further into the future. Alarmed at the prospect
of a teacher shortage (not surprisingly, in the context of this chapter) and
the demand on the teachers' pension fund, the Government introduced more
stringent regulations governing early retirement in 1997. The Chair of the
Association of Heads of Grant Maintained Schools comments (Phipson, quoted
in MacLeod 1996):

> It seems strange if you are trying to improve standards in schools to do
> it by keeping those people who feel worn out and want to retire. It is
> going to be hard not to have a number of disgruntled people.

Younger teachers trained within the National Curriculum are less at risk
in this respect. Their notions of career and outlook on the future have the
National Curriculum and other changes as their baseline. This is not to

forget that teachers in their first year often do have a hard time (Hanson and Herrington 1976). Nor that young teachers can rapidly become disillusioned. A 28-year-old teacher, after five years of teaching, was (Cusack 1993: 7)

> 'almost scared to do anything creative in case I fall foul of the law . . . I'm feeling overworked, under-valued and almost burned out. If this is how I feel at 28, what will I be like at 45?'

Such is the personal identification with the role, and the feeling of conscientiousness, that blame is frequently internalized when aims and demands are not met (see, for example, Chris in Chapter 4). Confessions abound in the pages of the educational press (see also Chapter 3):

> 'I felt totally useless and inadequate, and perhaps worst of all, guilty about it and very, very ashamed.'

> (Sloan 1996: 30)

> 'I frequently feel guilty because I know that I should do more marking, and preparation, and give more feedback to do justice to my pupils, but I simply cannot.'

> (Want 1996: 30)

An ex-primary headteacher who had recently suffered burn-out, after reading this paper, commented on the theme of guilt:

> 'I do believe this is a central theme. It is certainly a feeling which I consistently experienced as a teacher and as a head and it is a feeling which stays with you. It is very much part of the continuous contestation [because I think that is what it feels like] between what one feels one should be achieving in the job and the attempt to maintain the self. The sense of guilt becomes stronger as one increasingly feels that one is no longer able to achieve what one sees as necessary, thus putting the self under strain . . . We [i.e. heads] feel that we are the ones who should be capable of adapting to what we see as necessity and to perform accordingly. If we fail, we naturally have to take the personal responsibility for that failure. This is particularly true in relation to our responsibilities towards children whom we would view as especially vulnerable to the consequences of our failures.'

Status

Teachers have suffered an assault on their professional status in recent years. Teachers lost a long and bitter struggle with the Thatcher Government over pay in the 1980s. They were blamed for an alleged decline in educational standards, and had a National Curriculum and national assessment forced upon them, without consultation. They have been subjected to a 'discourse of derision' in the national media directed toward their pedagogy and their achievements (Wallace 1993). The polemical rhetoric of politicians and the press lambasted teachers in the early 1990s, engendering a 'moral panic' over educational standards and teaching methods, and swamping rationality (Woods and Wenham 1995). Not for the first time, teachers were the scape-goats for national decline. The powerful new inspection body of Ofsted has adopted a model of confrontation rather than collaboration, as we have seen in Chapters 3 and 5. One 'no longer feels that one is doing a job that society values' (MacFarlane 1989: 19). This was the major factor in Walsh-Harrington's (1990) survey of ex-teachers. Morale within the profession sinks lower, guilt levels rise (A. Hargreaves 1994a). One ex-head remarked, 'The culture of blame is pervasive, and it's a very nasty little atmosphere' (Haigh 1996: 4). A *Times Educational Supplement* leader (31 May 1996: 16) declared:

> The constant drip-drip of public criticism and the vaunting of parental rights over professional judgements cannot fail to lower the public esteem for schools.

In general, status is important in organizations because it grants authority to do things and the ability to get things done. Status is most often given to those who can be relied upon to do the job properly. It also reinforces the ego and provides incentive. Further, it promotes in individuals a sense of responsibility and dependability. Deprivation of status works in the opposite direction. The one benefit low status usually has – a guarantee of protection against exorbitant demands being made – most resoundingly does not apply in this case.

Values

On values, one early retiring primary head, reported by Dean and Rafferty (1996: 6) commented:

> 'We are losing sight of the important things in life.'
>
> (Jeremy Dicker)

Grace (1995: 150) states:

> [Together with the increase in problem, what has also changed are] the moral codes and moral certainties which headteachers could invoke in constructing a response to value dilemmas.

Teaching is a matter of values. People teach because they believe in some-thing. They have an image of the 'good society'. So do politicians. As reported in Chapter 1, the reforms of the late 1980s and early 1990s in England and Wales were informed by values of marketism, consumerism, managerialism and traditionalism. Where teachers are in sympathy with these ideas, as with

James in Chapters 3 and 5, their work and careers may well receive a boost. Where teachers are opposed, it makes it difficult to adjust to new roles and work patterns. As we have seen, many primary school teachers do subscribe to different values from those behind the reforms. These teachers prefer a different model of 'good teaching', one based on child-centred principles. Core features are full and harmonious development of the child, a focus on the individual learner rather than the whole class, an emphasis on activity and discovery, curriculum integration, and environmentally-based learning (Sugrue 1997). There is also a studied attention to the emotional aspects of learning and an emphasis on 'caring'. Nias (1995: 3) argues that this derives from a moral sense of responsibility towards their pupils. Interpersonal relationships are of fundamental importance to them. Yet,

> recent government policies take little account of teachers' views. Instead they emphasize their formal relationships and legal accountability. Teachers sense that they have a personal relationship with and moral obligation to children and their parents is constantly overridden by an official spirit of contractualism which they do not endorse and over which they have little control. In simplistic terms, they feel that the traditional service ethic of education has been replaced by one of consumerism.

The very nature of these beliefs, apart from their standing in opposition to government policy and preference, makes teachers vulnerable. As one primary head told us (Woods 1995: 85)

> As teachers wanting to be tender to others and have that tenderness returned to you . . . we are exceedingly thin-skinned . . . and that makes it easy for people to injure you . . .

Esther, a 'sinker' from Chapter 3, feels that

> 'the way they're going, they'll be no individuality left in classrooms, no way to be kids or encourage them or direct them or lead them the way you feel is best. If an Inspector walked in here and saw us building a city of Rome with kids standing on tables and chairs, seven hills and kids everywhere and "You are a house, stand still you are a house, where's your chimney?" They roar with laughter but they never get out of hand. I use children to show growth of city. It looks awful but it is creative.'

In a survey of teachers who had left, or who were on the point of leaving the profession (Walsh-Harrington 1990: 27), one 'just couldn't cope any longer, the emotional demands of the job were exhausting'. Another 'would come home emotionally drained, unable to give my own children the attention they deserved'. An ex-teacher told Croall (1995: 7) that

'The head felt we shouldn't get emotionally involved with the children, that we should stay behind the barrier of authority, that a more informal relationship left you in no-man's land. He also said that if we were 100 per cent dedicated it was too much like hard work, and we would burn ourselves out. But I'm not that kind of person.'

A daughter writes an open letter to her father, burnt out after thirty years' teaching (Anon 1993: 2):

... You are a giving, sensitive and caring person and until recently you have been able to channel your qualities to a large degree into your job. People like you always get exploited because you don't put a price on what you give to others ... Teaching is being restructured in a way that stifles your ability to care for and stimulate your students ... but also prevents you attending to yourself ...

All the pressures are on teachers to find new roles within teaching; but this would be a betrayal of all that many believe in. Unable to proceed forward or back, feelings of anomie develop (see Chapter 5). The central element in this, according to Rose (1962: 545) is that

life is meaningless. This entails a sense of worthlessness, a loss of motivation, a belief in one's inability to achieve anything worthwhile ... The result is a persistent psychological beating of the self with a circular intensification of the process. Soon the individual is no longer able to control his feelings of anxiety and depression.

In order to recover, Rose goes on (1962: 548), the individual needs to develop a positive attitude towards the self, and

must *do* those things which are in accord with his own values and which reflect the values of some social group that he rates highly. He must be able to congratulate himself occasionally and receive congratulations from esteemed others.

An ex-headteacher who experienced burn-out comments,

'This is a recurrent problem among headteachers. The position of being a head leads to a form of isolation which precludes the opportunity for assurance. One can get that assurance from other headteachers but the new managerialism has tended to breed a culture of cope or bust.'

Personal life

'I can't blame it all on the job, of course. I've had a pretty difficult year in my home life.'

(Want 1996: 30)

We have noted earlier how complications in one's personal life can become bound up with problems at work. Thus, one teacher experiencing stress during a school inspection compared her feelings to those felt during a recent bereavement (Jeffrey and Woods 1996: 335–6):

> 'My mother died a year ago and the stress that I feel now is not the same, but it's equivalent to the pressure that I felt under. She died in September and that first term was awful for me, getting through it . . . On my way to school I often think about things. I'm not exactly crying, but you know how you get when your eyes well up. Ofsted is like that time when my mother died, the world is not really there because you are concentrating so much on it. The pressure of visiting her and the guilt is just like Ofsted. It will be difficult getting back to reality.'

In another school in the same research, where teachers similarly were undergoing stress, hardships in their private lives were a notable factor (Woods 1996: 109):

> 'terrible times', 'anniversary of her mother's death', 'home becoming prison', 'suffered tremendously from a brutal father', 'one of her cats had died', 'aging parent recovering from alcoholism', 'nervous breakdown'.

The problems of value-clash experienced by Frances at Meadowfields 'just so happened to coincide with my marriage break-up as well. It was very unfortunate, I lost three stone in ten weeks'. The very fact of having a personal life, more usually considered a stress-reliever, can turn into a stress-producer because of the demands that it makes. We saw in Chapters 4 and 5 how Chris's work ate into her family life, and how she treads a thin line between coping and breakdown. Evans *et al.* (1994: 168) found that, for their infant teachers experiencing the worst stress, it was their personal and domestic lives which generally suffered the most. They point out that it was even worse for those who 'shouldered traditional female domestic and family responsibilities'. They cite David (1991), who asserts that the restructuring of the last decade has failed to take into account changes that have occurred in family life over the past thirty years or so. Women may be working double or treble shifts with work, home and childcare (Acker 1994). Despite this (Acker 1995: 24, quoted in Nias 1995: 6),

> women are less likely than men to look after themselves as long as they feel that there are others who need to be cared for, especially when there are social expectations that 'women's caring work should blur the distinction between labour and love'.

Nias (1995: 6) argues that, in common with others in the caring professions, teachers ignore their own needs. She has 'repeatedly been struck by teachers' neglect of their own physical and emotional health and their willingness to sacrifice these to the perceived needs of their children'. Given their multiple role and its nature that disposes them primarily towards the needs of others, women are especially disadvantaged by the service ethic that encourages teachers to disregard the early stages of stress (Veninga and Spradley 1981). By the time stress becomes a real problem, therefore, it is often too late.

SITUATIONAL FACTORS

There are a number of situational factors that appear to be relevant, notably school and neighbourhood characteristics, teacher and occupational culture, and pupil characteristics.

School and neighbourhood characteristics

There are, first, certain objective indices, such as level and size of school, though there are no data available regarding their connection with stress. With regard to the former, it might be argued that a lower school teaching children of 4–7 years is less pressurized than a middle school teaching children of 8–12 years, and certainly much less so than a school covering the whole range of 4–11 years. This is because not only are the latter schools larger, but test results at age 11 have to be published, and this is seen as more of a critical juncture in the pupils' career, involving movement to secondary school.

There are a range of factors connected with level of resource, such as poor physical working conditions, large class size (French 1993), and lack of materials and equipment. An increase in organizational support in the form of additional staffing, resources, money, and time is high on the list of Travers and Cooper's (1996: 161) alleviators of stress, for 'there is nothing more demoralizing for pupils and teachers alike than shabby rooms and poor equipment' (Butler 1996: 2). Nonetheless, that is what many schools have. An Ofsted report (1993b) on one of our case study schools described it thus:

> The school site and accommodation are well managed. Much has been done by the parents, staff and governing body to bring about minor improvements. However, the nine temporary classrooms have no running water and some of the teaching spaces are small. As a result practical work in, for example art and science is difficult to carry out. The scattered nature of the accommodation hinders liaison and the development of cooperative work within some year groups. The hall is small and storage space is limited. Many of the pupils have to go outside to visit the lavatory and in wet weather this may entail crossing areas of the playground which are flooded.

Osborn *et al.* (1996: 151) record that, in their study, schools in different types of catchment area experienced very different pressures as a result of the changes. Thus, in 'many schools in disadvantaged inner-city areas, anxiety centred on the difficulty of adapting teaching to the personal needs of the individual children'. The National Curriculum was not seen as relating well to the children's needs. In middle-class areas, teachers were more likely to see the National Curriculum as enhancing their teaching qualities. Osborn *et al.* (1996: 152) conclude that, as the effects of the educational market continue to operate, teaching in the inner city becomes a harder and less rewarding job.

A related factor is school ethos, which is likely to be as significant in the production of stress as it is in encouraging school effectiveness (Rutter *et al.* 1979; Galloway *et al.* 1982; Mortimore *et al.* 1988). The history of the school, for example, certainly seems a factor in successful adaptation to the National Curriculum (Ball and Bowe 1992), especially where it shows success in previous curriculum reform. There might also be a strong 'relational idea' (Bernstein 1975) which serves to integrate the curriculum and unite the staff. Alliances are important, as where a school has established a strong role within the community earning passionate support from all involved (Woods 1995); or is a member of a consortium of schools, linked in mutual support. Above all, perhaps, is the loss of 'fun' in teaching:

> 'The atmosphere has changed. There never seems to be any praise; and there were always extra things that I should have been doing. In my own subject, for example, teaching methods are more and more laid down in a politically correct way. There is no fun.'
>
> (Miller 1996: 35)

> 'I used to feel a much happier, comfortable, confident teacher and now I've become uptight. Now I feel "You've got to get this done, you've got to get that done," "don't talk to me, go away," and I hate it. Yet I'm working harder than I've ever done before . . . but not doing class work. In the past I would stay after school, potter around, get my resources ready, think about what I'm going to do, have everything ready, much more leisurely, and next day be well prepared, and it was all nice. But the balance is wrong now. This weekend I did about seven hours work that had nothing to do with the way I was going to teach on Monday morning. I was doing minutes for language meeting, minutes for staff meeting, summary of the half-term reports. I had to do a reference for a teacher who left. I had to do my reading samples and write them up, my reports . . .'
>
> (Woods and Jeffrey 1996b: 47)

The area that a school serves is also of crucial importance. Those serving deprived areas, for example, not only have to minister to a large number of intractable social problems, but up until recently have had their results compared with other schools in the 'league tables' without any compensation or 'value-added'. Inevitably, they feature towards the bottom of the lists, appearing to the world at large as 'failing' schools, even though they may have had uncommon success in their own terms. This, therefore, is a double blow for the staff, showing the typical stress-producing disjuncture. How this can affect a school in a disadvantaged area is indicated by Richardson (1995: 63):

> In the first year that league tables were published, my school's intake measured at the age of 13 had 73 per cent of pupils with a reading age below their chronological age but, by the time they were 16, 27 per cent had achieved grades of A–C in GCSE [General Certificate of Secondary Education] English. This is something to celebrate; instead we were the 'worst' school in the area. To come bottom in the league, even if only in one's own local education authority, is to feel not only failure but the threat of impending closure. The sense of failure afflicts the students as well as their teachers.

Teacher and occupational culture

The new managerialism in schools is bringing profound changes to the organizational structure of schools and how they are managed – another prominent factor in Travers and Cooper's (1996) research. Some heads are simply incompetent. Evans *et al.* (1994: 158) conclude 'the part played by headteachers in creating or reducing stress should not be underestimated', and quote from one of their teachers, who '[knows] quite clearly that the stress I'm under is caused by inadequate leadership, inadequate management of the school'. Some have been heads for a long time, and find it difficult coping with the changes and their leadership requirements. Tim Peskett retired at fifty after a headship of twenty years, since 'after a time I couldn't get the buzz, because of the longevity'. Given the added pressures of recent years, another primary head finds it increasingly difficult to restart each school year. 'Sometimes I feel I've given so much I've been bled dry and I find it harder to go back in September.' Haigh (1996: 4) concludes that 'many of our schools are being led by people who are finding it increasingly difficult to reinvent themselves'.

D.H. Hargreaves (1994) argues that a 'new professionalism' is emerging, characterized by a shift in the values and practices of teachers and a synthetic relationship between professional and institutional development. Significant developments in the changing teacher culture are, he claims, as follows: a move from individualism to collaboration; from hierarchies to teams; from supervision to mentoring; from in-service training to professional development; from authority *vis-à-vis* parents to contract. D.H. Hargreaves (1994: 426) asserts,

Older teachers who found the changes too stressful took early retirement; those remaining now divide into those who increase stress by trying to persist with the old structures and culture and those who are, sometimes reluctantly and painfully, generating a more collaborative culture built on new social structures.

Hargreaves points the way to the need for more 'collaborative cultures', and, indeed, where these are genuine, that is to say democratic, antihierarchical, where the motive force comes from the group, there is a good record of educational success (Nias 1989; Nias *et al.* 1994), and of successful political resistance (Woods 1995). However, we have seen in previous chapters how stress can be induced by those striving to collaborate. Also, we have noted the appearance of 'contrived collegiality' (A. Hargreaves 1994a) – enforced collaboration from above in the interests of managerialism rather than the interests of the group – in some of the primary schools in our studies. Where a head is skilled in micropolitics, as James in Chapters 2 and 4, he can carry it off with some aplomb, though even here there may be some confusion, as two teachers at James's school attest:

> 'It's got more involved. Since the inspectors were here we seem to spend most of our time going round in circles . . . We were trying to decide something but somebody isn't there so you've got to go away and see them and come back, and report back. I also think we are trying to run before we can walk because you feel this pressure on you to get things up and running whereas you need time. That's probably why some of the things we're having to do again because we are rushed into them in the first place. Sometimes our fault, and sometimes outside pressure . . .'
>
> (Elizabeth)

> 'All the meetings aren't voluntary. If you didn't have parent surgeries, if you didn't attend staff meetings, if you didn't have team meetings . . . This week we've got a science INSET tomorrow which doesn't finish till six o'clock; and he [the headteacher] wants us all to go on Thursday to a language INSET which doesn't finish till six o'clock. Well everybody's rebelling against that!'
>
> (Frances)

The less skilled a headteacher is, the more bullying might be used as a resource, as a kind of hidden survival strategy. The incidence of bullying among teachers in schools has indeed escalated. The pressures get handed down through the hierarchy through what one teacher union calls 'cascade bullying'. Such are the pressures that teachers may not always realize what they are doing when they bully – another sign of alienation. A recent report claimed that 10 000 teachers experienced bullying at the hands of colleagues, and that it was the biggest cause of stress-related illness in the profession.

Headteachers in their forties were the biggest perpetrators, followed by deputy heads and heads of department. Victims were often the most experienced and strongest personalities, with women in their mid-forties and primary school deputy heads particularly at risk. Tactics include (Whitehead 1996: 6):

> 'constant criticism, public humiliation, undermining of the victim's confidence and setting unreasonable performance targets. Bullies also resort to shouting at the victim in front of colleagues or pupils, arbitrary removal of responsibilities, threats, intimidating use of discipline or isolation . . . It's a pretty desperate situation. You're fighting for your survival, constantly looking over your shoulder. It's a drip-drip-drip effect which creates feelings of intense worthlessness.'

It could be argued that a similar syndrome attends Ofsted inspections. Though most inspectors themselves may be models of politeness, inspections on our evidence on the whole are hierarchical, confrontational, unfeeling, narrowly technically minded and condemnatory. They are bullying in their effects, if not in their intent. Again, women seem the most at risk. Punch and Tuettemann (1990) found that men tend to reach a stress plateau which women may exceed. The point of departure for women may have arrived with Ofsted inspections. Research in secondary schools (Brimblecombe *et al.* 1996: 34) shows the extent to which women classroom teachers felt more exposed to the Ofsted process in comparison with their mostly male managers. They state:

> In the case of inspection, it may be that men are already experiencing stress from other aspects of teaching, and that inspection coming on top of that makes little difference. For women, however, the stresses of teaching have not yet caused such high levels of stress; inspection comes as the last straw.

The combination of managerialism and inspection can disrupt the collegiality amongst staff, and bring some to cause hurt to others without their realizing it. Thus, one of our teachers, Nina, photocopied some more statistics for coordinators to consider a week prior to their inspection, and one particular teacher, whom she liked and worked well with, reacted particularly emotively, as she bitterly observes:

> 'Tears came to her eyes, and I thought, "Oh God, I've done it again!" It's in my management role, I've got no choice, I appreciate the timing is bad but I couldn't do anything about it. I thought I was actually being quite helpful by going away at 7.30 in the morning and photocopying these bits of paper. I totally realize her reaction wasn't to do with me. It was to do with feeling very, very worried and concerned about presenting the stuff to inspectors but what I'm saying is that the end result of me trying to be helpful and efficient and giving teachers things, was

to make somebody feel really, really upset and say, "I know I'm going to make a mess of this".'

(Nina)

Menstrual cycles have been disrupted, weight lost, demotivation felt, even if a school has been given a good report (Budge 1996).

'Bullying', therefore, seems part of the general culture of policy implementation and surveillance. Under genuine participatory styles, this form of behaviour is less likely to occur. Once again, arguably, intensification and the Government's policy are creating the pressures that lie behind the rising incidence of bullying. But organizational structure can affect how those pressures are played out.

Pupils

In general, in situations where teachers otherwise feel under pressure, the one thing that keeps them going is their relationship with the pupils (Campbell *et al.* 1991a; Walsh-Harrington 1990), and dedication to the cause of their needs. Equally, they can be a major stressor. Freeman (1987) concludes that teachers need to perform effectively, and whatever gets in the way of this is potentially stressful, whether it be misbehaviour or simply poor motivation. 'Poor attitudes to work' are a major problem (Kyriacou and Sutcliffe 1978; Kyriacou and Roe 1988). But there are also some fearsome tales of deteriorating behaviour among pupils. Two-thirds of the teachers questioned in a poll for the Association of Teachers and Lecturers in 1995 said deteriorating pupil behaviour and violence were a growing factor in stress (reported in *The Guardian*, 12 April 1995: 7). It has driven some out of teaching. Croall (1995: 6), for example, interviewed an ex-teacher who taught at a deprived inner-city school:

> 'Over the three years I was there I became exhausted, drained, depressed and cynical . . . Some of the children's problems were horrendous. In every classroom we had three or four who were living in extreme poverty or very difficult family circumstances.'

Overcrowding, parental abuse and/or neglect, malnutrition, overwork in the home were rife.

> These conditions obviously affect the children's behaviour in school. They were unable to concentrate and unwilling to work, they disrupted others, and they were constantly seeking attention because they were so emotionally needy.

Other testimony (Owen 1990: 25) has strains of a 'blackboard jungle':

> 'Kids mill about, walking in and out of the room. If you try to interrupt their conversations they turn on you. Sporadic fights break out.

> Someone is kicking, pinching, stealing, lighting matches. Textbooks, scarce now, are ripped up, chucked around. While the girls comb their hair and put on mascara, the boys play cards, flick catapults and pass cigarettes to each other. In front of me I see pornographic cartoons . . . where French verbs should be'.

Women teachers may be subjected to more direct sexual harassment (Mahoney 1985; Lock 1986). Male teachers are not immune, though they do not appear to be as distressed by the experience (Dubberley 1988).

While some of these examples are from secondary schools, there is evidence that the age of onset of disruptive behaviour is getting earlier, and that the problem is increasing (Lawrence and Steed 1986). There has been a concomitant increase in pupil exclusions. Parsons (in Gardiner 1996) points to a steady overall rise between 1991 and 1996 (nearly 13 600 in 1995 in England and Wales; *Times Educational Supplement* 13 December 1996), with primary exclusions growing, though they form a slightly diminishing proportion of the total. Even so, exclusions from primary schools have quadrupled over these years. One researcher comments (Hayden, cited in Young 1996),

> What we found was an awful lot of stress. In the majority of cases, parents had split up, in the majority pupils had identifiable special educational need. They were not just a load of unruly, naughty kids. There is a real rise in exclusions, and the main reason is stress. All-round stress in schools, stress in families.

There have been instances recently – a new phenomenon – at both primary and secondary schools, of teachers threatening strike action if the exclusion of certain pupils has not been confirmed. Here, the marketing ideology which forces schools to compete with each other (and hence predisposes them to exclude children who pull the school's performance down significantly) combines with and exacerbates the stress levels felt in dealing with such pupils. The fight for exclusion can itself be stressful, as potentially opposing forces to any particular exclusion – parents, governors, local educational authorities – might put up strong resistance.

Are teachers becoming less tolerant? Not according to Collette Drifte (1996: 23), an ex-deputy head of a large, inner-city primary school who has retired 17 years early. She points to, among other things,

> many more EBD [emotional and behavioural difficulties] children remaining in mainstream education, with less support and fewer resources. Mainstream staff have been expected to carry an ever-increasing load of special needs children without the necessary backup.

The causes of pupil deviance and disruption are complex. Arguably, however, some of the major factors are trends associated with developments in society at large, which have seen the decline of the inner cities, and for some people, have brought long-term unemployment, poverty and the destruction of the family. Pupils and their teachers are living out the consequences of this in some of our schools, and impacting against marketization and managerialism at the same time.

BEYOND BURN-OUT

Burn-out might be regarded as one of the products of the liminal stage of unscheduled status passages. There is no awareness of an 'anticipation' phase in these cases. The person is unprepared, and all the expectations are that one will continue in role. Socially, however, the stress-inducing factors multiply, disjunctures occur and deepen, the self becomes more and more damaged, and is precipitated against its will into liminality. But if liminality has its darker, confused, disorienting side, it also has a brighter, revelatory one. For it is not uncommon for those who go through such an experience to rebuild the fractured self, or even to emerge with a new-found self in the 'reincorporation' phase, launched on a new career either in or outside teaching. Shula, in Chapter 5, is one example of this. Millard (1995), having related the factors that forced his early retirement at age 52, hopes it will be a time which 'will prove to be early re*tyre*ment. New treads are badly needed and . . . I can't help feeling that I still have miles to go before I sleep!' Another ex-teacher (Mersh 1991) has set up business as a consultant in stress management. 'I've moved on to a new phase in my life,' he said. Sloan (1996: 30) is going 'back to school next term. I won't be beaten by this but life will never be quite the same again. I don't think I will ever in future take myself and my abilities for granted. The simplest things take on monumental proportions when you are depressed; now I value the ability to do those things. My faith in God has deepened . . . My husband, my children and all those people who showed their love for me are all infinitely more valuable now.' Bob Nicholson's quality of life (as reported in the *Times Educational Supplement* 15 March 1996: 7) has improved since he took early retirement:

> 'I used to work an 80 hour week as a head and 30 or 40 hours on top of that for everything else. I lived on five hours sleep per night for 20 years. Now I have time to reappraise, to be a bit more sensible and to do things with a bit more grace . . . Value in life should not be equated with being paid for it. Once I took the plunge I relaxed. Society thrives on fear about the future but if you can't afford to buy a new car you buy a second-hand one or you walk. I now cycle and walk as much as I can. Although I enjoyed my career, I did not enjoy the nonsense of the last 15 years.'

Anne Jarvis (1993) is 'glad to be going [and] can't wait to be free' after thirty years as a class teacher. She comments:

'Once I have caught up on sleep and culture, on garden and kitchen, on travel, family and friends, I will also be free to play an active part in political life – yet another restricted area for most working teachers. May all who are retiring this year share in the rejuvenation which is so noticeable on the faces and in the step of those who have already escaped their classroom chains and said goodbye to school!'

Graham Went (1996: 35), an ex-head who retired early following a critical Ofsted report on his school is looking forward to 'taking a break':

'I need time to consider what I want to do. It would be nice to have a job that you don't bring home, but I haven't ruled out a return to teaching or even headship at some time in the future. In the short term, supply teaching might be good for me. After 20 years in the same school, as deputy and then head, there is a danger of tunnel vision.'

The ex-headteacher of 34 years' experience is currently 'trying to raise public awareness about the parlous state of an education system controlled by ministers who consistently show ignorance of children as learners' (S. Ball 1994: 21). A 50-year-old 'burned out' ex-head from our previous research is studying for a postgraduate degree, researching into the problems of, and provision for, young bilingual learners, and acting as a consultant for local schools. Another is writing and researching, and has been prevailed upon to undertake some supply teaching. Helping one teacher with a National Curriculum project on 'The Romans' – a topic in which he has specialist knowledge – he has rediscovered the zest that went into topic work, at which he excelled.

What about the educational system beyond burn-out? From a managerialist viewpoint, the disturbances in the profession of the last ten years or so might be considered functional on the basis of 'no gain without pain'. Many teachers are adapting, others are unable to and eventually leave, to be replaced by new recruits trained in the new order. Radical change, from this viewpoint, needs trauma. The educational system is in such a parlous state, and the forces of conservatism within it so powerful, the argument runs, that it needs a major 'shake-up'. If some experience terminal stress as a consequence, this may be unfortunate, but ultimately to the benefit of the new system, which in turn will ensure the promotion of educational standards. This is the managerialist discourse. But it leaves out of account that many of the best teachers experience stress, rather than those who might be considered the weaker teachers (who have become experienced in survival strategies); that young teachers are not coming into or staying in the system in sufficient numbers and quality; that the inhumanity involved in such an approach casts a stark light on the values behind the managerialist discourse; and that there is, as yet, little real sign of the end of the liminality. That, it seems, would require more changes, but of a different order.

CONCLUSION

The rise in incidence of teacher stress is associated with a complexity of factors operating at a number of levels. At the micro level, there are factors concerning teacher commitment, career and role, values, status and personal lives. At the meso level, there are factors to do with type of school, school ethos, neighbourhood, teacher and student cultures. At the macro level, there is the restructuring and intensification of teachers' work, and its particular manifestation at national level in government policy. However, intensification cannot account for everything that occurs in schools or educational changes in process, and we have noted the existence of powerful contrary forces. In Chapter 4, in fact, we noted an 'extensification' syndrome, a new empowerment of self, fully legitimated in the new system. In fact, teachers may experience feelings of enhanced professionalism and stress at the same time. What pushes them in one direction or the other, one might argue, is the particular conjuncture of other factors that apply, and the balance between intensification and professionalization, as mediated perhaps through national policy. Over the last decade the general balance in the UK has been shifted from professionalization and towards intensification, and there has been an increasing incidence of stress. It may be that, over the next decade, the balance will shift back again, if, for example, an approach to restructuring such as has been adopted in the United States is taken (see Chapter 1). In that event, we might expect stress and burn-out to diminish. However, it is still too early to say, and we might equally have to learn to live with ambivalence.

It might be argued that there is an easier route to stress reduction. If 'personal adjustment' happens on a large scale, then there might be a system-wide realignment. In other words, if the reforms are successful in ushering in a new technical–rationalist age in education, many teachers will become little more than technicians, operating a prescribed National Curriculum in stipulated ways, their work closely monitored by the national inspectorate. Others will become 'managers', working the system to good effect, and deriving considerable intrinsic rewards from their endeavours. Such a system, with such compliance, is almost proof against stress and burn-out. But the education purveyed would be narrow-minded, conformist and uncreative. A better recipe for educational improvement, we would argue, entails a strongly motivated, well rewarded, widely respected, critically minded, professional teaching body. If 'the teaching force . . . is the major single determinant of the quality of education' (Department of Education and Science 1983: para. 1), that force needs to be empowered and its professionalism enhanced.

Restructuring schools is well under way. The reconstruction of teachers is long overdue.

References

Acker, S. (1990a) Managing the drama: the headteacher's work in an urban primary school. *The Sociological Review*, 38(2): 247–71.

Acker, S. (1990b) Teachers' culture in an English primary school: continuity and change. *British Journal of Sociology of Education*, 11(3): 257–73.

Acker, S. (1994) *Gendered Education: Sociological Relections on Women, Teaching and Feminism.* Buckingham: Open University Press.

Acker, S. (1995) Carry on caring: the work of women teachers. *British Journal of Sociology of Education*, 16(1): 21–36.

Al-Khalifa, E. (1989) Management by halves: women teachers and school management, in H. De Lyon and F.W. Migniuolo (eds) *Women Teachers: Issues and Experiences.* Buckingham: Open University Press.

Alexander, R. (1984) *Primary Teaching.* Eastbourne: Holt, Rinehart and Winston.

Alexander, R. (1992) *Policy and Practice in Primary Education.* London: Routledge.

Alexander, R. (1995) *Versions of Primary Education.* London: Routledge.

Alexander, R., Rose, J. and Woodhead, C. (1992) *Curriculum Organisation and Classroom Practice in Primary Schools: A Discussion Paper.* London: HMSO.

Angus, L. (1994) Sociological analysis and education management; the social context of the self-managing school. *British Journal of Sociology of Education*, 15(1): 79–91.

Anon (1993) Dear dad, no one can fight forever. *The Times Educational Supplement*, 17 September: 2.

Apple, M.W. (1986) *Teachers and Texts: A Political Economy of Class and Gender Relations in Education.* New York: Routledge and Kegan Paul.

Apple, M.W. and Jungck, S. (1992) You don't have to be a teacher to teach this unit: teaching, technology and control in the curriculum, in A. Hargreaves and M. Fullan (eds) *Understanding Teacher Development.* London: Cassell.

Argyris, C. and Schon, D.A. (1974) *Theory in Practice: Increasing Professional Effectiveness.* San Francisco: Jossey-Bass.

Arnot, M. and Barton, L. (eds) (1992) *Voicing Concerns: Sociological Perspectives on Contemporary Education Reforms.* Wallingford: Triangle.

Audit Commission for Local Authorities in England and Wales (1984) *Improving Economy, Efficiency and Effectiveness in Local Government in England and Wales.* Audit Commission Handbook. London: Audit Commission.

Ball, D. (1972) Self and identity in the context of deviance: the case of criminal abortion, in R.A. Scott and J.D. Douglas (eds) *Theoretical Perspectives on Deviance.* New York: Basic Books.

Ball, S. (1994) A shameful time for education. *The Guardian,* 8 September: 21.

Ball, S.J. (1990) *Politics and Policy Making in Education: Explorations in Policy Sociology.* London: Routledge.

Ball, S.J. (1994) *Education Reform: a critical and post-structural approach.* Buckingham: Open University Press.

Ball, S.J. and Bowe, R. (1992) Subject departments and the 'implementation' of National Curriculum policy: an overview of the issues, *Journal of Curriculum Studies,* 24(2): 97–115.

Barthes, R. (1976) *The Pleasure of the Text* (trans. Richard Miller). London: Cape.

Barton, L., Barrett, E., Whitty, G., Miles, S. and Furlong, J. (1994) Teacher education and teacher professionalism in England: some emerging issues, *British Journal of Sociology of Education,* 15(4): 529–43.

Bash, L. and Coulby, D. (1989) *The Education Reform Act: Competition and Control.* London: Cassell.

Becker, H.S. (1977) Personal change in adult life, in B. Cosin *et al.* (eds) *School and Society* (2nd edn). London: Routledge and Kegan Paul.

Bell, J. (1995) Teachers coping with change, in J. Bell (ed.) *Teachers Talk About Teaching.* Buckingham: Open University Press.

Berlak, A. and Berlak, H. (1981) *The Dilemmas of Schooling.* London: Methuen.

Berlak, A., Berlak, H., Bagenstos, N.T. and Mikel, E.R. (1976) Teaching and learning in English primary schools, in M. Hammersley and P. Woods (eds) *The Process of Schooling: A Sociological Reader.* London: Routledge.

Bernstein, B. (1975) *Class, Codes and Control. Volume 3: Towards a Theory of Educational Transmissions.* London: Routledge and Kegan Paul.

Billig, M. (1988) *Ideological Dilemmas.* London: Sage.

Biott, C. and Nias, J. (eds) (1992) *Working and Learning Together for Change.* Buckingham: Open University Press.

Blease, D. and Lever, D. (1992) What do primary headteachers really do?, *Educational Studies,* 18(2): 185–99.

Bowe, R. and Ball, S.J. with Gold, A. (1992) *Reforming Education and Changing Schools: Case Studies in Policy Sociology.* London: Routledge.

Boyd, W.L. (1996) 'The new institutionalism', paper presented at the School of Education, The Open University, 10 June.

Brimblecombe, N., Ormston, M. and Shaw, M. (1996) Gender differences in teacher response to school inspection, *Educational Studies,* 22(1): 27–40.

Brimblecombe, N., Ormston, M. and Shaw, M. (1995) Teachers' perceptions of school inspection: a stressful experience. *Cambridge Journal of Education,* 25(1): 53–61.

Broadfoot, P. and Osborn, M. (1988) What professional responsibility means to teachers: national contexts and classroom constants, *British Journal of Sociology of Education,* 9(3): 265–88.

Broadhead, P. (1987) A blueprint for the good teacher? The HMI/DES model of good primary practice, *British Journal of Educational Studies,* 35(1): 57–72.

Budge, D. (1996) Inspections can be the last straw for women. *The Times Educational Supplement,* 31 May: 12.

Butler, C. (1996) Why we are alienated. *The Times Educational Supplement 2,* 13 September: 2.

Caldwell, B. and Spinks, J. (1988) *The Self-Managing School.* London: Falmer Press.

Campbell, R.J. (1988) Conflict and strain in the postholder's role, in R. Glatter, M. Preedy, C. Riches and M. Masterson (eds) *Understanding School Management.* Milton Keynes: Open University Press.

Campbell, R.J. (1993) The National Curriculum in primary schools: a dream at conception, a nightmare at delivery, in C. Chitty and B. Simon, *Education Answers Back: Critical Responses to Government Policy.* London: Lawrence and Wishart.

Campbell, R.J. and St J. Neill, S. (1990) *Thirteen Hundred and Thirty Days.* Final report of a pilot study of teacher time in Key Stage 1, commissioned by the Assistant Masters and Mistresses Association.

Campbell, R.J. and Southworth, G. (1992) Rethinking collegiality: teachers' views, in N. Bennett, M. Crawford and C. Riches (eds) *Managing Change in Education: Individual and Organisational Perspectives.* London: Paul Chapman.

Campbell, R.J. and St J. Neill, S. (1994a) *Curriculum Reform at Key Stage 1: Teacher Commitment and Policy Failure.* Harlow: Longman.

Campbell, R.J. and St J. Neill, S.R. (1994b) *Primary Teachers at Work.* London: Routledge.

Campbell, R.J., Evans, L., St J. Neill, S.R. and Packwood, A. (1991a) *Workloads, Achievements and Stress: two follow-up studies of teacher time in Key Stage 1.* Policy Analysis Unit, Department of Education, University of Warwick.

Campbell, R.J., Evans, L., St J. Neill, S.R. and Packwood, A. (1991b) 'The use and management of infant teachers' time – some policy issues', paper presented at Policy Analysis Unit Seminar, Warwick University, 15 November.

Carr, W. and Kemmis, S. (1986) *Becoming Critical.* Lewes, Falmer Press.

Casey, C. (1995) *Work, Self and Society after Industrialism.* London: Routledge.

Chubb, J. and Moe, T. (1992) *A Lesson in School Reform from Great Britain.* Washington: The Brookings Institute.

Clarke, K. (1991) Primary education – a statement. Text of a statement made by the Secretary of State for Education and Science, 3 December. London: DES.

Clegg, D. and Billington S. (1994) *Making the Most of Your Inspection.* London: Falmer Press.

Cohen, A.K. (1976) The elasticity of evil: changes in the social definition of deviance, in M. Hammersley and P. Woods (eds) *The Process of Schooling: A Sociological Reader.* London: Routledge.

Cook, A. and Mack, H. (1972) The headteacher's role. *British Primary Schools Today,* 2, London: Macmillan.

Cooper, P. and McIntyre, D. (1996) *Effective Teaching and Learning: Teachers' and Students' Perspectives.* Buckingham: Open University Press.

Coopers and Lybrand (1988) *The Local Management of Schools: A Report to the DES.* London: Coopers and Lybrand.

Corrie, L. (1995) The structure and culture of staff collaboration: managing meaning and opening doors, *Educational Review,* 47(1): 89–99.

Coulson, A.A. (1976) The role of the primary head, in R.S. Peters *The Role of the Head.* London: Routledge and Kegan Paul.

Cox, T., Boot, N., Cox, S. and Hanson, S. (1988) Stress in schools; an organizations perspective, *Work and Stress,* 2: 353–62.

Croall, J. (1995) Some of the children's problems were horrendous; the stories they told made you want to weep. *The Guardian,* 7 February: 6–7.

Cunningham, S. (1994) Women teachers: career identity and perceptions of family constraints, *Research Papers in Education,* 9(1): 81–105.

Cusack, I. (1993) Looking back in anger, aged 28, *The Times Educational Supplement*, 8 January: 7.

Dale, R. (1989) *The State and Education Policy*. Milton Keynes: Open University Press.

Darling, J. (1993) The end of primary ideology, *Curriculum Studies*, 1(3): 417–26.

David, M. (1991) A gender agenda: women and family in the new era?, *British Journal of Sociology of Education*, 12(4): 433–46.

David, T., Curtis, A. and Siraj-Blatchford, I. (1992) *Effective Teaching in the Early Years: Fostering Children's Learning in Nurseries and in Infant Classes*. Stoke-on-Trent: Trentham.

Davies, A.F. (1989) *The Human Element: Three Essays in Political Psychology*. Harmondsworth: Penguin.

Davies, L. (1987) The role of the primary school head, *Educational Management and Administration*, 15(1): 43–7.

Day, C. and Hadfield, M. (1995) 'Metaphors for movement: accounts of professional development', paper presented to the 7th Biennial Conference of the International Association on Teacher Thinking, Brock University, St Catherines', Ontario, Canada, July 30–August 3.

Dean, C. (1996) More heads quit capital primaries, *The Times Educational Supplement*, 24 May.

Dean, C. and Rafferty, F. (1996) Heads search in vain for good staff, *The Times Educational Supplement*, 6 September: 4–5.

Denicolo, P.M. (1995) 'Productively confronting dilemmas in educational practice and research', paper presented at the 7th Biennial Conference of the International Study Association on Teacher Thinking, Brock University, St Catherines', Ontario, Canada, July 30–August 3.

Densmore, K. (1987) Professionalism, proletarianisation and teachers' work, in T. Popkewitz (ed.) *Critical Studies in Teacher Education*. Lewes: Falmer Press.

Department of Education and Science (DES) (1983) *Teaching Quality*. London: HMSO.

Department of Education and Science (DES) (1985) *Better Schools. Cmnd 9469*. London: HMSO.

Department of Education and Science (DES) (1992a) *Curriculum Organisation and Classroom Practice in Primary Schools: A Discussion Paper*. London: DES, Information Branch.

Department of Education and Science (DES) (1992b) *School Teachers' Pay and Conditions Document 1992*. London: HMSO.

Donaldson, P.R. (1970) Role expectations of primary school headteachers. Dissertation Diploma in Child Development. London: University of London.

Drifte, C. (1996) The last goodbye, *The Times Educational Supplement*, 13 September: 23.

Dubberley, W. (1988) Humour as resistance, *International Journal of Qualitative Studies in Education*, 1(2): 109–23.

Dunning, G. (1993) Managing the small primary school: the problem role of the teaching head. *Educational Management and Administration*, 21: 79–89.

Easen, P. (1994) 'Planning to collaborate and collaborating to plan: moving beyond the contractual to the contributive', paper presented to the British Educational Research Association Conference, Oxford, September 8–11.

Evans, L., Packwood, A. St J. Neill, S.R. and Campbell, R.J. (1994) *The Meaning of Infant Teachers' Work*. London: Routledge.

Evans, J. and Penney, D. (1994) Whatever happened to good advice? Service and inspection after the Education Reform Act, *British Educational Research Journal,* 20(5): 519–33.

Evetts, J. (1989) The internal labour market for primary teachers, in S. Acker (ed.) *Teachers, Gender and Careers.* London: Falmer Press.

Evetts, J. (1994) *Becoming a Secondary Headteacher.* London: Cassell.

Fisher, P. (1995) Conditions are the key to discontent, *The Times Educational Supplement,* 27 January: 12.

Fitz, J. (1994) Implementation research and education policy: practice and prospects, *British Journal of Educational Studies,* 42(1): 53–69.

Freeman, A. (1987) Pastoral care and teacher stress, *Pastoral Care in Education,* 5(1): 22–8.

French, N.K. (1993) Elementary teacher stress and class size, *Journal of Research and Development in Education,* 26(2): 66–73.

Friedman, A. (1977) *Industry and Labour: Class Struggles at Work and Monopoly Capitalism.* London: Macmillan.

Fullan, M. (1988) Change processes in secondary schools: towards a more fundamental agenda, University of Toronto (mimeo).

Fullan, M. (1991) *The New Meaning of Educational Change.* New York: Teachers College Press.

Furlong, J. (1992) Reconstructing professionalism: ideological struggle in initial teacher education, in M. Arnot and L. Barton (eds) *Voicing Concerns: Sociological Perspectives on Contemporary Education Reforms.* Wallingford: Triangle.

Gardiner, J. (1996) Exclusions rise relentlessly, *The Times Educational Supplement,* 8 November.

Gewirtz, S. (1996) 'Post-welfarism and the reconstruction of teachers' work', paper presented at the British Educational Research Association Conference, Lancaster University, 12–15 September.

Gipps, C., Brown, M., McCallum, B. and McAllister, S. (1995) *Intuition or Evidence? Teachers and National Assessment of Seven-Year-Olds.* Buckingham: Open University Press.

Glaser, B.G. and Strauss, A.L. (1971) *Status Passage.* Chicago: Aldine.

Goffman, E. (1959) *The Presentation of Self in Everyday Life.* Garden City, Doubleday.

Goffman, E. (1961 and 1968) *Asylums: Essays on the Social Situations of Mental Patients and Other Inmates.* Harmondsworth: Penguin.

Goffman, E. (1972) *Interaction Ritual: Essays on Face-to-Face Behaviour.* Harmondsworth: Penguin.

Goffman, E. (1983) The interaction order, *American Sociological Review,* 48: 1–17.

Gouldner, A. (1965) *Wildcat Strike.* New York: Harper.

Grace, G. (1972) *Role Conflict and the Teacher.* London: Routledge and Kegan Paul.

Grace, G. (1985) Judging teachers: the social and political contexts of teacher evaluation, *British Journal of Sociology of Education,* 6(1): 3–16.

Grace, G. (1995) *School Leadership: Beyond Education Management; An Essay in Policy Scholarship.* London: Falmer.

Graddol, D. (1994) Three models of language description, in D. Graddol and O. Boyd-Barrett (eds) *Media Texts: Authors and Readers.* Clevedon: Multilingual Matters.

Griffith, A. and Smith, D.E. (1991) Constructing cultural knowledge: mothering as discourse, in J. Gaskell and A. McLaren (eds) *Women and Education* (2nd edn). Calgary: Detselig.

Habermas, J. (1976) *Legitimation Crisis*. London: Heinemann Educational Books.

Haigh, G. (1993) Trapped by trivia?, School Management Update, *The Times Educational Supplement*, 3 June: 16–17.

Haigh, G. (1995a) To be handled with care. *The Times Educational Supplement*, 10 February: 3–4.

Haigh, G. (1995b) Guiding light for first-time heads, *The Times Educational Supplement*, 8 September: 7.

Haigh, G. (1996) 50 and out, *The Times Educational Supplement*, 25 October: 4.

Hanson, D. and Herrington, M. (1976) *From College to Classroom: The Probationary Year*. London: Routledge and Kegan Paul.

Hargreaves, A. (1985) The micro–macro problem in the sociology of education, in R.G. Burgess (ed.) *Issues in Educational Research: Qualitative Methods*. Lewes: Falmer Press.

Hargreaves, A. (1989) *Curriculum and Assessment Reform*. Milton Keynes: Open University Press.

Hargreaves, A. (1990) Teachers' work and the politics of time and space, *International Journal of Qualitative Studies in Education*, 3(4): 303–20.

Hargreaves, A. (1991) Contrived collegiality: the micropolitics of teacher collaboration, in J. Blase (ed.) *The Politics of Life in Schools*. London: Sage.

Hargreaves, A. (1994a) *Changing Teachers, Changing Times: Teachers' Work and Culture in the Postmodern Age*. London: Cassell.

Hargreaves, A. (1994b) Restructuring restructuring: postmodernity and the prospects for educational change, in P.P. Grimmett and J. Neufeld (eds) *Teacher Development and the Struggle for Authenticity*. New York: Teachers College Press.

Hargreaves, A. and Dawe, R. (1989) Paths of professional development: contrived collegiality, collaborative culture, and the case of peer coaching, *Teacher and Teacher Education*, 6(3): 227–41.

Hargreaves, A. and Tucker, E. (1991) Teaching and guilt: exploring the feelings of teaching, *Teaching and Teacher Education*, 7(5/6): 491–505.

Hargreaves, D.H. (1972) *Interpersonal Relations and Education*. London: Routledge and Kegan Paul.

Hargreaves, D.H. (1980) The occupational culture of teachers, in P. Woods (ed.) *Teacher Strategies*, London: Croom Helm.

Hargreaves, D.H. (1983) The teaching of art and the art of teaching: towards an alternative view of aesthetic learning, in M. Hammersley and A. Hargreaves (eds) *Curriculum Practice: Some Sociological Case Studies*. Lewes: Falmer Press.

Hargreaves, D.H. (1994) The new professionalism: the synthesis of professional and institutional development, *Teaching and Teacher Education*, 10(4): 423–38.

Hargreaves, D.H. and Hopkins, D. (1991) *The Empowered School: The Management and Practice of Development Planning*. London: Cassell.

Harvey, D. (1990) *The Condition of Postmodernity*. Oxford: Basil Blackwell.

Haviland, J. (1988) *Take Care Mr Baker*. London: Fourth Estate.

Hawes, L. (1995) Teachers blamed for putting children first. *Observer*, 12 February.

Hayes, D. (1993) Learning to live with the National Curriculum: a case study of a headteacher's dilemmas, *The Curriculum Journal*, 4(2): 201–13.

172   *Restructuring Schools, Reconstructing Teachers*

Hellawell, D. (1990) Some effects of the national dispute on the relationships between head teachers and school staffs in primary schools, *British Journal of Sociology of Education*, 11(4): 397–410.

Helsby, G. (1995) Teachers' construction of professionalism in England in the 1990s, *Journal of Education for Teaching*, 21(3): 317–22.

Her Majesty's Inspectorate (HMI) (1978) *Primary Education in England: A Survey by HM Inspectors of Schools.* London: HMSO.

Hill, T. (1994a) *Developing a Career in Primary Education.* London: David Fulton.

Hill, T. (1994b) Primary headteachers: their job satisfaction and future career aspirations. *Educational Research*, 36(3): 223–35.

Hooper, L. (1996) Trapped with all escape routes blocked, *The Times Educational Supplement 2*, 7 June: 2.

House of Commons Education, Science and Arts Committee (1986) *Achievement in Primary Schools, Third Report, Session 1985–86: HC 40–1, Volume, 1.* London: HMSO.

Hoyle, E. (1974) Professionalility, professionalism and control in teaching, *London Educational Review*, 3(2): 15–17. Also (1975) in V. Houghton, R. McHugh and C. Morgan (eds) *Management in Education: The Management of Organizations and Individuals.* London: Ward Lock Educational in association with Open University Press.

Hoyle, E. (1980) Professionalization and deprofessionalization in education, in E. Hoyle and J. Megarry (eds) *World Yearbook of Education 1980: Professional Development of Teachers.* London: Kogan Page, pp. 42–54.

Hoyle, E. (1986) *The Politics of School Management.* London: Hodder and Stoughton.

Hughes, M.G. (1973) The professional as administrator: the case of the secondary school head, *Educational Administration Bulletin*, 2(1): 11–23.

Inglis, F. (1989) Managerialism and morality, in W. Carr (ed.) *Quality in Teaching: Arguments for a Reflective Profession.* Lewes: Falmer.

Jarvis, A. (1993) Why I'm glad to be going, *The Times Educational Supplement*, 20 August.

Jeffrey, B. and Woods, P. (1995a) 'Reconstructions of reality: schools under inspection', paper presented at the European Conference on Educational Research, Bath University, 14–17 September.

Jeffrey, B. and Woods, P. (1995b) 'The role of humour in constructing a discourse', paper presented at the International Society for Humour Studies Conference, Birmingham, 31 July–4 August.

Jeffrey, B. and Woods, P. (1996) Feeling deprofessionalized: the social construction of emotions during an Ofsted inspection, *Cambridge Journal of Education*, 26(3): 325–43.

Kelly, A.V. (1990) *The National Curriculum: A Critical Review.* London: Paul Chapman.

Kickert, W. (1991) 'Steering at a Distance: a new paradigm of public governance in Dutch higher education', paper for the European Consortium for Political Research, University of Essex, March.

Kyriacou, C. and Roe, H. (1988) Teachers' perceptions of pupils' behaviour problems at a comprehensive school, *British Educational Research Journal*, 14(2): 167–73.

Kyriacou, C. and Sutcliffe, J. (1978) Teacher stress: prevalence, sources and symptoms, *British Journal of Educational Psychology*, 48: 159–67.

Lacey, C. (1977) *The Socialization of Teachers.* London: Methuen.

Lauder, H. (1996) Extended review: the dilemmas of leadership and the virtues of policy scholarship, *British Journal of Sociology of Education*, 17(1): 99–101.

Lawlor, S. (1990) *Teachers Mistaught: Training in Theories or Education in Subjects.* London: Centre for Policy Studies.

Lawn, M. (1988) Skill in schoolwork: work relations in the primary school, in J. Ozga, (ed.) *Schoolwork: Approaches to the Labour Process of Teaching.* Milton Keynes: Open University Press.

Lawn, M. (1991) Social constructions of quality in teaching, in G. Grace and M. Lawn (eds) *Teacher Supply and Teacher Quality: Issues for the 1990s.* Clevedon: Multilingual Matters.

Lawn, M. (1995) Restructuring teaching in the USA and England: moving towards the differentiated, flexible teacher, *Journal of Education Policy*, 10(4): 347–60.

Lawrence, J. and Steed, D. (1986) Primary school perception of disruptive behaviour, *Educational Studies*, 12(2): 147–57.

Lawton, S. (1992) Why restructure? An international survey of the roots of reform, *Journal of Education Policy*, 7(2): 139–54.

Lock, L. (1986) Cited by M. Godfrey, Telling tales out of school, *The Guardian*, 12 March: 22.

Lortie, D.C. (1975) *Schoolteacher.* Chicago: University of Chicago Press.

Mac An Ghaill, M. (1992) Teachers' work: curriculum restructuring, culture, power and comprehensive schooling, *British Journal of Sociology of Education*, 13(2): 177–99.

Mac an Ghaill, M. (1996) Sociology of education, state schooling and social class: beyond critiques of the New Right hegemony, *British Journal of Sociology of Education*, 17(2): 163–76.

MacFarlane, E. (1989) Down and out, *The Times Educational Supplement*, 21 July: 19.

MacGregor, J. (1990) *National Curriculum and Assessment: A Summary of Messages from Recent Speeches to Teacher Associations.* London: DES.

McHugh, M. and McMullan, L. (1995) Headteacher or manager? Implications for training and development, *School Organisation*, 15(1): 23–34.

Macleod, D. (1996) Heads attack retirement curbs, *The Guardian*, 12 November.

Macleod, D. and Meikle, J. (1994) Education changes 'making heads quit', *The Guardian*, 1 September: 6.

Maguire, M. (1995) Dilemmas in teaching teachers: the teachers' perspective, *Teachers and Teaching: Theory and Practice*, 1(1): 119–31.

Mahoney, P. (1985) *Schools for the Boys.* London: Hutchinson.

March, J.G. and Olsen, J.P. (1976) *Ambiguity and Choice in Organisation.* Bergen: Universitetslaget.

Menter, I., Muschamp, Y. and Ozga, J. (1995a) 'Public collusion, private trouble: the discursive practices of managerialism and their impact on primary teachers', paper presented at the European Conference on Educational Research, Bath, 14–17 September.

Menter, I. with Muschamp, Y., Nicholls, P., Pollard, A. and Ozga, J. (1995b) Still carrying the can: primary-school headship in the 1990s, *School Organisation*, 15(3): 301–12.

Mersh, C. (1991) Turning the tables on stress, *Northampton Chronicle and Echo*, 13 February.

Millard, A. (1995) Tired out from the weight of my armour, *The Times Educational Supplement*, 10 February: 20.

Miller, J. (1996) Too much work, too little praise – I've had enough, *The Times*, 6 September: 35.

Miller, P. (1994) Perspectives on the recognition and resolution of dilemmas within an educational framework. PhD thesis, University of Surrey.

Mills, C.W. (1959) *The Sociological Imagination.* New York: Oxford University Press.

Moore, R. (1996) Educational discourse and social change, Unit 5 of Course EU208 *Exploring Educational Issues.* Milton Keynes: The Open University.

Morrison, M. (1996) 'Supply teaching and discontinuous employment: the social construction of personal and professional worlds', paper presented at the ISA Conference on Occupations and Professions, University of Nottingham, September.

Mortimore, P., Sammons, P., Lewis, L. and Ecob, R. (1988) *School Matters: The Junior Years.* London: Open Books.

Murphy, J. and Evertson, C. (eds) (1991) *Restructuring Schools: Capturing the Phenomena.* New York: Teachers College Record.

Musgrave, P.W. (1972) *The Sociology of Education* (2nd edn). London: Methuen.

Musgrove, F. (1974) Education of teachers for a changing role, in J.D. Turner and J. Rushton (eds) *The Teacher in a Changing Society.* Manchester: Manchester University Press.

National Governors' Association (1989) *Results in Education.* Washington: NGA.

Nias, J. (1987) One finger one thumb: a case study of the deputy head's part in the leadership of a nursery/infant school, in G. Southworth (ed.) *Readings in Primary School Management.* London: Falmer Press.

Nias, J. (1989) *Primary Teachers Talking: A Study of Teaching as Work.* London: Routledge.

Nias, J. (1991) Changing times, changing identities: grieving for a lost self, in R.G. Burgess (ed.) *Educational Research and Evaluation.* London: Falmer Press.

Nias, J. (1993) 'Primary headteachers' use of school assemblies to promote whole school curriculum development', paper presented at the British Educational Research Association Conference, University of Liverpool, 10–13 September.

Nias, J. (1995) 'Teachers' moral purposes, sources of vulnerability and strength', paper presented at the Conference on *Teacher Burnout,* Johann Jacobs Foundation, Marbach, Germany, 2–4 November.

Nias, J., Southworth, G. and Yeomans, A. (1989) *Staff Relationships in the Primary School.* London: Cassell.

Nias, J., Southworth, G. and Yeomans, A. (1994) The culture of collaboration, in A. Pollard and J. Bourne (eds) *Teaching and Learning in the Primary School.* London: Routledge.

Nixon, J. and Rudduck, J. (1993) The role of professional judgement in the local inspection of schools: a study of six local education authorities, *Research Papers in Education,* 8(2): 135–48.

Ofsted (1993a) *The Handbook for the Inspection of Schools.* London: HMSO.

Ofsted (1993b) *Meadowfields Primary School: A Report from the Office of Her Majesty's Chief Inspector of Schools.* London: Ofsted.

Ofsted (1994) *Primary Matters: A Discussion on Teaching and Learning in Primary Schools.* London: Ofsted.

Ofsted (1995) *The Handbook for the Inspection of Nursery and Primary Schools.* London: Ofsted.

O'Leary, J. (1996) Why are our teachers leaving?, *The Times,* 6 September: 35.

Osborn, M. (1995) 'Not a seamless robe: a tale of two teachers' responses to policy change', paper presented to the European Conference on Educational Research, Bath University, 14–17 September.

Osborn, M. and Black, E. (1994) Developing the National Curriculum at Key Stage 2: The Changing Nature of Teachers' Work. Report commissioned by NASUWT, Bristol, University of West of England at Bristol.

Osborn, M. and Broadfoot, P. (1992) The impact of current changes in English primary schools on teacher professionalism, *Teachers College Record*, 94(1): 138–51.

Osborn, M., Abbot, D., Broadfoot, P., Croll, P. and Pollard, A. (1996) Teachers' professional perspectives: continuity and change, in R. Chawla-Duggan and C.J. Pole (eds) *Reshaping Education in the 1990s: Perspectives on Primary Schooling*. London: Falmer Press.

Owen, M. (1990) School for scandal, *The Guardian*, 1 May: 25.

Ozga, J. and Lawn, M. (1988) Schoolwork: interpreting the labour process of teaching, *British Journal of Sociology of Education*, 9(3): 323–36.

Peters, T.J. and Waterman, Jr., R.H. (1982) *In Search of Excellence*. New York: Warner Books.

Plowden Report (1967) *Children and their Primary Schools*, Report of the Central Advisory Council for Education in England. London: HMSO.

Plummer, K. (1975) *Sexual Stigma*. London: Routledge and Kegan Paul.

Pollard, A. (1985) *The Social World of the Primary School*. London: Holt, Reinhart and Winston.

Pollard, A. (1987) Primary school teachers and their colleagues, in S. Delamont (ed.) *The Primary School Teacher*. London: Falmer.

Pollard, A. (1991) *Learning in Primary Schools*. London: Cassell.

Pollard, A. (ed.) (1994) *Look Before You Leap? Research Evidence for the Curriculum at Key Stage 2*. London: Tyrell Press.

Pollard, A., Broadfoot, P., Croll, P., Osborn, M. and Abbott, D. (1994) *Changing English Primary Schools? The Impact of the Education Reform Act at Key Stage 2*. London: Cassell.

Postman, N. and Weingartner, C. (1971) *Teaching as a Subversive Activity*. Harmondsworth: Penguin.

Purkey, S. and Smith, M. (1985) School reform: the district policy implications of the effective schools literature, *The Elementary School Journal*, 85: 353–89.

Richards, C. (1987) Primary education in England: an analysis of some recent issues and developments, in S. Delamont (ed.) *The Primary School Teacher*. London: Falmer.

Richardson, G. (1995) Leaving the profession, in J. Bell (ed.) *Teachers Coping With Change*. Buckingham: Open University Press.

Riley, K. (1994) *Quality and Equality: Promoting Opportunities in Schools*. London: Cassell.

Riseborough, G.F. (1981) Teacher careers and comprehensive schooling: an empirical study, *Sociology*, 15(3): 352–81.

Riseborough, G.F. (1993) Primary headship, state policy and the challenge of the 1990s: an exceptional story that disproves total hegemonic rule. *Journal of Education Policy*, 8(2): 155–73.

Rose, A.M. (1962) A social-psychological theory of neurosis, in A.M. Rose (ed.) *Human Behaviour and Social Processes: An Interactionist Approach*. London: Routledge.

Rudduck, J. (1991) *Innovation and Change: Developing Involvement and Understanding*. Milton Keynes: Open University Press.

Rudduck, J. (1992) Practitioner research and programmes of initial teacher education, in T. Russell and H. Munby, (eds) *Teachers and Teaching*. London: Falmer Press.

Rudow, B. (1995) 'Stress and burnout in the teaching profession in European studies, issues and research perspectives', paper presented at the Conference on *Teacher Burnout*, Johann Jacobs Foundation, Marbach, Germany, 2–4 November.

Rutter, M., Maugham, B., Mortimore, P. and Ouston, J. (1979) *Fifteen Thousand Hours*. London: Open Books.

Seddon, T. (1991) Restructuring teachers and teaching: current Australian developments and future prospects, *Discourse*, 12(1): 1–23.

Sikes, P., Measor, L. and Woods, P. (1985) *Teacher Careers: Crises and Continuities*. Lewes: Falmer Press.

Sloan, V. (1996) Way beyond the end of the road, *The Times Educational Supplement*, 30 August: 30.

Smilansky, J. (1984) External and internal correlates of teachers satisfaction and willingness to report stress, *British Journal of Educational Psychology*, 54(1): 84–92.

Smithers, A. (1989) Where have all the teachers gone?, *The Times Educational Supplement*, 12 May: A17.

Smyth, J. (1991) International perspectives on teacher collegiality: a labour process discussion based on the concept of teachers' work, *British Journal of Sociology of Education*, 12(3): 323–46.

Southworth, G. (1993) 'A closer look: an ethnographic study of a primary headteacher', paper presented at the British Educational Research Association Conference, University of Liverpool, 3–10 September.

Steedman, C. (1985) The mother made conscious: the historical development of a primary school pedagogy, *History Workshop Journal*, 20: 149–63.

Sugrue, C. (1997) *Complexities of Teaching: Child-Centred Perspectives*. London: Falmer Press.

The Times Educational Supplement (1996) Primary class sizes up again. 5 July: 6.

Toffler, A. (1990) *Powershift*. New York: Bantam Books.

Tooley, J. (1993) *A Market-led Alternative for the Curriculum: Breaking the Code*. London: Institute of Education.

Travers, C.J. and Cooper, C.L. (1993) Mental health, job satisfaction and occupational stress among UK teachers, *Work and Stress*, 7(3): 203–19.

Travers, C.J. and Cooper, C.L. (1996) *Teachers Under Pressure: Stress in the Teaching Profession*. London: Routledge.

Troman, G. (1996a) The rise of the new professionals? The restructuring of primary teachers work and professionalism, *British Journal of Sociology of Education*, 17(4): 473–87.

Troman, G. (1996b) Models of the good teacher: defining and redefining teacher quality, in P. Woods (ed.) *Contemporary Issues in Teaching and Learning*. Milton Keynes: Open University Press.

Troman, G. (1996c) 'Stepping' into the future: new forms of organisation in the primary school, *Journal of Education Policy*, 11(5): 611–24.

Turner, R.H. (1962) Role-taking: process versus conformity, in A.M. Rose (ed.) *Human Behaviour and Social Processes*. London: Routledge and Kegan Paul.

Turner, V.W. (1969) *The Ritual Process*. London: Routledge and Kegan Paul.

Van Gennep, A. (1960) *The Rites of Passage*. London: Routledge and Kegan Paul.

Veninga, R. and Spradley, J. (1981) *The Work–Stress Connection*. Boston: Little-Brown.

Vulliamy, G. and Webb, R. (1993) Progressive education and the National Curriculum: findings from a global education research project, *Educational Review*, 45(1): 21–41.

Walker, S. and Barton, L. (eds) (1987) *Changing Policies, Changing Teachers*. Milton Keynes: Open University Press.

Wallace, M. (1988) Towards a collegiate approach to curriculum management in primary and middle schools, *School Organization*, 8(1): 25–34.

Wallace, M. (1991) Coping with multiple innovations in schools: an exploratory study, *School Organization*, 11(2): 187–209.

Wallace, M. (1993) Discourse of derision: the role of the mass media within the education policy process, *Journal of Education Policy*, 8(4): 321–37.

Walsh-Harrington, J. (1990) Out on a low note, *The Times Educational Supplement*, 26 January: 26–7.

Want, C. (1996) An occupational hazard, *The Times Educational Supplement*, 30 August: 30.

Warren-Little, J. (1987) Teachers as colleagues in V. Richardson-Koehler (ed.) *Educators' Handbook: A Research Perspective*. London: Longman.

Webb, R. and Vulliamy, G. (1996) *Roles and Responsibilities in the Primary School*. Buckingham: Open University Press.

Weinstock, A. (1976) I blame the teachers, *The Times Educational Supplement*, 23 January.

Went, G. (1996) Pressure that led the head to quit, *The Times*, 6 September: 35.

Werner, W. (1982) *Evaluating Program Implementation (School Based), Final Project Report*. Vancouver: Centre for the Study of Curriculum Instruction, University of British Columbia.

Whitehead, M. (1996) The drip-drip-drip despair that slowly destroys lives, *The Times Educational Supplement, School Management Update*, 10 May: 6.

Wilcox, B. and Gray, J. (1994) Reactions to inspection: a study of three variants, *Cambridge Journal of Education*, 24(2): 245–59.

Wilson, B.R. (1962) The teacher's role: a sociological analysis, *British Journal of Sociology*, 13(1): 15–32.

Winterton, J. and Barlow, A. (1994) 'Multiskilling: social construct or workplace reality?', paper presented to the Annual Labour Process Conference, Aston University, 24 March.

Woodhead, C. (1996) *Chief Inspector's Annual Report*, London: Ofsted.

Woods, P. (1979) *The Divided School*. London: Routledge and Kegan Paul.

Woods, P. (1989) Stress and the teacher role, in M. Cole and S. Walker (eds) *Teaching and Stress*. Buckingham: Open University Press.

Woods, P. (1990) *Teacher Skills and Strategies*. Lewes: Falmer Press.

Woods, P. (1993) *Critical Events in Teaching and Learning*, London: Falmer Press.

Woods, P. (1995) *Creative Teachers in Primary Schools*. Buckingham: The Open University Press.

Woods, P. (1996) *Researching the Art of Teaching*. London: Routledge.

Woods, P. and Jeffrey, R.J. (1996a) A new professional discourse? Adjusting to managerialism, in P. Woods (ed.) *Contemporary Issues in Teaching and Learning*. London: Routledge.

Woods, P. and Jeffrey, R.J. (1996b) *Teachable Moments: The Art of Teaching in Primary Schools*. Buckingham: Open University Press.

Woods, P. and Wenham, P. (1995) Politics and pedagogy: a case study in appropriation, *Journal of Education Policy*, 10(2): 119–41.

Worsley, P. (1977) *Introducing Sociology* (2nd edn). Harmondsworth: Penguin.

Young, S. (1996) Primary exclusions blamed on stress. *The Times Educational Supplement*, 31 April.

Name index

Subject index

ROLES AND RESPONSIBILITIES IN THE PRIMARY SCHOOL
CHANGING DEMANDS, CHANGING PRACTICES

Rosemary Webb and Graham Vulliamy

- How are teachers planning and implementing the National Curriculum at Key Stage 2?
- How have the recent policy and legislative changes affected the roles and responsibilities of class teachers, curriculum coordinators, deputy headteachers and headteachers?
- How are primary schools managing the current plethora of innovations and what can be learned from their experience?

Based on qualitative research in 50 schools throughout England and Wales, this book portrays teachers' work as it is currently experienced in the post-ERA context of multiple innovations. It examines the impact of the National Curriculum and assessment on classroom practice, curriculum organization and planning at Key Stage 2. Drawing on the wealth of ideas and successful practices shared with the authors by the teachers in the study, it demonstrates how class teachers, curriculum coordinators, deputy headteachers and headteachers are tackling the new demands of their expanding roles. An analysis of the management of change reveals a growing tension between collegial and top-down directive managerial styles, which is fundamentally affecting the culture of primary schools. Through presenting what is actually happening in primary schools in contrast to prescribed educational orthodoxies, this book makes a vital contribution to the debate on the future of primary education.

Contents
Introduction and methodology – The changing context of primary education – Changing demands on classroom practice – Changing curriculum organization and planning – The changing role of the curriculum coordinator – The changing role of the deputy headteacher – The changing role of the headteacher – Managing whole school change in the post-ERA primary school – References – Index.

192pp   0 335 19472 9 (Paperback)   0 335 19473 7 (Hardback)

TEACHABLE MOMENTS
THE ART OF TEACHING IN PRIMARY SCHOOLS

Peter Woods and Bob Jeffrey

Creative teaching is an art form – aesthetic, intuitive and expressive. The recent proliferation of new educational policies and the related increase in tensions and dilemmas facing schools, combined with the growing demand for a wider range of skills and knowledge among children mean that there is an even greater need for creative teaching than before the National Curriculum.

This book addresses this need by:

- exploring the features of creative teaching with a focus on the day to day practice of primary teachers;
- showing how teachers use emotion, create atmosphere and stimulate imagination to enhance their teaching;
- examining the ways in which teachers have managed the National Curriculum and developed a new professional discourse in response to government pressures.

This book is a sequel to *Creative Teachers in Primary Schools* (Open University Press 1995) and builds upon this work to provide new insights into the art of teaching.

Contents

Preface – Creative teaching and its significance – Creative teachers – A new professional discourse? Adjusting to managerialism – The emotional side of teaching and learning – Creating atmosphere and tone – Stimulating the imagination through story – Managing the curriculum – References – Index.

176pp   0 335 19373 0 (Paperback)   0 335 19374 9 (Hardback)

CREATIVE TEACHERS IN PRIMARY SCHOOLS

Peter Woods

Is creative teaching still possible in English schools? Can teachers maintain and promote their own interests and beliefs as well as deliver a prescribed National Curriculum?

This book explores creative teachers' attempts to pursue *their* brand of teaching despite the changes. Peter Woods has discovered a range of strategies and adaptations to this end among such teachers, including resisting change which runs counter to their own values; appropriating the National Curriculum within their own ethos; enhancing their role through the use of others; and enriching their work through the National Curriculum to provide quality learning experiences. If all else fails, such teachers remove themselves from the system and take their creativity elsewhere. A strong theme of self-determination runs through these experiences.

While acknowledging hard realities, the book is ultimately optimistic, and a tribute to the dedication and inspiration of primary teachers.

The book makes an important contribution to educational theory, showing a range of responses to *intensification* as well as providing many detailed examples of collaborative research methods.

Contents

Introduction: Adapting to intensification – Resisting through collaboration: A whole-school perspective of the National Curriculum – The creative use and defence of space: Appropriation through the environment – The charisma of the critical other: Enhancing the role of the teacher – Teaching, and researching the teaching of, a history topic: An experiment in collaboration – Managing marginality: Aspects of the career of a primary school head – Self-determination among primary school teachers – References – Index.

208pp   0 335 19313 7 (Paperback)   0 335 19314 5 (Hardback)

MAKING SENSE OF PRIMARY INSPECTION

Ian Sandbrook

- What *really* happens in an inspection of a primary school?
- What are the effects of inspections on primary schools and teachers?
- How do inspectors feel about the inspection process?

Making Sense of Primary Inspection provides a unique insight into these and many other issues. Based on a series of case studies, the book examines what really happens in inspections both in technical and in emotional terms. It explores tensions between judgement and development, myth and reality, evidence and interpretation, and the institution and the individual. It raises issues about power, professionalism, objectivity, credibility and confidence and reveals the internal workings of inspection as conditional, negotiated and dominated by human nature.

This book will be invaluable reading for all primary school headteachers, teachers and governors who have either undergone or are preparing for inspection. It will also be of great interest to school inspectors.

Contents

Introduction – The changing culture of inspection – Expectations and preconceptions – Gathering evidence – Roles and reliability – Feedback – Patterns of emotional response – Relationships and rituals – Outcomes of inspection – Professionalism and inspection – Inspection illuminated – Appendix: The case studies – Bibliography – Index.

160pp   0 335 19664 0 (Paperback)   0 335 19665 9 (Hardback)